CHINESE GRAND STRATEGY
AND
MARITIME POWER

CASS SERIES:
NAVAL POLICY AND HISTORY
Series Editor: Geoffrey Till
ISSN 1366-9478

This series consists primarily of original manuscripts by research scholars in the general area of naval policy and history, without national or chronological limitations. It will from time to time also include collections of important articles as well as reprints of classic works.

CHINESE
GRAND STRATEGY
and
MARITIME POWER

THOMAS M. KANE
University of Hull

FRANK CASS
LONDON • PORTLAND, OR

First published in 2002 in Great Britain by
FRANK CASS PUBLISHERS
Crown House, 47 Chase Side, Southgate
London N14 5BP

and in the United States of America by
FRANK CASS PUBLISHERS
c/o ISBS, 5824 N.E. Hassalo Street
Portland, Oregon, 97213-3644

Website: www.frankcass.com

British Library Cataloguing in Publication Data

Kane, Thomas M.
 Chinese grand strategy and maritime power. – (Cass series.
 Naval policy and history; 16)
 1. Sea-power – China 2. China – Strategic aspects 3. China –
 Foreign relations – 1976 –
 I. Title
 327.5′1′00905

ISBN 0-7146-5282-2 (cloth)
ISSN 1366-9478

Library of Congress Cataloging-in-Publication Data

Kane, Thomas M., 1969–
 Chinese grand strategy and maritime power / Thomas M. Kane
 p. ; cm. – (Cass series – Naval policy and history, ISSN 1366-9478; 16)
 Includes bibliographical rerferences and index.
 ISBN 0-7146-5282-2
 1. Sea-power – China – History. I. Title. II. Series.

VA633 .K36 2002
359′.00951 – dc21

 2002018815

Printed in Great Britain by MPG Books Ltd., Bodmin, Cornwall

With love to my father and mother, Norman E. Kane and Jean M. Kane. Warm, clear-sighted and educated. People who understood freedom and managed to achieve it. Parted only by death. From them I learned to think, to write and to accomplish. My greatest teachers and my closest friends.

Contents

Series Editor's Preface

This book establishes beyond doubt that China is building up maritime power in all its dimensions. The main units of its sea-going Navy are expanding in number, reach and military capacity. China's fishing and merchant fleet is now huge, and its leaders are developing the shore-side infrastructure to match.

Thomas Kane shows that while these developments may be relatively new in contemporary terms, they actually fit into the pattern of centuries rather more easily. It has often been remarked that the Chinese navy of the period AD 1000–1500 was almost certainly the world's largest and technically most advanced maritime force. After this period, though, China failed to keep abreast of contemporary technological advances (especially in the radical transformation brought about by the development of naval artillery). This simple fact is a salutary reminder that the exclusive association of maritime thinking with Western experience, and largely British and American experience at that, can be profoundly misleading. In his exploration of Chinese maritime thinking, Thomas Kane implicitly hammers this vital point home.

Investigating a navy also often offers a window into the internal development of the country that it is designed to defend. A navy illustrates the country's social and economic strengths and weaknesses; more to the point perhaps, it provides a means of assessing the strategic and international perspectives of the country's leaders.

This is the main reason why so many people are interested in Chinese maritime thinking. China will be pivotal to strategic developments in the Asia Pacific in the twenty-first century and it is hard to exaggerate the attention with which its many neighbours look for clues as to its future intentions in their area. Moreover, the fact that the on-going disputes over the South China Sea and with Taiwan are primarily maritime in nature reinforces the centrality of naval developments to this kind of sometimes fevered investigation.

In this book, Thomas Kane offers a calm and dispassionate review that will be of interest both to maritime analysts and to the world's China watchers. He concludes that China is indeed building up its maritime power, with the intent of propelling itself once more among the foremost of the great powers, and ends with some stimulating reflections on how the West and China's neighbours should respond to this development. In strategic terms, the Asia-Pacific region is overwhelmingly maritime in orientation. The economies of the area, now so crucial to the effectiveness of the world economy as a whole, depend absolutely on sea trade. Marine resources, fish, oil and gas are essential to the prosperity of many countries in the region.

The sea is the strategic space among the area's key players, the United States, Japan, Southeast Asia, the Koreas and Australasia. Unsurprisingly, jurisdiction over sea areas is in contentious dispute throughout the region. For all these reasons, Thomas Kane's review of the Chinese approach to maritime power is both apposite and timely. Its appearance is to be warmly welcomed.

Geoffrey Till
Series Editor

Acknowledgements

My deepest gratitude to Mr Brian Auten, Mr Adam Baddeley, Dr Eric J. Grove, Dr Timothy Huxley, Dr Lawrence Serewicz and Ms Isoko Sunakawa.

Abbreviations

AEW	airborne early warning (radar)
AMRAAM	advanced medium-range air-to-air missile
ASEAN	Association of South-East Asian Nations
ASW	anti-submarine warfare
AWAC	airborne warning and control
C4I	command, control, computers and intelligence
CMIC	Chinese Military–Industrial Complex
COSTIND	Committee for Science and Industry for National Defence
DoD	Department of Defense
DRV	Democratic Republic of Vietnam (Communist)
DWT	dead-weight tons
Ekranoplan	a surface-skimming craft, similar to a hydrofoil
GED	General Equipment Department
GPS	global positioning system
LCM	landing craft, mechanised
LCU	landing craft, utility
LSM	landing ship, medium
LST	landing ship, tank
MSDF	Maritime Self-Defence Force
PAP	People's Armed Police
PLA	People's Liberation Army
PLAAF	People's Liberation Army Air Force
PLAN	People's Liberation Army Navy
PNG	Papua New Guinea
PRC	People's Republic of China
RMA	revolution in military affairs
ROC	Republic of China (Taiwan)
RRF	Rapid Reaction Force
RVN	Republic of (South) Vietnam
SAM	surface-to-air missile
SEZ	Special Economic Zones
SPLA	Sudanese People's Liberation Army
USTND	University of Science and Technology for National Defence

1

China to the Sea

'There lies a sleeping giant', Napoleon Bonaparte said of China. 'Let him sleep, for when he wakes, he will shake the world.'[1] Over the second half of the twentieth century, China appears to have awakened. Indeed the People's Republic of China (PRC) has called for changes in the international system, which its own leaders describe as nothing less than a 'new order'.[2] China's attempts to create such an order must lead to friction, for, in the words of one expert, on no single strategic issue are China and the West on the same side.[3]

If China wishes to claim a leading role in international politics, it must become a seapower. Maritime strength is a fundamental part of global strategic leverage for any nation, but it is particularly important for the PRC.[4] Although China is hardly an island, the regions of greatest importance to its national destiny are most accessible to it by sea. Two of Beijing's strongest potential rivals and wealthiest potential trading partners, Japan and the United States, are separated from China by water. The PRC's disputes in the Taiwan Straits and the South China Sea are entirely maritime.

Although there are overland routes between China and the rest of Eurasia, the Chinese will find it far cheaper to trade with Europe, Southeast Asia and the Middle East by water. China's rivalry with India is partially land-oriented, but also partially naval. For these reasons and others, it is no surprise that China has devoted great resources to improving its navy and commercial fleet, or that Western analysts have paid special attention to this development. Seapower is not the only factor which will determine whether the PRC realizes its potential to become a global power, but it ranks alongside economic development and political stability as one of the most critical. In the past two decades, not surprisingly, the road to promotion in the Chinese armed forces has led through military academies that emphasize the importance of the navy.[5]

China clearly needs seapower, and influential members of the Beijing establishment recognize that need. These facts raise the questions of whether the PRC is able to build a powerful navy, and how it might go about so doing. Not only are these questions interesting for their inherent drama, but they are critical to any debate over how other countries should respond to Beijing's international debut. History is full of examples of how dangerous it can be to underestimate a rising power, but as the China expert Gerald Segal noted, it may be perilous to overestimate the PRC as well.[6] Citizens and policymakers throughout the world must assess the PRC accurately, and must understand as much as possible about both what China is trying to achieve and what this might mean for their own countries.

As one investigates these questions, one sees that advocates of Chinese naval power will have to overcome formidable economic and technical obstacles, and perhaps important political obstacles as well. Nevertheless, such an investigation also indicates that China's naval strategists know what they are doing. Although Beijing's means are limited, it is using them intelligently to work itself into a position from which it will be able to exercise far more influence in the future. In other words, China's leaders appear to be pursuing a consistent and well-founded grand strategy, which has put them on a course toward realizing their most ambitious political goals. Maritime development is one of the most prominent and most challenging goals of the PRC's strategy, and it reveals the techniques Beijing is using in its larger strategic enterprise.

GRAND STRATEGY DEFINED

What does it mean to follow a 'grand strategy'? Carl von Clausewitz defined strategy as 'the use of engagements for the object of the war', and this author continues in that vein to define grand strategy as the use of political, economic and military actions to achieve the objectives of the regime.[7] Success at either kind of strategy depends on one's ability to make effective combinations: to assemble seemingly discrete endeavors such as battles, industrial programs or diplomatic initiatives into an overall pattern of victory. Plato compared the art of statesmanship to the art of weaving separate threads into a whole piece of cloth, and the analogy is apt.[8]

This definition of grand strategy is open-ended. A state leader may incorporate any imaginable activity into his or her plans, as long as it furthers the aims of the regime. Likewise, grand strategy may unfold over any period of time. One tends to associate the concept with long-term plans. Books on the grand strategy of the Roman Empire, for instance, routinely hypothesize about political gambits which are supposed to have evolved over the course of centuries.[9] Nevertheless, state policy can have specific objectives, and there are specific moments in history when states bring their plans to fruition, often through swift action and the decisive use of violence.

Historically, assorted leaders have written detailed political blueprints that lay out their grand strategies in detail. Many have intended for their plans to unfold over many decades. In the seventeenth century, for instance, Cardinal Richelieu wrote a testament to help future generations of French statesmen continue what he had begun.[10] Frederick William I of Prussia entrusted his son Frederick with a similar document, and the young man realized his father's goals effectively enough to earn the sobriquet 'the Great'.[11]

However, there are limits to what even the most far-sighted statesmen can plan in advance. The elder Moltke's maxim, 'no plan of operations can look with certainty beyond the first meeting with the major forces of the enemy', is as valid in grand strategy as it was on the nineteenth-century battlefield.[12] In statecraft, the metaphorical 'major forces of the enemy' can appear in many guises and at the most unexpected times. The fact that few governments can sustain a consensus about even their own interests and policies makes it yet more difficult for leaders to map out long-term strategies in detail.

These difficulties need not stop state leaders from practicing grand strategy, any more than the proverbial fog of war stops military commanders from practicing strategy on the battlefield. What Clausewitz said about combat applies to statecraft as well.

> Nowhere, in consequence, are differences of opinion so acute … and fresh opinions never cease to batter at one's convictions. No degree of calm can provide enough protection: new impressions are too powerful, too vivid, and always assault the emotions as well as the intellect.[13]

Plans fall to pieces in such an environment, but one would be foolish to rely on *ad hoc* reactions to these innumerable and frequently contradictory 'impressions' as well. Those who merely react are apt to dither aimlessly, hurting their own cause as often as they help it, until finally the tide of events overwhelms them. In an earlier comment, Clausewitz suggested that '[a]ction can never be based on anything firmer than instinct'.[14] Instinct alone, however, is clearly not enough – it must be grounded in 'a sensing of the truth'.

How, then, can one sense the truth amidst chaos? Clausewitz suggests a solution: 'Only those general principles and attitudes that result from deep understanding can provide a *comprehensive* guide to action' (emphasis in original). In a military campaign, principles, attitudes and understanding can belong to an officer who possesses that 'sense of unity' and 'power of judgment' that Clausewitz describes as genius.[15] Even dictatorships seldom place their entire foreign policy in the hands of a single leader, but 'principles', 'attitudes', 'understanding' and a 'sense of unity' can provide a comprehensive guide to action for collectives in the same way that they provide such a guide for individuals.

One can best illustrate the way grand strategy takes shape amid the chaos of international affairs by means of an example. Within 20 years of its defeat in the First World War, Germany had put itself back in a position to overrun western Europe. The Germans accomplished this by pursuing active, consistent and mutually supporting programs in all the dimensions of statecraft. Germany's return to power involved interlocking fiscal policies, industrial policies and diplomatic policies, as well as the putatively secret rearmament policy itself.

This book has defined grand strategy as 'the use of political, economic and military actions to achieve the objectives of the regime', and Germany's return to power is a clear example of such a strategy in action. Clearly, the German feat required well-conceived and purposeful action. Nevertheless, not only did the Germans face turmoil and unforeseeable setbacks in the 1920s and 1930s, it seems unlikely that they were following any kind of detailed plan until the process was nearly complete. The first steps in the rearmament program began, not with Hitler, and not even under the Weimar regime, but in 1917, with the First World War nearly a year from its end and the Kaiser still in power.[16] It seems highly unlikely that an official state program would have survived these two revolutionary changes in government, but the general predilections that allowed German leaders to carry on a coherent policy did.

Formally and informally, German society had indoctrinated its leaders with what Clausewitz called a 'deep understanding' of their country's political situation, and with the 'principles' and 'attitudes' they needed to achieve national goals. This allowed them to practice a large-scale version of what their field officers might have called *Auftragstatik*. This is a military doctrine in which higher commanders state their goals in general terms, and allow their subordinates to accomplish them in whatever way the situation requires. In grand strategy, the overall goals often come from geographical understandings, overall political sentiments and a nation's historical aspirations rather than explicit military commands, but the concept remains the same.

ON STUDYING GRAND STRATEGY

For these reasons, it is a mistake to limit one's understanding of grand strategy to formal strategic blueprints. Master plans to take over the world have existed, but they are most common in the realms of thriller movies and conspiracy theory. To understand grand strategy in its more common and possibly more effective form, one must try to think like a grand strategist. Just as state leaders weave their policies one thread at a time, following general principles rather than detailed blueprints, so must analysts study the way the threads cross over each other, following general principles in an attempt to see the pattern as it emerges on the loom. This process involves speculation, but it is one of reasoning rather than guesswork.[17]

In investigating grand strategy, one must allow for the fact that no one can ever fully know another's mind. The fact that even relatively libertarian governments shroud many of their military and diplomatic activities in secrecy compounds this situation, and the fact that many governments are willing to lie in pursuit of their ends complicates matters yet further. For these reasons, one must also ground one's studies in what one knows about how a particular government tends to operate. One must place some faith in the principles that the past is the prologue in international affairs, and that the truth, in some form, will eventually out. The fact that grand strategy relies so heavily on generally taught principles helps the researcher here, because the attitudes a nation teaches all its people throughout their lives are difficult to keep secret.

Analysts may take advantage of the fact that strategy most often involves material things operating in material environments. Therefore, although one cannot know precisely how strategists in another country will approach a problem, one can know the general sorts of action they will have to take. The physical realities of geography, industrial procedures and military capabilities have similar effects on everyone, and these effects change remarkably slowly over time. History can help identify such physical realities, not because history repeats itself *per se*, but because similar causes produce similar effects at any time. Alfred Thayer Mahan both observed this principle and also provided an example of such analysis in his *The Influence of Seapower Upon History, 1660–1783*:

> To impress more strongly the truth that history both suggests strategic study and illustrates the principles of war by the facts which it transmits, two more instances will be taken, which are more remote in time than the period specially considered in this work. How did it happen that, in two great contests between the powers of the East and of the West in the Mediterranean, in one of which the empire of the known world was at stake, the opposing fleets met on spots so near each other as Actium and Lepanto? Was this a mere coincidence, or was it due to conditions that recurred, and may recur again? [Here, Mahan notes that the more recent battle of Navarino, between Turkey and the Western Powers, also took place in the same region.] If the latter, it is worth while to study out the reason; for if there should again arise a great eastern power of the sea like that of Antony or of Turkey, the strategic

questions would be similar. At present, indeed, it seems that the centre of seapower, resting mainly with England and France, is overwhelmingly in the West; but should any chance add to the control of the Black Sea basin, which Russia now has, the possession of the entrance to the Mediterranean, the existing strategic conditions affecting seapower would all be modified. Now were the West arrayed against the East, England and France would go at once unopposed to the Levant, as they did in 1854 and as England alone went in 1878; in case of the change suggested, the East, as twice before, would meet the West half-way.[18]

To probe another country's grand strategy, it is necessary to study the statements that reflect that nation's principles, the organizations which are capable of translating these principles into action, the physical realities which shape that state's capabilities, and the events which indicate how these factors will come together in practice. One must look for themes and directions. Although the significance of particular events will seldom be known in precise detail, continual observation of these events will often reveal an underlying pattern. This is no more than a version of the way diplomats and intelligence analysts have always operated. Such methods have fallen into disuse among academic political scientists, which may be one reason why foreign-service veterans such as George Kennan were able to foresee the eventual demise of the Soviet Union whereas international relations scholars were not.[19]

GRAND STRATEGY IN MODERN CHINA

In the 1990s, several China specialists denied that the PRC had any kind of coherent foreign policy.[20] These scholars argued that the Chinese merely responded to problems as they arose, not thinking beyond the immediate future and not caring how contradictory or ultimately self-destructive their short-sighted reactions might be. If this were true, it would follow that China had no grand strategy worthy of the name. This contention, however, rests on questionable evidence. Furthermore, it is at odds with Chinese attitudes, Chinese activities and China's general pattern of foreign-policy success.

Those who question the coherence of China's foreign policy point to the complexity of China's government, the absence of consensus within that government and historical oscillations in China's diplomatic alignments.[21] None of these things, however, necessarily indicates aimlessness or incompetence. All governments are complex, and all feature arguments between people with different points of view. The Roman republic, to pick an example from antiquity, had a highly convoluted constitution, but this did not stop its polity from conquering the world. No one can deny that the Beijing government contains labyrinthine formal and informal institutions, many of which have competing interests, but this need not overshadow the equally undeniable facts that China has continually improved its military and diplomatic position over the past few decades, and that such improvements are rarely the result of pure good luck.

China's leaders have certainly attempted to develop institutions that will allow them to conduct sound foreign policy on a systematic and consistent basis. The Cultural Revolution set back Beijing's efforts to establish smoothly functioning government agencies. Nevertheless, throughout the 1980s, the Chinese worked to promote professionalism and coordination in their growing foreign-affairs bureaucracies.[22] Although the PRC continued to face difficulties, Western scholars noted that even the most developed countries experienced many of the same problems.[23] China's foreign-policy bureaucracy is not perfect, but it appears to be competent.

One must indeed keep in mind that there is no uniform Chinese point of view on many issues, and that there are passionate disagreements within China's government.[24] This, however, need not mean that the Beijing regime cannot make decisions when necessary, or that these decisions will not support broader national goals. Chinese communists have traditionally seen properly channelled debate, not as an obstacle to policymaking, but as a way of improving it.[25] The democratic system of government is deliberately designed to give as many people as possible a chance to express their point of view, and although this may have hampered democracies in certain periods, the overall history of Western countries in their struggles with Nazi Germany and the Soviet Union indicates that it is not necessarily a fatal handicap.

Those who question the coherence of China's foreign policy point to the fact that the PRC oscillated between alignment with the United States and the Soviet Union during the Cold War.[26] This, however, does not necessarily indicate inconsistency – it implies only that Beijing's foreign policy goals were not myopically ideological. Mao Zedong formed a temporary alliance with his opponent Chiang Kai-Shek during the Chinese Civil War, and exhorted his followers to forge similar united fronts with outsiders whenever such unions proved expedient, discarding them the moment they lost their utility.[27] During the Cold War, China's shifting alliances helped it to protect itself from invasion, attract aid from abroad, and resolve two Asian wars to its liking. When viewed in this light, Beijing's policies were consistent, successful and clearly defined.

One cannot know another's state of mind, but it appears indubitable that China's leaders have the kind of understandings that would both inspire and enable them to practice grand strategy. They have certainly received a lifelong education in such principles. The Sinologist Alistair Johnston argues that strategic thinking is integral to Chinese culture. In Johnston's eyes, China's traditional approach to statecraft 'predisposes those socialized in it to act more coercively against an enemy as relative capabilities become more favorable'.[28]

Not only does Chinese tradition encourage leaders to use violence, it encourages them to use it intelligently. From the Spring and Autumn Period onward, Chinese literature has featured numerous classics on war and statecraft, of which Sun Tzu's well-known work is only the most popularized.[29] These works teach a variety of methods, but all are based on the premise that there is a knowable art of war, and that those who master it enjoy a great advantage over those who do not. Many of these works specifically address the issue of long-term grand strategy involving economics, espionage, diplomacy, and political subversion. Sun Tzu, among others, argues that this upper level of statecraft is more significant than purely military maneuvering.[30]

China's traditional historical accounts support a similar attitude toward war and politics. The Chinese have always been impressed, for instance, by the way the country of Ch'in systematically overcame the other kingdoms of the Warring States Period, and eventually united China into a single empire. Ch'in's conquest involved centuries of deliberate action. From the Warring States Period onward, Chinese thinkers have studied the political maxims that allowed Ch'in to realize its strategic vision, most of which bear great similarity to what Clausewitz might have called 'general principles and attitudes'. Ch'in's approach to statecraft remains a topic of great interest in contemporary China.[31]

Johnston points out that 'within the China field there seems to be little controversy about the proposition that "deep" history and culture are critical sources of strategic behavior'.[32] In other words, Sinologists agree that the Chinese take their traditions seriously. One can safely assume that Chinese leaders will act on the basis of their cultural beliefs. Certainly, contemporary Chinese leaders read the classic works on strategy and claim to take them seriously – more seriously than they take contemporary Western works on international relations.[33] Clausewitz is also popular among the Chinese elite, and it seems reasonable to conclude that his ideas influence them as well.[34]

Mao Zedong not only relied on the classics, but rearticulated their assumptions about the importance of grand strategy. 'Conscious activity is man's characteristic', Mao wrote. 'This characteristic is most strongly manifested in man at war.'[35] Mao emphasized the importance of planning throughout every aspect of military operations, and he suggested that plans are particularly important at the grand strategic level.[36] As a communist, Mao was acutely aware of the concept that economic and social factors play a critical role in statecraft as well.[37]

These concepts of strategy persist in early twenty-first-century China. Although Chinese strategists have updated Mao's ideas over time, they acknowledge his work as the foundation of their own.[38] Some tributes to Mao may have more to do with political conformity than actual intellectual influence, nevertheless, there is a clear line of development from Mao's thought to the Chinese strategic writings of the 1990s.[39]

Like Mao himself, more recent Chinese leaders have conceived of statecraft in terms of cunning, long-term strategy. 'Tao guang yang hui', Mao's successor Deng Xiaoping advised his compatriots. Let us 'conceal our abilities and bide our time'.[40] Such attitudes appear likely to guide Chinese policy for the indefinite future. Indeed, continuity and respect for traditional approaches are themselves key parts of China's strategic culture. Certainly, older generations of Chinese leaders make a conscious effort to choose successors who share their approach to strategic affairs.[41]

These facts, combined with the PRC's continued successes, led many observers to reconsider doubts about Beijing's strategic competence. In the mid-1990s, the international relations scholar Thomas J. Christensen published work which showed that the PRC had historically practiced a grand strategy which corresponded to formal models of rational behavior.[42] At the close of the twentieth century, the RAND Corporation released reports drawing upon the expertise of impeccably credentialed China scholars which argued that the PRC was engaged in an ambitious grand strategy and that the West would have to respond accordingly.[43]

The RAND reports concur with Johnston's opinion that the Chinese will use force intelligently, to whatever degree they are able. Michael D. Swaine and Ashley J. Tellis, writing in one report, characterize the PRC's current approach as a 'calculative' strategy. These authors believe that China has reached a point at which it will be difficult for it to 'replicate its traditional goal of controlling or at very least pacifying new periphery regions beyond the expanded heartland', particularly without economic development.[44] For these reasons, they suggest, the Chinese have chosen to avoid international confrontations and focus on building up their economy.

> The notion of calculative strategy is defined in *substantive* terms as a pragmatic approach that emphasizes the primacy of internal economic growth and stability, the nurturing of amicable international relations, the relative restraint in the use of force combined with increasing efforts to create a more modern military, and the continued search for asymmetric gains internationally. The reasons for this new strategy are ultimately rooted in the fact that China today requires high levels of undistracted growth in economic and technological terms, and hence significant geopolitical quiescence, to both ensure domestic order and well-

being and to effectively protect its security interests along the periphery and beyond.[45]

These authors go on to note:

> The ascent to power [through economic means] thus comes at the cost of limitations on Beijing's freedom of action and although it appears that this is a price China is by and large willing to pay, at least in the near term, it only makes the question of what Beijing's long-term directions would be – that is, the directions that can be pursued once the constraints relating to external dependency in the near term diminish – even more interesting.[46]

Even in the short term, however, these authors anticipate that China will attempt to offset its growing dependency on trading partners by gaining strategic leverage over them. In the longer term, Swaine and Tellis believe that China will move toward an 'assertive' strategy, using force to achieve 'geopolitical pre-eminence on a global scale'.[47] Other RAND studies present similar arguments and again emphasize that China has significant differences both with specific nations and with the existing international system, which it will wish to redress as soon as it can.[48] If one accepts any part of these propositions, one becomes acutely interested in the question of when China is likely to shift toward openly aggressive policies.[49]

Swaine and Tellis acknowledge that '[t]he key to assessing the natural longevity of the calculative strategy lies in examining more closely why the strategy was devised to begin with'.[50] A close examination has other advantages as well. Since, as the RAND authors noted, China's shift to an overall strategy of assertiveness may not be clear-cut even in retrospect, one needs to be able to assess the significance of the PRC's more tangible actions.[51] One needs to be able to apply one's general understandings to the specific activities that make up political and strategic intercourse on a day-to-day basis. The devil, as the saying goes, is in the details.

A close study of China's strategy also helps outsiders decide how 'assertive' their own policies must be. Although China and the Western nations have sharp differences of opinion, they need not be mortal enemies on every issue. Most commentators agree that the commonly presented alternatives of 'engaging' China with economic cooperation and 'containing' China with force are both inadequate.[52] The more Western observers understand about the details of China's strategy, the easier it will be for them to discriminate between cases in which their countries can accommodate the PRC's aspirations fruitfully and cases in which any compromise would be foolhardy.

Studying China's approach to strategy, increases our ability to see how current events fit into unfolding patterns. This helps to avoid both the temptation to overestimate Beijing's present capabilities and to underestimate Beijing's ability to exploit the capabilities it actually has. Such enquiries also help in shaping a long-term strategy for one's own nation. Western countries must develop such a strategy to avoid the risk that China will eat away the existing world order 'as the silkworms devour mulberry leaves', which is to say, slowly, silently and one bite at a time.

Furthermore, close knowledge is interesting from an academic standpoint. By studying the details of how the PRC's statecraft works, one learns more about China and more about the art of strategy. Beijing has made great progress in developing its economy and increasing its political influence. Many of its methods may work equally well in other cases, even for those whose ideas of happy political life and acceptable international conduct are less Machiavellian. Other nations may have much to learn from China.

Although the RAND reports acknowledge the importance of close study, they address broad questions and provide a correspondingly broad analysis. One of these reports touches upon the significance of China's military development for the US Air Force, but neither look at the details of how the PRC might develop its military means to support its national ends, and neither devotes specific attention to China's fleet. These studies also tend to rely on the abstract propositions of Neo-Realist international relations theorists rather than actual Chinese ideas or actual Chinese actions. This book advances their work by examining the specifics of China's attempts to become a seapower, with an emphasis on the art of strategy and in as much detail as the sources allow.

STRUCTURE OF THE BOOK

Having explored basic concepts in Chapter 1, this book goes on to explore China's maritime strategy as follows. Chapter 2 discusses the history of Chinese seapower. This indicates the origins of contemporary events, suggests what China's geographical and cultural position may allow, and summarizes incidents which the Chinese themselves may find instructive. The fact that the Chinese traditionally pay close attention to historical examples makes a historical study particularly rewarding.

Chapter 3 considers what the ideas of dominant Western naval theorists imply for China's future as a seapower. If one accepts the idea that there are objective principles in strategy, one can conclude that these principles of seapower apply as much to China as to any other place. Therefore, these theories indicate the sort of problems the PRC will face and the range of solutions the PRC will have to consider, whether or not the strategists in Beijing base their work on this particular set of writers. Recent history tends to confirm these theorists' statements.

Chapter 4 looks at how recent Chinese leaders have perceived their strategic situation, and how this has led them to seek maritime power. Chapter 5 discusses Chinese naval thinking in greater detail, and goes on to describe how the PRC has put its maritime doctrine into practice. Chapter 6 shows how the military side of China's naval strategy fits into Beijing's larger diplomatic initiatives. A concluding chapter summarizes main findings and notes points of particular interest to Westerners interested in crafting a prudent response.

NOTES

1. R.P. Khanua, 'Impact of China's Ambition To Be a Regional Superpower', *Asian Defence Journal*, Vol. 6, No. 9 (Aug. 1999), p. 9.
2. Anon., 'Full Text of China–Iran Joint Communique', *BBC Summary of World Broadcasts*, FE/3876 (26 June 2000), p. G/1.
3. Gerald Segal, 'Does China Matter?', *Foreign Affairs*, Vol. 78, No. 5 (Sept.–Oct. 1999), p. 31.
4. For a discussion of the importance of seapower in the modern world, see Colin S. Gray, *The Leverage of Seapower: The Strategic Advantage of Navies in War* (New York: Free Press, 1992), *passim*.
5. Tseng Hui-Yeh, 'Shandong Faction Reportedly Controls Military', *FBIS-CHI-94-204* (21 Oct. 1994), p. 34.
6. Segal, 'Does China Matter', p. 31.
7. Carl von Clausewitz, *On War*, trans. and ed. Michael Howard and Peter Paret (Princeton, NJ: Princeton University Press, 1976), p. 128.
8. Plato, *Plato's Statesman*, trans. J.B. Skemp (London: Routledge & Kegan Paul, 1952), p. 763.
9. Susan P. Mattern, *Rome and the Enemy: Imperial Strategy in the Principate* (Berkeley, CA: University of California Press, 1999), *passim*; Edward N. Luttwak, *The Grand Strategy of the Roman Empire* (Baltimore, MD: Johns Hopkins University Press, 1976), *passim*.
10. Alfred Thayer Mahan, *The Influence of Seapower Upon History, 1660–1783* (Boston, MA: S.J. Parkhill, 1890), p. 70.
11. Dennis E. Shoalwater, *The Wars of Frederick the Great* (Harlow: Longman, 1996), pp. 3–4.
12. Hajo Holborn, 'The Prusso-German School: Moltke and the Rise of the General Staff', in Peter Paret (ed.), *Makers of Modern Strategy from Machiavelli to the Nuclear Age* (Princeton, NJ: Princeton University Press, 1986), p. 289.
13. Clausewitz, *On War*, p. 108.
14. Ibid.
15. Ibid., p. 112.
16. Harold W. Rood, *Kingdoms of the Blind* (Durham, NC: Carolina Academic Press, 1980), p. 22.
17. For a discussion of these concepts, see Deborah A. Stone, *Policy Paradox and Political Reason* (New York: HarperCollins, 1988), *passim*.
18. Mahan, *The Influence of Seapower*, p. 13.
19. John L. Gaddis, 'International Relations Theory and the End of the Cold War',

International Security, Vol. 17, No. 3 (Winter 1992–93), pp. 5–58; John L. Gaddis and Ted Hopf, 'Getting the End of the Cold War Wrong', *International Security*, Vol. 18, No. 2 (Fall 1993), pp. 202–10.

20. David Shambaugh, 'China's Security Strategy in the Post-Cold War Era', *Survival*, Vol. 34, No. 2 (Summer 1992), p. 132; Gerald Segal, 'East Asia and the "Constrainment" of China', *International Security*, Vol. 20, No. 4 (Spring 1996), p. 132.

21. Shambaugh, 'China's Security Strategy', p. 132; Segal, 'East Asia and the "Constrainment" of China', p. 132.

22. A. Doak Barnett, *The Making of Foreign Policy in China: Structure and Process* (London: I.B. Tauris, 1985), pp. 2–3.

23. Ibid., p. 4.

24. Michael Pillsbury, 'PLA Capabilities in the 21st Century: How Does China Assess its Future Security Needs?', in Larry M. Wortzel (ed.), *The Chinese Armed Forces in the 21st Century* (Carlisle, PA: Strategic Studies Institute, 1999), p. 92.

25. Murray Scot Tanner, 'The Erosion of Communist Party Control Over Lawmaking In China', *China Quarterly*, No. 138 (June 1994), p. 386.

26. Shambaugh, 'China's Security Strategy', p. 132; Segal, 'East Asia and the "Constrainment" of China', p. 132.

27. Mao Zedong, *Selected Works of Mao Tse-Tung, Volume Two* (London: Lawrence & Wishart, 1954), pp. 218–22.

28. Alastair Ian Johnston, *Cultural Realism: Strategic Culture and Grand Strategy in Chinese History* (Princeton, NJ: Princeton University Press, 1995), p. x.

29. For a discussion of ancient Chinese strategic writings, see Ralph D. Sawyer, *One Hundred Unorthodox Strategies: Battle and Tactics of Chinese Warfare* (Boulder, CO: Westview Press, 1996), *passim*.

30. Sun Tzu, *Sun Tzu's Art of War*, trans. Yuan Shibing, commentary Tao Hanzhang (New York: Sterling, 1987), pp. 80–90.

31. Adda B. Bozeman, *Strategic Intelligence & Statecraft* (Washington, DC: Brassey's (US): 1992), p. 71.

32. Johnston, *Cultural Realism*, p. 22.

33. Bozeman, *Strategic Intelligence*, p. 71.

34. Paul H.B. Godwin, 'Chinese Concepts of Doctrine, Strategy and Operations in the Chinese People's Liberation Army 1978–87', *China Quarterly*, No. 112 (Dec. 1987), p. 573.

35. Mao, *Selected Works*, p. 156.

36. Ibid., p. 176.

37. Ibid., pp. 124–5.

38. Peng Guangqian, 'Deng Xiaoping's Strategic Thought', in Michael Pillsbury (ed.), *Chinese Views of Future Warfare* (Washington, DC: National Defense University Press, 1998), p. 3.

39. Shen Kuiguan, 'Dialectics of Defeating the Superior with the Inferior', in Michael Pillsbury (ed.), *Chinese Views of Future Warfare*, pp. 213–20.

40. Pillsbury, 'PLA Capabilities', p. 90.

41. Li Cheng, 'Jiang Zemin's Successors: The Rise of the Fourth Generation of Leaders in the PRC', *China Quarterly*, No. 161 (Mar. 2000), p. 1.

42. Thomas J. Christensen, *Useful Adversaries: Grand Strategy, Domestic Mobilization and Sino-American Conflict, 1947–1958* (Princeton, NJ: Princeton University Press, 1996), *passim*.

43. Michael D. Swaine and Ashley J. Tellis, *Interpreting China's Grand Strategy: Past, Present and Future* (Santa Monica, CA: RAND, 2000), *passim*; Zalmay M. Khalizad, Abram N. Shulsky, Daniel L. Byman, Roger Cliff, David T. Orletsky, David Shlapak, and Ashley J. Tellis, *The United States and a Rising China:*

13

Strategic and Military Implications (Santa Monica, CA: RAND, 1999), *passim*.
44. Swaine and Tellis, *Interpreting China's Grand Strategy*, pp. 6, 101–6.
45. Ibid., pp. 97–8.
46. Ibid., pp. 104–5.
47. Ibid., pp. 104, 201–2.
48. Zalmay, *The United States and a Rising China*, pp. 1–32.
49. Swaine, *Cultural Realism*, p. 152; Zalmay, *The United States and a Rising China*, p. 3.
50. Swaine, Cultural Realism, p. 152.
51. Zalmay, *The United States and a Rising China*, p. 3.
52. Ibid., p. 72.

2

The History of Chinese Seapower

Throughout history, China has possessed timber reserves, navigable rivers, secure harbors, and several thousand miles of heavily populated coastline. Thus, for as long as there has been a Chinese state, that state has had the potential to be a great power at sea. Some of China's rulers have realized that potential, while others have knowingly refused to do so. In every era, however, Chinese leaders have understood that the oceans were vital to their national aims and have developed sophisticated – if occasionally misguided – policies to reflect that awareness.

The following chapter narrates the naval history of China from ancient times to the twentieth century. This account helps us identify enduring cultural, economic and geographical influences which will continue to shape China's maritime policy in the future. Not only does this narrative provide us with a foundation of facts to support the more general propositions about Chinese seapower in Chapter 3, it helps us understand those propositions more fully. When we look at the details of how factors such as culture, economics and geography have affected state policy in earlier eras, we gain a clearer sense of how they might affect it in our own.

This chapter is not a comprehensive history of China, but a summary which focuses on the question of how Chinese statesmen in different periods have viewed the role of navigation in state policy. For this reason, not only does it gloss over events upon the land, but it omits many of China's most important technical innovations in navigation, naval tactics, naval weaponry and nautical engineering. However, it includes these details where they reveal turning points in Chinese thought and the scale of China's maritime enterprises. The chapter focuses on the overall policies China has implemented and the factors which caused Chinese leaders to adopt them.

FIRST CHINESE FLEETS

Chinese civilization emerged on the inland plains around the Yellow River. This body of water is not well suited for navigation, but the prehistoric Chinese invented a variety of rafts and swimming-floats for crossing it. People in coastal regions gradually developed these craft into ships, and, in the process, came up with a number of design innovations, notably watertight bulkheads and battened sails, which made their vessels safer and more maneuverable than those available in the West at that time. Nevertheless, there is little archeological evidence that the Chinese engaged in long-range seafaring in this era, and Chinese texts say little about navies or maritime commerce for the first two millennia of China's existence.[1]

For the rulers of China's Hsia, Shang and Chou Dynasties (prehistory to 800 BC), the sea had relatively little to offer. The Chinese ideal of government featured a centralized state modeled on the family, in which a benevolent emperor managed the country for the collective good of its inhabitants, with the aid of expert advisors. The Chou emperors modified this system by dividing their territory into numerous small fiefdoms, each administered by a nobleman, who, in turn, owed allegiance to the ruler. Nevertheless, the basic ideals of government remained unchanged.

During this era, economic prosperity was mainly a matter of grain production. China's rulers saw their chief economic problem as being that of irrigating fields and regulating the flow of streams in order to maximize the fertility of the land. Long-range trade involved only luxury products such as pearls and jade, and many condemned such indulgences as a waste of society's resources.[2] Emperors mobilized armies of conscript workers to build levees and canals, but although these projects required great feats of organization and engineering, they did not create a national requirement for foreign trade, nor did they foster the spirit of independence and personal initiative which leads private individuals to seek their fortune at sea.

Armies during this period were relatively small, and had correspondingly small logistical requirements. The aristocratic warriors who led these forces prided themselves more on their personal chivalry than on their ability to exploit strategic opportunities. A passage from the annals of the period describes how, when the nobleman Hua Pao shot his bow at an enemy charioteer and missed, his opponent reminded him that it would be cowardly not to take turns.[3] Hua Pao had already fitted another arrow to his string, but he accepted the admonition and did not fire. His opponent, who apparently was a better marksman, shot him dead.

Owing to the relatively small size of armies, military commanders in this era seldom needed to carry supplies by sea and were not inclined to use amphibious operations in order to gain advantages in position. The fact that China's coastline is mainly convex ensured that the shortest routes between rival Chinese fiefdoms would almost always be overland rather than over the water. It is not surprising, therefore, to learn that Chinese commanders tended to use ox carts, not ships, for transportation.[4]

The ancient Chinese had legends about a race of immortals who dwelled in islands to the east, but they had no regular contact with overseas civilizations, nor were they particularly inclined to seek it.[5] The traditions of China's dominant Han ethnic group encouraged people to view foreigners with suspicion. The Chou Dynasty word for the peoples who lived northeast of China, *ch'uan-jung* ('barbarian dogs') captures the way the Chinese felt about outsiders. China's leaders in this period had neither military, economic or scientific reasons to devote resources to navigation.

Between 800 BC and 400 BC, all of the circumstances which had prevented China from becoming a seapower changed. During this era, known as the Spring and Autumn Period, China went through a combination of agricultural, metallurgical, economic, cultural, intellectual, political and military transformations. The trend toward change became apparent in 771 BC, when the reigning emperor of the Chou Dynasty humiliated his wife by paying undue attention to a concubine. The emperor's wife's relatives joined forces with the horse nomads of the northwest to attack the imperial capital. Another prominent nobleman intervened to save the crown prince, but, from then on, the Chou emperors depended on powerful vassals to protect them from other feudal lords. As the position of emperor dwindled to a merely symbolic role, the lords of the feudal fiefdoms declared themselves to be rulers of independent states and went on to fight incessant wars with each other.

Meanwhile, Chinese metalworkers learned how to smelt iron. Previously, ordinary people had made most of their tools from wood and stone, but the new metal was cheap enough for general use. Iron ploughs allowed farmers to work more land more efficiently, and maximized the benefits of other new agricultural techniques, such as the use of manure for fertilizer and improved systems of crop rotation. As agriculture became more productive, it became possible for a smaller number of farmers to feed a larger number of people. The population of China increased dramatically during this period, and this provided manpower for new kinds of economic enterprise and for new kinds of warfare.[6]

Trade sprang up, not only in luxuries, but in such necessities as salt, cloth, wood, hides, metal goods and grain. This led to an explosion in finance, as both rulers and merchants minted coins to facilitate commerce. The monetary economy allowed people to save or borrow capital and then use that wealth to set up enterprises of unprecedented size and complexity. Entrepreneurs built business empires which incorporated mines, workshops, market stalls, wagon caravans and fleets of ships. Rulers formed alliances with businessmen in order to finance state projects, so that the lines between business and government began to blur.

Meanwhile, the Chinese became more open to other cultures. The growing class of merchants had an obvious interest in finding new markets and new sources of valuable goods. This was the period when Chinese silk first reached India.[7] Traders did business with peoples in Korea, Manchuria and Siberia, often by sea.[8]

The Chinese also began to borrow foreign inventions, even when they violated traditional sensibilities. In one notorious incident, military commanders in the state of Chao replaced chariot forces with mounted cavalry, despite the fact that the new method of fighting required soldiers to abandon traditional clothing and adopt the barbarian practice of wearing pants.[9] On a more grisly note, the rulers of certain Chinese principalities took up the nomadic practice of making cups out of the skulls of their defeated enemies.[10]

The Han people never abandoned their prejudice against other ethnic groups, but they found themselves forced to accept neighboring kingdoms as part of their social and political world. This had important consequences for the development of Chinese seapower, because several of these states had long coastlines, strong traditions of seafaring, and disputes with maritime rivals. The most significant of these states was the southern kingdom of Ch'u, which controlled most of the Yangtze delta, along with much of the river itself. By the late 600s Ch'u had started to participate in the struggles between China's warring principalities. In 606 BC, the Chou emperor, who still retained a great deal of moral authority, honored Ch'u by calling on its king to defend all of China against an invasion of nomadic horsemen from the north. After this, it was difficult for anyone to deny that Ch'u was a part of China.

The Chinese way of war changed during this period as well. As the lords of the contending kingdoms struggled to 'roll up all-under-heaven like a mat and tie the four seas in a bag', they became increasingly pragmatic. This is the era in which Sun Tzu wrote his *Art of War*, and those who are familiar with this work will recall that it emphasizes, not gallantry, but rational planning, flexible methods and efficient use of resources. New weapons, notably the crossbow, led to changes in tactics, and the new economy allowed rulers to build armies and fortifications on a previously unimaginable scale.

Conditions were ripe for Chinese rulers to start developing navies. The growth of trade had made sea travel more important economically, the opening to foreign innovations had made it more acceptable culturally, the incorporation of Ch'u had brought ports and seafaring peoples into China, economic growth had given both rulers and private individuals the resources they needed to build fleets, and the changes in

18

warfare had produced military commanders who were capable of appreciating the strategic advantages of seapower. If these factors were not enough, this happened to be a period in which outside peoples made the Chinese forcibly aware of the value of amphibious tactics. There was a primitive kingdom on the southern side of the Yangtze delta called Wu. Between 600 BC and 500 BC, the warriors of Wu began to attack the Ch'u coastline using seagoing canoes.

These raids wreaked havoc. Ch'u's army took to the water in similar craft to fend off the invasions, leading both sides to develop more advanced vessels and more effective tactics for maritime warfare. By 486 BC, Wu's forces were deploying purpose-built warships with deck castles for use by archers. Meanwhile, the Chinese noted the fact that yet another barbarian potentate of the south, the king of Yueh, placed great store by his fleet of 300 'halberd-boats', which carried a force of 8,000 marines. Modern historians believe that the halberd boats were probably large sailing-rafts. The king of Yueh also had another 3,000 marines, who traveled in more conventional decked warships.[11]

By 400 BC, the Spring and Autumn era gave way to the age known as the Warring States Period. The seven most successful Chinese principalities developed into large and well-organized countries, which continued to struggle for supremacy. China's burgeoning armies began to carry supplies by water. The seven kingdoms also maintained navies and continued to develop more effective military vessels. Records from the Han empire (206 BC to AD 220) indicate that Warring States' navies included sailing vessels of up to 120 feet in length, although modern scholars believe that figures of 50 feet and 70 feet are more likely.[12]

Over a 200-year period, the kingdom of Ch'in wore down its opponents and conquered them one by one. Ch'in's greatest strengths were the organizational skills of its administrators and the ruthlessly utilitarian political philosophy of its rulers, which allowed it to harness China's demographic, technological and economic revolutions for the sole purpose of achieving military power. Although Ch'in itself was landlocked, its rulers understood the importance of water transportation. When they acquired the means to do so, they incorporated fleets into their repertoire of military tools.

Ch'u's vast size, large population and economic vigor made it one of Ch'in's most difficult conquests. In 312 BC, Ch'in began a series of campaigns to weaken its southern opponent. One of Ch'in's famous administrators, a man named Chang I, recognized that the easiest way to move large forces into Ch'u was by river and assembled an invasion fleet which reputedly consisted of 100,000 double-hulled boats, each of which carried 50 armed men. Chang I supported this force with a further 10,000 transport vessels, each of which carried approximately 16 tons of grain.[13] Although the numbers of boats and troops are almost certainly exaggerated, they still indicate the scale of Ch'in's amphibious operations.

In 221 BC, Ch'in conquered the last of its opponents and united China into a new empire. This realm was more than a successor to the Chou Dynasty – it covered far more territory and included far more people from many more ethnic backgrounds than any state that East Asia had ever seen. The new emperor, Shih-Huang-ti, crushed the remnants of the feudal nobility and introduced a centralized bureaucracy, which allowed him to mobilize the human and material resources of the entire empire in much the same way that Ch'in's rulers had always exploited their own state. These policies allowed him to carry out public works, which included building a network of roads which spanned the empire, and constructing the first Great Wall. When a clique of scholars protested against the new government's cruelty and lack of respect for tradition, the emperor had them buried alive and issued a decree ordering officials to burn all the privately owned books in China, excepting only those containing knowledge deemed useful to the state.

Ch'in continued to use amphibious tactics to expand its realm in the south. In 219 BC, for instance, imperial troops invaded Yueh in a fleet of 'war boats with deck castles'.[14] The Ch'in Empire established outposts along the East Asian coast as far south as Hanoi.[15] Furthermore, the emperor was obsessed by the fear of death, and sent explorers into the Pacific Ocean to search for herbs which would allow him to live for ever. The following anecdote from the works of the Han Dynasty historian Ssu Ma-Chien indicates the number of ships and people involved in these ventures.

> Ch'in Shih Huang Ti also sent out [the explorer] Hsu Fu to search for magical beings and strange things. [When Hsu Fu returned having failed to find anything worthwhile,] he invented excuses, saying: '[On an island] in the midst of the ocean, I met a great Mage who said to me 'are you an envoy of the Emperor of the West?,' to which I replied that I was. 'What have you come for?' said he, and I answered that I sought for those drugs which lengthen life and promote longevity [yen nien i shou yao]. 'The offerings of your Ch'in king,' he said, 'are but poor; you may see these drugs but you may not take them away'. Then going south-east we came to Pheng-Lai, and I saw the gates of the Chih-Chheng Palace, in front whereof there was a guardian of brazen hue and dragon form lighting the skies with his radiance. In this place I did obeisance to the Sea Mage twice, and asked him what offerings we should present to him. 'Bring me young men,' he said, 'of good birth and breeding, together with apt virgins, and workmen of all the trades; then you will get your drugs'. Ch'in Shih Huang Ti, very pleased, set three

thousand young men and girls at Hsu Fu's disposal, gave him [ample supplies of] the seeds of the five grains, and artisans of every sort, after which [his fleet again] set sail. Hsu Fu [must have] found some calm and fertile plain, with broad forests and rich marshes, where he made himself king – at any rate, he never came back to China.[16]

The historian goes on to suggest that Hsu Fu founded a colony in Japan. There is, in fact, a tomb shrine in the explorer's honor at Shingfu, on Japan's southern coast. The fact that Ssu Ma-Chien's histories circulated freely in Japan, however, casts doubt on the authenticity of this site. More recent writers speculate that some of Shih-Huang-ti's explorers reached the Americas.[17]

SECURING FOREIGN TRADE

The Ch'in Empire alienated its subjects through its harsh laws and its rejection of traditional political ideals. When Shih Huang-Ti died in 210 BC, intrigues broke out in the imperial court and an assortment of rebels took advantage of the central government's weakness to stage uprisings throughout the country. After eight years of civil war, a peasant leader named Liu Pang defeated his various rivals and established himself as the emperor of a new dynasty, the Han. The new rulers tended to be more moderate, more traditional and more popular than Shih-Huang-ti, but they governed the same territory which Ch'in had united, and they had a similar state bureaucracy at their disposal.

Trade flourished in the early Han Dynasty. This was as much a political phenomenon as an economic one, since the imperial government conducted much of this business itself and used commerce as a tool, not only for acquiring wealth, but for establishing desirable relations with neighboring peoples. Chinese emperors demanded 'tribute' from foreign rulers, thus asserting their authority, but gave those rulers 'gifts' of equal or even greater value in return; thus, they hoped, winning goodwill through their magnanimity and encouraging so-called barbarian rulers to become dependent upon their largesse. These exchanges were not merely symbolic – by AD 91, the empire was spending between 30 per cent and 40 per cent of its annual revenue on gifts.[18] The nomadic horsemen known in Europe as the Huns and in China as the Hsiung-nu stepped up their raids during this period, making it all the more important for the Han rulers to maintain allies and buy friendship from potential enemies.

As commerce became increasingly vital and the threat of Hsiung-nu banditry grew greater, the Han emperors resolved to protect their trade. This led the Chinese to explore the trails and sea lanes by which their goods reached distant markets, and then to establish outposts at points which dominated those routes.[19] In the process, the Chinese learned a great deal about the world around them, and became even more deeply involved in external affairs. In the northwest, the Han emperors ended up mounting a series of campaigns which took them to the borders of Persia, but their expansion in the oceans to their southeast was no less dramatic.

The Chinese became newly conscious of the fact that their trade routes extended to Java, Borneo, Cambodia, Ceylon (Sri Lanka) and India. Simultaneous explosions of seafaring and trade in India, Persia and the Middle East made commerce across the Indian Ocean more valuable than ever before. Meanwhile, the Chinese had been moving into the fertile regions of the south for some time. These factors led the Han Dynasty to settle much of what has become Southern China and establish colonies throughout northern Vietnam. Chinese troops built strategic ports in places such as Guangdong, the peninsula of Lei-chou in modern Kwangtung and on the Gulf of Tonkin.[20] These campaigns forced the Han Dynasty to transport armies hundreds of miles by sea, and to fight battles upon the water.

The Chinese began to build vessels with two and more decks, in order to gain the advantage of height in ship-to-ship combat. Han Dynasty warships also used catapults and rams in naval battles. Meanwhile, China's rulers came to recognize navies as an independent military instrument, and not merely an adjunct to land forces. Han Dynasty rulers began to award naval commanders titles such as Lou Chhuan Chiang-Chun (Commander of the Embattled Ships), Fu Po Chiang-Chun (Wave-Subduing Commander) and Ku Chhuan Chiang-Chun (Fighting-Ship Commander), thus acknowledging the distinctive nature of war at sea.[21]

China's drive to control the Indian Ocean trade routes involved land campaigns as well as amphibious operations. During a journey which lasted from 139 to 126 BC, the explorer Chang Ch'ien discovered Indian goods in Bactriana. From this, he determined that there was a road which led from India to Central Asia through Burma. When Chang Ch'ien informed the Han government of this fact, it promptly seized territory in the west in order to dominate those routes.[22]

POWER POLITICS AT SEA

Palace intrigues, widespread poverty and seditious religious cults weakened the Han Dynasty until it collapsed completely in AD 220. In AD 221–222, the empire split into three rival kingdoms, the northern state of Wei and the southern realms of Wu and Shu. The Yangtze River cut through the borderlands which separated these states, and the southern kingdoms preserved their independence primarily through their control of the river.[22] Although the key battles among the three kingdoms took place well inland, engagements between fleets of riverboats played a critical role in the fighting.

The kingdom of Wu, which incorporated most of the southern Chinese coast, continued the Han Dynasty policy of colonizing strategic points along trade routes by seizing outposts in Formosa (Taiwan) and Hainan. Wu also sent a diplomatic mission to the kingdom of Funan, in modern Cambodia, knowing that this state was a center of trade for merchants from as far away as Arabia.[24] As maritime trade became increasingly important, Indian ideas, notably Buddhism, spread throughout southern China. This influx of foreign beliefs served to widen the cultural rifts between China's different regions.

Meanwhile, the kingdoms of Wei and Wu sought to outflank each other in the Pacific. Wu seized the island of Quelpaert, off the southern coast of Korea, while Wei re-established a number of Han Dynasty outposts on the Korean mainland. Wu also sent fleets around Korea to Manchuria so that its troops could join forces with nomads hostile to Wei. The largest of these armadas reputedly consisted of 100 ships and carried 8,000 men.[25]

These ventures drew Japan into China's conflicts. Chinese documents from the period contain the first known descriptions of the sea routes from Korea to Japan via the Tsushima and Iki islands. Archeologists have found evidence that Wei traded extensively with the Japanese. By the fifth century, however, Japan had united with Wu's successor states in order to protect their allies in southwestern Korea from a coalition which included both north China and the powerful Korean kingdom of Koguryo.[26]

The rise and fall of the Sui and Tang Dynasties dominated Chinese history from the sixth to the eleventh centuries. Invasions from Central Asia played a critical role in Chinese politics, and, owing to geographic proximity, these incursions had their greatest effects in the north. Meanwhile, in the early seventh century, sailors from China discovered Africa. Chinese texts from AD 860 contain detailed descriptions of Berbera, a region on the Gulf of Aden.[27]

THE NEW GREAT WALL

By the eleventh century, China was a united empire again, under a dynasty known as the Sung. This was another period of rapid economic development in China and, like the Spring and Autumn era, it raised seafaring to new levels of importance in Chinese affairs. From the eighth century onward, new techniques of rice farming had allowed the people

23

of the Yangtze region to produce progressively greater harvests. In 1012, the Sung government imported a superior strain of rice called *hsien* from Champa (southern Vietnam) and systematically distributed it throughout China. *Hsien* ripened quickly, allowing farmers to reap two harvests per year, and grew in poor soil, allowing farmers to double the amount of land under cultivation.[28]

'When the harvest of Su(-chow) and Ch'ang(-chou) [is] ripe', went a saying from that period, 'the world is satiated.' The abundance of food freed people to work in the hemp, silk, cotton, porcelain, tea, lacquer, paper, copper, iron, tin and lead industries. Industrialists introduced explosives for mining, coal for fuel, and hydraulic equipment to operate bellows. Trade became more important than ever, and much of it traveled along the coast in ships.[29]

Raiders from Central Asia had plagued China since prehistoric times, but during the Sung Dynasty, these attacks acquired a new character. In the past, the nomadic raiders had often been content to pillage the settled regions and then depart, but from the tenth century onward they began to seize land on a permanent basis and to found territorial states.[30] Imperial China could not hold back these invasions. In 1125, after a major defeat, the Sung emperors moved their capital city from K'ai-feng, in the north to Hangchow, in the south, and began turning more and more of their energies toward the sea.

The tribal kingdoms blocked China's overland trade routes and occupied China's fertile northern plains. Refugees from tribal attacks moved into the south, and since there was no unclaimed land there for them to work, they poured into the growing chain of cities along the coast. Urbanization led to yet greater expansion in industry and commerce. These facts made seaborne trade with distant markets more vital to China's economy than ever, and China's rulers recognized this fact.[31]

China's merchants responded to this fresh demand for trade. Chinese ships were considerably larger and more seaworthy than those of any other nation trading in the Indian Ocean, and China's merchants secured a near-monopoly on the freight and passenger business.[32] In order to maintain this trade, the Chinese established colonies abroad. In Africa, for instance, Chinese merchants founded commercial enclaves where traders from throughout the Indian Ocean region could do business without interruption by political developments in their home countries.[33]

As trade grew more important, the importance of the monetary economy grew proportionally. Since overseas trade was a principal source of coinage, this raised government interest in maritime affairs to new levels. The state itself owned businesses which profited from access to overseas markets. 'The profits from maritime commerce are very great', observed the Sung emperor, Kao Tsung in 1145. 'If properly managed they can amount to millions of strings of cash. Is this not better than taxing the people?'[34] In practice, the Chinese government did both, and overseas trade accounted for approximately 20 per cent of its monetary revenue.[35]

The Hangchow emperors also understood the purely military uses of the sea. By 1131, supporters of China's navy commonly observed that the sea and the Yangtze River had become China's new Great Wall against the barbarians, and that ships were the new watchtowers. In 1161, a tribal state known as Jurchen actually attempted to cross this 'great wall' and invade Sung China by sea. The Chinese Navy destroyed the invasion fleet off Shantung.[36]

Against those who wished to raise armies and drive back the barbarians on land, the navalists countered that this policy would allow the tribal peoples to exploit their superior cavalry. In naval warfare, on the other hand, it was the Chinese who had the advantage. As one political pamphlet put it, 'to use our navy is to use our strong arm to strike at the enemy's weakness'.[37] The historian Jung-Pang Lo offers the following description of the Sung navy.

> The navy of Southern Sung had the distinction of being the first national navy to be established on a permanent basis and to function as an independent service. It was the first navy to be administered by a special agency of the government, the Imperial Commissioner's Office for the Control and Organization of the Coastal areas [Yen-hai chih-chih shih-ssu] which was established in 1132 with headquarters at Ting-hai, one of the islands in the Chusan group. The fleet steadily grew in strength. In 1130, there were eleven squadrons with three thousand men; in 1174, fifteen squadrons with twenty-one thousand men; and in 1237, the Southern Sung navy had grown to be an effective fighting force of twenty squadrons manned by nearly fifty-two thousand men. The largest base was at Hsu-p'u, which guarded the entrances to the Yangtze River and protected a flourishing port, soon to be known as Shanghai. Ting-hai, the second largest base, defended the capital, Hangchow.
>
> By the first half of the thirteenth century, the Sung navy ranged unchallenged over the East China Sea. As a member of the Privy Council [Shu-mi Yuan], Wu Ch'ien pointed out in a memorial, 'the area of control of our navy extends westward to Hsu-p'u, southward to Fukien, northward to Korea and eastward to Japan, an area of over ten thousand li. The navy is used for scouting, the navy is used for patrolling, and the navy is used for the defense of strategic points. . .
>
> But, [Wu Chien] went on, the navy was 'only strong enough to

check the Japanese and the Koreans,' and he and other ministers who shared his views urged the further expansion of the navy and its transformation into a weapon of offense. The adoption of a strong naval policy had been advocated by many Sung officials since 1129 when a bold scheme was conceived for the invasion of Korea by naval forces and the use of Korea as an advance base for seaborne attacks on the Chin empire. Others suggested the extension of Chinese naval power into the South China Sea. But, because of insufficient resources and preoccupation with border wars, the Sung court did not heed these proposals. It remained for the Mongols to take the next step of employing the navy as an instrument of aggression.[38]

The success of China's merchants contributed directly to the success of its navy. Not only did businessmen provide the government with funds and military supplies, they made ships and trained seamen available for the military; 338 merchantmen, for instance, took part in a war in 1161. Private artisans also came up with many of Sung China's most important pieces of naval technology, often spurred on by the promise of government rewards for useful inventions.[39]

THE MONGOLS ADOPT SEAPOWER

Between 1206 and 1279, the Mongols overran the tribal kingdoms in northern China and went on to conquer what remained of the Sung Empire itself. Despite their background as inland horsemen, these invaders saw the value of seapower and lost little time in acquiring a navy of their own. In 1268, Mongol generals considered launching an amphibious invasion to outflank China's defenses from the sea. Although the Mongols ultimately decided to attack by land instead, Sung ships managed to delay them in river battles. The Mongols used captured Chinese vessels, captured Chinese shipyards and captured Chinese personnel to deploy a fleet which went on to defeat the Sung navy in 1279.[40]

After conquering China, the Mongols used Chinese artisans to build ships at a rate which reached 4,000 per year in 1283.[41] Kublai Khan carried out similar programs of naval construction in Korea. These fleets allowed the Mongols to invade Japan twice, first with 23,000 men and later with 140,000 men.[42] Although these invasions failed, Kublai Khan successfully captured Champa and Tongking by sea, and went on to launch expeditions against Java. The Mongols also used ships to carry tribute, mostly grain, from their southern colonies to the north.[43] In 1329, the tribute fleet carried a record 247,000 tons of cargo.[44]

SEAPOWER REGAINED, SEAPOWER REJECTED

In 1368, Chinese patriots drove out the Mongols, overcame their internal rivals and founded the Ming Dynasty. The new Chinese government maintained active diplomatic relations with overseas kingdoms, resumed the Han Dynasty policy of seizing territory in Central Asia, and took measures to ensure that it would remain a naval power. Envoys from Korea, Japan, Vietnam and Champa came to Nanking in 1369, and representatives from Cambodia and Siam arrived the year after.[45] In 1391, the Chinese government had more than 50 million trees planted in the Nanking area, to provide timber for its future navies. Fourteen years later, the Ming rulers began to dispatch fleets of ships under the command of a eunuch named Cheng Ho to visit the maritime states of East Asia, East Africa, India, the Red Sea and the Persian Gulf.

Emperor Cheng Tsu initially sent Cheng Ho to sea to search for one of his political rivals, whom he feared had fled abroad to plot revenge. The eunuch took 62 ships on this voyage, along with 37,000 men. Although Cheng Ho found no trace of the fugitive, he proclaimed the virtue and majesty of his emperor wherever he went, and numerous foreign kings offered submission to China.[46] In Java, he intervened in a succession struggle between rival princes, and in Palembang (south-eastern Sumatra), he settled a dispute between the local government and Chinese colonists.

The Chinese government saw that Cheng Ho's voyage had increased its influence abroad, and sent him on six more such expeditions. In the course of his career, he erected steles (stone tablets) in Calicut, Cochin, Ceylon and Malacca, declaring that those kingdoms were vassal states of the Ming Empire.[47] In several instances, he overthrew and imprisoned foreign rulers in their own countries, the most notable being the king of Ceylon. Cheng Ho also brought back drugs, curiosities, exotic animals and large quantities of wealth to the Chinese court.[48]

One can measure the seapower of the early Ming dynasty more directly by looking at how the Chinese navy dealt with piracy. In the 1400s, Japanese pirates known as *wokou* began to raid China's coast and attack coastal shipping. The Ming government deployed fleets to patrol the Yangtze delta and established diplomatic contact with Japan. China's rulers made it clear that, if necessary, they would invade Japan and take control of the regions which the pirates used as havens.[49] These measures caused the Japanese government to suppress the *wokou* more assiduously, and effectively eliminated pirate activity for nearly a century.[50]

In the mid-1400s, however, China's bid for seapower fell victim to court politics. The Confucian scholars who ran China's bureaucracy were traditionally hostile to seafaring, both because Confucius himself had depicted merchants as social parasites and because the court eunuchs who controlled the fleet were their political rivals. In 1424, a scholar-official named Hsia Yuan-Chi urged Emperor Jen Tsung to cancel all missions to foreign countries and stop building sea-going ships. Jen Tsung died before he could act on this suggestion, and the next emperor dispatched Cheng Ho on yet another voyage, but this ruler died shortly thereafter as well, and his successors followed Hsia Yuan-Chi's advice. At some point between 1465 and 1487, other scholar-officials burned the reports which Cheng Ho had made after his voyages.[51]

Maritime trade declined in economic importance as well. China's currency collapsed during the mid-1400s, forcing Chinese merchants to pay for their goods in gold and silver. Officials who might once have seen trade as a valuable source of revenue began to perceive it as a dangerous drain on China's reserves of precious metals. The Ming Dynasty constructed a series of canals which made inland water transport cheaper and safer than coastal shipping.[52] Meanwhile, invasions from Central Asia distracted officials from maritime affairs.

China's foreign trade shriveled, its shipbuilding industry disintegrated and its navy fell apart. By 1474, only 140 of the fleet's original 400 warships were left. The anti-maritime faction grew continually stronger in court. Chinese officials feared allowing private merchants to gain excessive wealth, and they also deplored the influence of foreign cultural ideas within China. In 1525, the emperor ordered coastal officials to destroy all ships with more than one mast, and in 1555, the government declared that simply going to sea in such a ship was a crime equivalent to espionage.[53]

Within a few decades, the government relaxed these laws and began to license a limited amount of trade.[54] Nevertheless, China remained a country of landsmen. When the *wokou* re-appeared in the mid-1500s, the Chinese generally defended themselves with ground troops, after the raiders had landed. On occasions when the *wokou* vessels fought Chinese warships, the pirates normally won with little difficulty.[55]

In 1644, a people known as the Manchus overran Ming China with aid from a treacherous Chinese general, and established their own dynasty. Patriotic Chinese took to the sea, and fought back against the invaders with piracy and coastal raids. Survivors of the Ming royal house went so far as to grant one particularly successful raider, the half-Japanese freebooter Cheng Ch'eng-kung, the right to bear their family name. Cheng appealed to the rulers of Japan to help him free coastal China from the invaders, but the Japanese refused.[56] On a different occasion, Cheng and his supporters considered invading the Philippines to punish Spanish colonists who had massacred Chinese citizens there, but decided that the expedition would be too difficult.[57]

Cheng was a businessman as well as a pirate, and he made himself a middleman between Chinese merchants and the rest of the world. The people of southern China willingly cooperated with him. In this way, Cheng reaped a share of the profits from China's overseas trade, which gave him enough wealth to support his fleet. As one imperial edict put it:

> Recently we have heard that a bandit, Hung, a subordinate of the pirate-traitor, Cheng Ch'eng-kung, has allied himself with that treacherous bandit and has set up trading stations at Sha-ch'enf and other places in Fukien and along coastal regions. The merchants of the Interior engaged in intrigues with him to profit in mutual trade in fir, timber, t'ung-oil, iron articles, sulphur, Hu-chou-silk, silk gauze and floss, grain, rice and all kinds of necessary commodities; everything boldly bought and sold to supply the pirate-traitor Cheng Ch'eng-kung. Everywhere along the coast those who join the pirate-traitor and secretly communicate with merchants and peddlers like this fellow, Hung, are numerous. Again, We heard that the inhabitants of the coastal regions, as well as the merchants, sail their ships as they please and communicate with the bandit on intimate terms.[58]

In 1656, the imperial government banned all sailing and made traffic with the rebels punishable by death.[59] Six years later, the Manchus razed much of China's southern coast to punish the inhabitants for consorting with Cheng, and to deny him their support. Since Cheng needed a new base, he invaded Formosa with a fleet of 900 ships and 25,000 men. In the process, he drove out Dutch colonists who had been there since 1624. The rebels raided China from Formosa until 1683, when the Manchus staged an amphibious landing and conquered the island.[60]

FACING THE WEST

An imperial edict of 1713 noted that pirates preferred to attack Asian ships rather than European ships, because the European ships carried vastly superior weapons.[61] The Chinese discovered the full strategic significance of Western military technology a little more than a century later, in the Opium War. This conflict began in 1839 when Chinese officials destroyed over 20,000 chests of opium belonging to British traders in Canton. In a subsequent skirmish, a single British vessel, HMS *Volage*, defeated a squadron of 29 Chinese warships. The *Volage* blew one Chinese ship to pieces immediately and sank three more in later fighting.[62]

In 1840, a British detachment of 16 warships sailed to China with orders to compel the Chinese to compensate the traders for their loss, cede one or more islands to Britain and relax their restrictions on foreign trade. This force managed to capture the Chusan Islands, blockade the Chinese coast and force the Manchu rulers to surrender. Lin Tse-hsu, the far-sighted and patriotic governor of Canton observed that if China had used but one-tenth of its customs revenue from foreign trade to build a Western-style navy, it would not have suffered such embarrassment.[63]

Others took up Lin's ideas, and in the 1860s, local authorities in China's coastal provinces began to study Western techniques, open naval academies, establish factories capable of producing European-style naval guns, and build experimental warships. A leading modernizer named Li Hung-chang explained the importance of these reforms in terms of global strategy. Li argued for naval development on the grounds that China faced a situation which was unprecedented in its 3,000 years of history, in which European countries had advanced step by step from India to Southeast Asia to China. Only a technological navy, Li felt, could protect China from this juggernaut. Li also noted that, if the Manchu regime allowed Japan to acquire a powerful navy first, the Japanese would be in a position to take advantage of China.[64]

The Manchu Empire, however, lacked the will and the administrative efficiency to realize the reformers' ideas. Although individual officials procured steam-powered warships with relatively modern armaments, the central government failed to organize these vessels into an effective national navy.[65] France defeated the Chinese at sea in the Sino-French war of 1884–85, and although this prompted the Manchus to reform their system of naval organization somewhat, the Japanese humiliated China's fleet again precisely ten years later.[66] The latter war left Japan in control of Formosa, the Pescadore Islands and the Liaotung Peninsula, thus consolidating Japanese supremacy in the seas around China.[67]

The Manchu Dynasty itself did not last much beyond the war with Japan. In 1911, a coalition of nationalist revolutionaries headed by Sun Yat-sen overthrew the Manchu Empire and established a republic, but internal strife plagued China throughout the first half of the twentieth century. When the Japanese invaded in 1937, the Chinese offered no significant naval resistance.

NOTES

1. Joseph Needham, Wang Ling and Lu Gwei-Djen, *Science and Civilisation In China, Volume 4* (Cambridge: Cambridge University Press, 1971), pp. 439–40.
2. Jacques Gernet, *A History of Chinese Civilization*, trans. J. R. Foster (Cambridge: Cambridge University Press, 1972), p. 72. For a detailed discussion of how Chinese thinkers of this period viewed the moral status of commerce, see p.144.
3. Frank A. Kierman Jr, 'Phases and Modes of Combat in Early China', in Frank A. Kierman Jr. and John K. Fairbank (eds), *Chinese Ways in Warfare* (Cambridge, MA: Harvard University Press, 1974), p. 43.

4. Richard Wilhelm, *A Short History of Chinese Civilization*, trans. Joan Joshua (London: George G. Harrap, 1929), p. 123.
5. Needham, Wang and Lu, *Science and Civilization in China*, p. 541.
6. Gernet, *History of Chinese Civilization*, p. 67.
7. Ibid., pp. 72, 73.
8. Needham, Wang and Lu, *Science and Civilization in China*, p. 441.
9. Gernet, *History of Chinese Civilization*, p. 66.
10. Wilhelm, *Short History of Chinese Civilization*, p. 131.
11. Needham, Wang and Lu, *Science and Civilization in China*, pp. 440, 441.
12. Ibid., pp. 440, 441.
13. Ibid.
14. Ibid.
15. Gernet, *History of Chinese Civilization*, p. 126.
16. Needham, Wang and Lu, *Science and Civilization in China*, p. 553.
17. Ibid.
18. Gernet, *History of Chinese Civilization*, p. 132.
19. Ibid., p. 130.
20. Ibid., pp. 126, 127, 130.
21. Needham, Wang and Lu, *Science and Civilization in China*, pp. 441–2.
22. Gernet, *History of Chinese Civilization*, p. 130.
23. Ibid., p. 177.
24. Ibid., pp. 196, 197.
25. Ibid.
26. Ibid.
27. Needham, Wang and Lu, *Science and Civilization in China*, p. 494.
28. Gernet, *History of Chinese Civilization*, p. 319.
29. Ibid., p. 321.
30. Ibid., pp, 350–1.
31. Jung-Pang Lo, 'The Emergence of China as a Sea Power during the Late Sung and Early Yuan Periods', *Far Eastern Quarterly*, Vol. 14, No. 4, Special Issue on Chinese History and Society (Aug. 1955), p. 497; Needham, Wang and Lu, *Science and Civilization in China*, p. 488.
32. Ibid., pp. 499–500.
33. Needham, Wang and Lu, *Science and Civilization in China*, p. 496.
34. Ibid., p. 488.
35. Jung-Pang Lo, 'The Emergence of China as a Sea Power', p. 499, 502.
36. Ibid, p. 502.
37. Ibid.
38. Ibid., pp. 491–2, 499, 500.
39. Ibid., p. 499.
40. Ibid.
41. Ibid., p. 493.
42. George Samson, *A History of Japan to 1334* (London: Cresset Press, 1958), pp. 442, 448–9.
43. Jung-Pang Lo, 'The Emergence of China as a Sea Power', p. 493.
44. Needham, Wang and Lu, *Science and Civilization in China*, p. 478.
45. Gernet, *History of Chinese Civilization*, p. 399.
46. Needham, Wang and Lu, *Science and Civilization in China*, pp. 487–8.
47. Gernet, *History of Chinese Civilization*, p. 401.
48. Needham, Wang and Lu, *Science and Civilization in China*, pp. 489, 515–16.
49. Charles O. Hucker, 'Hu Tsung-hsien's Campaign against Hsu Hai, 1556', in Frank A. Kierman Jr and John K. Fairbank (eds), *Chinese Ways in Warfare* (Cambridge, MA: Harvard University Press, 1974), pp. 274–5.

50. Ibid., p. 275; Gernet, *History of Chinese Civilization*, p. 402.
51. Needham, Wang and Lu, *Science and Civilization in China*, pp. 524, 525.
52. Ibid., p. 526.
53. Ibid., pp. 526–7.
54. Ibid., p. 527.
55. Hucker, 'Hu Tsung-hsien's Campaign against Hsu Hai, 1556', p. 289 and *passim*.
56. Gernet, *History of Chinese Civilization*, 468.
57. Lo-Shu Fu, *A Documentary Chronicle of Sino-Western Relations (1644–1820)* (Tuscon, AZ: University of Arizona Press, 1966), pp. 31–2.
58. Ibid., p. 28.
59. Ibid., pp. 20–1.
60. Gernet, *History of Chinese Civilization*, pp. 468–9.
61. Lo-Shu fu, *A Documentary Chronicle*, p. 118.
62. Immanuel C. Y. Hsu, *The Rise of Modern China* (Oxford: Oxford University Press, 1970), p. 229.
63. Ibid., p. 233.
64. Ibid., pp. 336–40.
65. For a detailed discussion of this period, see John L. Rawlinson, *China's Struggle for Naval Development 1839–1895* (Cambridge, MA: Harvard University Press, 1967), *passim*.
66. Ibid., pp. 109–28, 167–97.
67. Hsu, *The Rise of Modern China*, pp. 407–8.

3

Principles of Chinese Seapower

Having considered the history of China's actual experiences with the sea, we can go on to search for the underlying principles that influenced China's actions and their consequences. This chapter discusses the implications of classic strategic theory for the development of the Chinese navy. Earlier sections use the writings of Alfred Thayer Mahan to discuss China's general strengths, weaknesses and needs as a seapower, whereas later sections use the work of Julian Corbett and Charles Callwell to discuss how China might make use of its naval assets in more specific terms.

VALIDITY OF MAHAN

'Mahan is, and will always remain, the point of reference and departure for any work upon "seapower"', writes the historian Paul Kennedy.[1] Although scholars have criticized Mahan for overestimating the effects of seapower on the course of history and underestimating the effects of commerce raiding on the conduct of naval operations, more recent commentators have noted that his detractors may have merely misunderstood his purposes. Jon Tetsuro Sumida, for instance, argues that Mahan proposed many of his ideas, not as prosaic statements of fact, but as provocations designed to spur readers on to greater understanding.[2] Certainly, Mahan's works reward those who use them in this fashion.

Captain Wayne P. Hughes of the US Navy, for instance, notes Mahan's failure to anticipate twentieth-century naval combat in all its detail, but still finds that Mahan provided a better guide to these events than any other theoretician, and concludes that Mahan 'paints a picture full of truth'.[3] Many have observed that, whatever Mahan's biases as a historian and a tactician, he had deep insights into the more conceptual realms of grand strategy and politics. The scholar John H. Mauer argues that Mahan's most seminal thoughts concerned these topics.[4] J. Michael Robertson notes that Mahan's geopolitical writings continue to reveal a great deal about world events, and that his ideas are particularly relevant to the politics of Asia.[5] Mahan, in short, is a theorist in the sense intended by Carl von Clausewitz, when he wrote that theory should be study, not doctrine:

> [T]hese principles and rules are intended to provide a thinking man with a frame of reference for the movements he has been trained to carry out, rather than to serve as a guide which at the moment of action lays down precisely the path he must take.[6]

'Above all else', Colin Gray notes, 'Mahan's treatment of "the elements of seapower", providing it is not treated as holy writ, remains incomparable and of enduring relevance.'[7] The following two sections draw on that treatment to discuss the maritime orientation of China.

PURPOSE OF CHINESE SEAPOWER

The fact that people live on solid ground means that naval power is valuable only when it can affect events upon the land. One way in which it can do this is by securing friendly maritime trade while denying such trade to one's enemies. The other obvious way is by facilitating assaults on enemy coastlines. With these truisms in mind, Mahan proposed two reasons why states deploy fighting fleets:

> The necessity of a navy, in the restricted sense of the word, springs, therefore, from peaceful shipping, and disappears with it, except in the case of a nation which has aggressive tendencies, and keeps up a navy merely as a branch of the military establishment.[8]

This statement applies to Chinese history, but only when one modifies it to account for imperial China's view of economics. Just as Mahan would have predicted, the eras in which China has maintained effective navies over long periods have been eras in which thriving maritime trade gave the Chinese government a clear reason to do so. When the importance of trade declined in the Ming period, anti-maritime courtiers were able to convince the emperor that the navy was a dangerous luxury that served only to embroil the state in unnecessary foreign struggles.[9] Nevertheless, when one studies China, it is a mistake to equate what Mahan called 'peaceful shipping' with private commerce in the modern Western sense. Chinese rulers have traditionally seen trade, not as a politically neutral occupation for individual citizens, but as a tool of state policy.

The three main philosophical doctrines of ancient China, Confucianism, Taoism and Moism, all condemned the pursuit of wealth for its own sake.[10] China's leaders disliked commerce for the more pragmatic reason that it placed resources in the hands of individual merchants, rather than the state.[11] There have been eras in which China's rulers have encouraged foreign trade as a source of revenue and eras in which the Chinese government has forbidden it as a source of corruption. Both policies, however, treat commerce as a means to grander political ends. These ends include, not only profit, but military advantage and diplomatic influence.

Chinese merchants have quietly gone on making money under governments that ignored and even banned their activities. Historically, however, China has only achieved that combination of robust trade and naval strength which constitute seapower under rulers who harnessed commerce to extend the influence of their empire. Han Dynasty rulers decided to secure their trade routes, not because they were profitable, but because they were vital to their policy of coopting so-called 'barbarian' leaders with gifts. The independent merchants of the Sui, Tang and Manchu Dynasties braved the seas with little official protection.[12] When cut off from the north, the people of southern China have often sustained themselves by maritime commerce, but even the Sung emperors praised trade, not so much as a way to achieve general prosperity, but as a way to raise state revenue.[13]

Cheng Ho became legendary throughout China as 'the Three-Jewel Eunuch who went down into the West', and imperial historians continued to write about him for hundreds of years[14] The Chinese appear to have paid comparatively little attention to the innumerable merchants who made similar voyages in earlier centuries.[15] Although modern scholars have been impressed by the size and technological sophistication of Cheng Ho's ships, his fame has more to do with the fact that he 'made known the proclamations of the Son of Heaven, and spread abroad the knowledge of his majesty and virtue', so that 'every country became obedient to the imperial commands'.[16] Cheng Ho's ships also exchanged vast quantities of valuables with the people he visited, and presumably realized either a profit or a loss, but his biographers seem to have considered this to be of secondary importance.

Mahan doubted that a country could sustain a navy without a base of merchant shipping.[17] 'History has proved that such a purely military seapower can be built up by a despot, as was done by Louis XIV; but though so fair seeming, experience showed that his navy was like a growth which having no root soon withers away.'[18] Over the course of centuries, China's navies have been notoriously prone to withering, but this has not stopped rulers from building navies as their more immediate policies demanded. Even the Manchus, who mistrusted the population of coastal China and had no maritime tradition of their own, deployed fleets to invade Formosa and to support campaigns against Russia.[19]

China's rulers repeatedly succeeded where Louis XIV failed. The Chinese, it seems, had a stronger state than the Sun King. Powerful emperors could draw upon national resources to re-route rivers and raise walls thousands of miles long, and they could draw upon those resources to build fleets as well. Thus, although the government itself had little incentive to field long-range navies during periods when trade was less significant, it was politics, not economic interest, that drove China's policies concerning the sea.

One cannot know how far these principles apply today. One can, however, note that imperial China's policies on this matter are certainly compatible with the doctrines of communism, which subordinates individual profit to collective interests and stresses the political implications of economic activity. Although China's leaders may now have tacitly abandoned the ideals of Marx, Lenin and Mao, they seem unlikely to have discarded a political tradition which offers them so much power to shape both internal and external affairs. The current Chinese regime certainly continues to mingle politics and economics to such an extent that the People's Liberation Army is a major business concern.[20]

SOURCES OF CHINESE SEAPOWER

Mahan identified six conditions which affect a nation's maritime power. These are geographical position, physical conformation, extent of territory, number of population, character of the people and character of the government.[21] This chapter will now consider China's maritime potential in terms of each of these factors.

Geography

Mahan points out that continental states are handicapped at sea. A country with land borders will always have to divide its resources between the army and the navy, with the consequence that neither will ever receive its full effort. China provides a textbook example of this principle in action. The fact that imperial China had to maintain large land armies to protect itself from the warrior peoples of Central Asia prevented the Chinese from building navies for long periods of history.[22] Since imperial Russia became active in the Far East, Moscow has had the potential to impede China in the same way.

In the Han and Ming Dynasties, however, powerful Chinese emperors managed to expand their realms by sea and land simultaneously. This required heroic efforts and expenditures of resources, but it promised equally great strategic returns. As the Han Dynasty explorer Chang

Ch'ien discovered, there are three main corridors between China and western Asia. These are the historical Silk Road, which runs north through Central Asia, the sea route which runs south around the Indonesian archipelago and a central land route which cuts through Burma. China has considerably more to gain by dominating all three of these routes at once than by controlling any one or two. The sum, in this case, is greater than the whole of its parts.

From a military point of view, as long as any of these routes lies outside Chinese control, China has an open flank, which exposes it to attack along long stretches of its border. For these reasons, China's more dynamic emperors preferred to control the routes by which invaders reach their country than to fight those invaders in China. When China has managed to secure its land borders, it has presumably had more resources available for its maritime forces, and vice versa, meaning that strength in one strategic environment can contribute to strength in the other.

When China controls these transportation corridors, it not only protects itself from threats, it gains positive advantages. Just as these routes allow outside powers to reach China, they allow China to reach potential rivals in the Indian Ocean region. The more of these corridors China can control, the more directions from which it can flank that area. This has obvious military benefits, and gives China considerable diplomatic leverage, even if it never chooses to go to war.

From a commercial point of view, many of the same principles apply. The more trade routes China can use, the more markets it can reach and the more easily it can reach them. This, in turn, improves its business position against foreign competitors. During periods of international harmony, China may be able to buy and sell freely regardless of which states occupy these transportation corridors, but throughout much of history, the surest way for China to guarantee its commerce has been through direct control of the trade routes.

Geography shapes China's bid for seapower in many more localized ways as well. Islands and peninsulas fragment East Asia's waters into a variety of distinct regions. China's rulers must contend with different military and diplomatic problems in each of the seas which wash their coasts. Beyond those waters lie two oceans which Chinese navies must negotiate as they move toward the other industrial centers of the world. Thus, for China to exercise maritime power beyond its coasts, it must establish its influence in a number of distinct regions, and the farther it wishes to go, the more regions it must master.

The Korean peninsula embraces the Yellow Sea, possesses ports on the Sea of Japan, and serves as the shortest route between mainland Asia and the Japanese archipelago. Korea is well positioned to control shipping in North Asian waters, to serve as a logistical base for land campaigns between Russia and Manchuria, and to facilitate invasions of China by Japan or vice versa.[23] Any power that wishes to dominate North Asia and its waters must keep Korea out of the hands of potential opponents. Thus, Korea has frequently been a battleground. The twentieth century was not the first time in history that Korea had broken up into contending states, nor was it the first time that outside powers had used those states as proxies in their own geopolitical maneuvers.

Just as the Korean peninsula dominates the waters of Siberia and North China, the Japanese archipelago dominates the waters of Korea. Thus, Japan is potentially the linchpin of North Asia. Historically, the fact that Korea has usually been weak and embattled has frequently allowed aggressive Japanese leaders to realize that potential. In eras when Japan has been less powerful or less expansionist, other states contending in the region have still needed to keep it out of the hands of their enemies. The diplomatic struggles between Wei, Wu and their Korean allies illustrate this point.

Korea and Japan also have access to the East China Sea, and the Ryukyu Islands provide a string of potential bases around these waters. If one follows the arc of the Ryukyus, one comes to Taiwan (Formosa), at the southern end of this body of water. The indigenous people of Formosa never developed a strong enough state to fend off invasions, but their island has enough resources to sustain a large population and support naval forces, which made it attractive as a new home for rebels from mainland China in the 1640s, and did so again 300 years later.[24] The island also straddles the northern approaches to the South China Sea, making it doubly important to China's maritime power.

Vietnam, Indonesia and the Philippines have direct access to the South China Sea, but all the maritime states of Southeast Asia have influence in this region. Large islands such as Hainan allow mainland countries to extend their naval influence outward into this body of water, and although the Spratly and Paracel islands are too small to support large-scale military activity, they have the potential to serve as outposts in the center of this navigationally and politically treacherous sea. The fact that all shipping going between the Indian Ocean and the Pacific must pass through the Indonesian straits or take a detour of several thousand miles to the south makes this area critical to all the maritime powers of the world, and the prosperity of Southeast Asia makes this region economically important in its own right. These statements were as true in ancient times as they are today. From the Han Dynasty onward, China has jockeyed for position in the complex and colorful politics of this region. China's geographical proximity to Southeast Asia means that this is another area in which it can use its land power and its seapower to reinforce each other.

For China to extend its influence as far as its interests, it must go beyond its coastal waters. The Indian Ocean and the Persian Gulf are particularly important to China, not only for commercial reasons, but because those waters allow China to reach Iran, India, Pakistan and other nations of concern to its foreign policy. In theory, of course, the Chinese have interests in every ocean of the world, if only to offset the influence of the United States. Although the Chinese would have to be quite ambitious to contemplate overt military adventures outside East Asia, one must still consider the strategic challenges which face them in these areas, both because, as Chapter 1 noted, grand strategy may take generations to reach fruition, and because the Chinese will have to cope with these geographical facts even if they restrict themselves to more subtle endeavors. A thorough discussion of geopolitics in every maritime region of the world would warrant a book in itself, but there are several areas which the Chinese may find particularly interesting, even at their current level of development.

The Indian Ocean is far from China, and therefore, if the Chinese are to sustain a naval presence there, they need local ports of call. Historically, the Chinese have found such harbors along the entire rim of South-Central Asia, notably in Sri Lanka (Ceylon) and on the East African coast. India's geographical position at the center of this ocean means that outside naval forces in the region must contend with whichever power controls the sub-continent. One notes that this fact makes Sri Lanka doubly valuable, since it overlooks the Indian shoreline.

Ever since the opening of the Suez Canal, Egypt and the Levant have been the gateway between Asian waters and the West. The disposition of these regions is critical to any maritime strategy which involves the Indian Ocean. China's naval power is inversely proportional to the power of any fleets that outside powers send to counterbalance it, and so, if China wishes to exert power in the Indian Ocean, it is likely to take measures to deter the passage of such fleets. China may also seek influence in the Persian Gulf, both because it has its own interests in that part of the world, and because of the leverage such influence would give it against Europe, the United States and Japan.

To its east, China confronts the United States. As long as China wishes to assert its independence from the United States, it must seek a way to interfere with US forces in the middle of the Pacific, before they can devastate China's coasts. Although the idea of China deploying a fleet which could out-fight the US Navy in open battle remains in the realm of science fiction, the idea that China might seek the means to threaten US shipping and thus push US leaders toward more accommodating policies does not. The island chains which dominated Pacific strategy in the Second World War are relevant to this struggle as well.

As Chinese leaders consider Pacific strategy, they may also look toward Latin America. A handful of Asians might conceivably have reached Central America on sailing-rafts in prehistoric times, and Chinese merchants traded with Spain's Mexican colonies during the late 1500s.[25] The Chinese may profit by participating in Latin America's emerging markets, while building credentials as a friend of developing countries at the same time. In the event of outright war with the United States, China would benefit from having access to ports on the eastern side of the Pacific, and from the opportunity to stage special operations overland against the continental United States.

Physical Conformation

Regional geography divides China into two regions, one maritime and the other not. In the northwestern plains, land is plentiful, if arid, and the Chinese have historically found ways to make them largely self-sufficient. The eastern provinces, by contrast, are smaller and tend to be hilly. These areas cannot support large populations without trade, and, fortunately enough, the Yangtze River and its tributaries make the ocean accessible even in the inland parts of this region.[26]

Southern China has many characteristics of an island. In the pre-modern era, the southern Chinese were able to use water barriers as their 'new Great Wall', and to deploy fleets as 'watchtowers' along it.[27] As the rulers of Ch'in, Wei and the Mongol Empire discovered, it was difficult for land powers to overrun this region without mastering amphibious warfare. Thus, nobody should be surprised that, during periods when southern China has been detached from the north, it has frequently oriented itself toward the sea.

Over millennia, these circumstances have conditioned people from different parts of China to adopt different ways of life. The coast tends to be urban, cosmopolitan and industrial, whereas the interior tends to be rural, conservative and agricultural. Modern technology blurs the material distinctions between these regions but may accentuate the importance of the cultural divide. Both regions now need trade to realize their economic potential, and motor transport makes it easier to carry goods between landlocked regions and ports, but the fact that people from different regions have such different economies and different attitudes compels the Chinese government to treat them as separate entities.[28] For the Chinese government to wield seapower effectively, it must unite the two parts of its country.

Extent of Territory

Taken as a whole, China has an abundance of land. Although the coastal provinces are more compact than the northwest plains, they have historically been more than adequate as a base for shipping. The wooded hills which reduce the amount of arable land available in this area have historically provided timber for ships.[29] These regions also have ample harbors and inland waterways, which allow mariners to take shelter both from storms and from human enemies. During periods when the coast has been in revolt, the southeast has repeatedly been able to sustain strong enough rebel fleets to threaten the central government, despite the fact that imperial forces have nominally controlled both the land and the sea.

Size of Population

Mahan notes that, when one estimates the effects of a country's population on its capacity for seapower, 'it is not only the grand total, but the number following the sea, or at least readily available for employment on ship-board and for the creation of naval material, that must be counted'.[30] When a country is home to people who live by the sea, Mahan notes, it can draw on their numbers to expand its fleet as much as its shipyards will allow, and to reconstitute its naval forces even after catastrophic losses.[31] China has had a large seafaring population throughout history, and leaders who have had the power to exploit it have had little difficulty using this pool of human talent to build and re-build navies, even on short notice. The Mongol period provides numerous examples of this fact.

One may doubt that the skills of a fisherman or merchant sailor remain as transferable to military purposes today as they were in Mahan's time. Nevertheless, the People's Liberation Army Navy (PLAN) undoubtedly benefits from having access to a reservoir of people who are comfortable with technology in general and ships in particular. Without the maritime cities of China's southeast, the Chinese navy would not enjoy this resource. One must also note that, in terms of grand strategy, a nation's capacity for merchant shipping is almost as important to seapower as the navy itself.

National Character

Mahan believed that countries develop naval power in proportion to their level of maritime trade. On these grounds, he argued that a specific aspect of a nation's culture – the way in which its people seek wealth – has a 'marked effect' on that people's ability to use the sea.[32] Historically, the Chinese have had, not one national attitude toward the acquisition of wealth, but several. Moist, Legalist, Confucian and communist thinkers disapproved of trade in principle, but often made exceptions when commerce served the political interests of the state. Nevertheless, from antiquity onward, China has produced energetic private merchants and industrialists.[33]

41

These contradictory cultural traditions have demonstrated the potential to alienate China's most productive entrepreneurs from the state. The fact that the commercial tradition tends to be strongest in the coastal southeast whereas many of China's rulers were northerners who founded their governments in the inland plains compounds makes this clash of attitudes yet more divisive. When China's rulers have been strong and cosmopolitan, as in the early Han and Ming periods, they have been able to exploit their country's mercantile tradition. Less dynamic governments have found trade to be a source of weakness and tried to reign it in, with deleterious consequences for their nation's seapower.

'A true hero knows how to duck punches', as the Chinese proverb goes, and given the fact that China's governments have suppressed trade as often as they have encouraged it, one should not be surprised to learn that China's merchants have developed a subculture which prizes cleverness, personal relationships, political influence and a certain stateless pragmatism. The best-known merchants in China's history are often those such as the infamous Lu Pu-Wei of the Warring States Period who used their wealth to bankroll the military and political ventures of their chosen factions. China's entrepreneurs have often moved abroad in search of supportive environments in which to do business, and, as a result, there are now enclaves of overseas Chinese throughout much of the world. Cosmopolitan Chinese governments have often sought ties to the overseas Chinese, whereas more insular regimes have washed their hands of them.

Just as a doctrinaire Confucian might have warned, this commercial subculture has the potential to undermine the state. On the other hand, traders and emigrants have given China international contacts and international interests. As Han Dynasty diplomats might have hoped, China's merchants have spread Chinese ideas across the globe. The overseas Chinese tend to stay in contact with their country of origin, and to send goods and money there. Cheng Ho, among others, used the presence of overseas Chinese as a pretext for intervening in the domestic politics of foreign countries.[34] Furthermore, just as Chinese merchants have traditionally sought personal influence in politics, Chinese leaders have traditionally used business connections to pursue state policy (most obviously in revolutionary politics). Thus, China's entrepreneurs have given China's leaders an abundance of so-called 'soft' power, should they choose to exploit it.

Character of the Government

Mahan states:

It would seem probable that a government in full accord with the natural bias of its people would most successfully advance its growth in every respect; and, in the matter of seapower, the most brilliant successes have followed where there had been intelligent direction by a government fully imbued with the spirit of its people and conscious of its true general bent.[35]

Although Mahan's belief that a government should maintain 'full accord with the natural bias of its people' is broadly compatible with the traditional Chinese concept that the emperor must rule by the Mandate of Heaven, neither imperial nor communist China has seen democracy as an ideal. The question of whether China could achieve greater seapower if it followed a liberal model of government is strictly hypothetical. Furthermore, China's people have more than one 'general bent'. All Chinese governments have faced the threat of national disintegration, although this danger has been far more acute in some periods than in others. For these reasons, the Chinese governments that have been the most successful at developing seapower have been those that managed to seize the initiative at home and abroad, taking an active role in channeling their nation's energies into maritime expansion.

Mahan acknowledges that 'despotic power, wielded with judgment and consistency, has created at times a great sea commerce and a brilliant navy with greater directness than can be reached by the slower processes of a free people. The difficulty in [this] case is to insure perseverance after the death of a particular despot.'[36] Over the course of centuries, China has suffered from precisely this difficulty. The episode in which Ming rulers voluntarily gave up their first-rate merchant fleet and navy bears out Mahan's point entirely. Nevertheless, during periods when China's ruling class had a deeper appreciation for seapower, notably the later Sung period, Chinese governments maintained dynamic maritime policies for numerous generations.

EXERCISE OF CHINESE SEAPOWER

Mahan's principles indicate that China has great maritime potential, but that its status as a seapower will always be shaky and that its fleet will often be inferior to the navies of more naturally seafaring states. History bears out Mahan's points. The past few centuries have been a low point in China's naval power, and, as of the early twenty-first century, the Chinese have taken only tentative steps toward recovery. What can China do with its limited seapower? I will discuss how a navy like the contemporary PLAN might operate.

If Mahan was right when he argued that decisive engagements between capital ships are 'the only really determining elements in naval war', China is currently incapable of asserting itself at sea.[37] There are, however, other ways to exercise seapower. Theorists such as Julian Corbett and C.E. Callwell have explored the principles behind a variety of maritime strategies, many of which offer alternatives to direct confrontation with the strongest elements of the enemy fleet. Perhaps because their works are less ambitious than Mahan's, they have attracted less controversy, although people have questioned their judgment on more technical matters such as the role of convoys.[38] These writers outline ways in which today's Chinese fleet might support the national strategies of today's Chinese state.

Since one can assume that the Chinese wish to use their navy effectively, one can assume that they will apply Corbett and Callwell's principles to one degree or another. One must, however, remember that China's leaders may come up with ideas that Corbett and Callwell never thought of, that no strategic concept applies in all times or under all circumstances, and that, even when a theory provides a clearly effective solution to a problem, the people who might be expected to put that theory into practice often make mistakes. The following section discusses the imperatives and opportunities which the Chinese will encounter, and thus it gives us clues about ways to interpret China's actions, but it does not imply that the PLAN will adopt one specific doctrine in any particular situation.

Applying the writings of Corbett and Callwell to contemporary China, one must remember that these authors' theories are approximately one hundred years old. Although the two writers' concepts remain valid in the early years of the twenty-first century, many of the points which they made in specific tactical terms are now more useful as general strategic analogies. Corbett, for example, makes some salient points about the constitution of a fleet, and discusses his ideas in terms of the division of labor between cruisers and battleships. Neither type of vessel plays the same role in the early twenty-first century that it played in the early twentieth century, but Corbett's points about the ultimate purpose of the navy and the way in which different types of ships carrying out different kinds of operations can work together to achieve that goal remain as true as they ever were. Indeed, modern communications and data-processing equipment have allowed dispersed fleets to achieve unprecedented levels of synergy.

One of the most sweeping changes in naval warfare has been the development of air power. One can find parallels between the principles of naval strategy in the gunnery age to the principles of naval strategy today. Just as shore batteries traditionally had an advantage over naval guns, for instance, carrier aircraft tend to be inferior to their land-based cousins.[39] Nevertheless, one must remain alert to the ways that any theorist's understanding of the strategic environment has become obsolete. Corbett and Callwell provide an invaluable guide to the principles of naval strategy, but their work is dated; the reader is warned.

Corbett outlines the principle which allows weaker navies to challenge stronger ones in his definition of seapower. 'The object of naval warfare', he writes, 'must always be directly or indirectly either to secure the command of the sea or to prevent the enemy from securing it.'[40] Most of the time, he goes on to note, neither side will have full control of the waters, nor does it need such absolute control to exert naval power.[41] It is a mistake to equate seapower with the conquest and occupation of land: 'command of the sea, therefore, means nothing but the control of communications, whether for commercial or military purposes'.[42] If a nation can slip its own transports past enemy ships, or, alternatively, if it can interfere with the enemy's shipping, it can use seapower for both offensive and defensive purposes, regardless of the overall balance of forces upon the water.

Even minuscule naval forces can achieve dramatic results by striking at enemy communications. As Wayne P. Hughes of the US Navy has noted:

> We have two modern examples of nations whose navies were utterly swept from the seas that still created the greatest difficulties for their opponents. One is Japan off Okinawa in 1945, whose Kamikazes destroyed ships of the US Navy at the rate of one a day. The other is Argentina, which, though isolated from the Falklands by sea, posed a frightening threat of air, missile, and even submarine attack (with an effective order of battle of one submarine!) throughout the war.[43]

Corbett notes that just as bridges, mountain passes and similar points can be critical to land campaigns, straits, strategically placed islands, shipping lanes approaching important parts of the theater of war and other definable geographical locations can be vital to naval operations.[44] The importance of these regions helps to neutralize the advantages of a superior navy. Since there are likely to be many such points within a theater of operations, the superior navy will not be able to cover them all without dispersing its fleet. The fact that it takes far more ships to patrol such sea lanes than it takes to raid them further increases the problems that even a considerably stronger navy will face in bringing its force to bear. For these reasons, Corbett advised admirals to disperse their fleets cunningly and take the initiative whenever possible. It is easier to upset the strategic status quo than to enforce it.

Thus, when Corbett discussed the concept of concentration as a principle of strategy, he offered a paradoxical definition of the term:

> [O]nce the mass is formed, concealment and flexibility are at an end. The further, therefore, from the formation of the ultimate mass

we can stop the process of concentration the better designed it will be. The less we are committed to any particular mass, and the less we indicate what and where our mass is to be, the more formidable our concentration. To concentration, therefore, the idea of division is as essential as the idea of connection. It is this view of the process which, at least for naval warfare, a weighty critical authority has most strongly emphasized. 'Such,' he says, 'is concentration reasonably understood – not huddled together like a drove of sheep, but distributed with a regard to a common purpose, and linked together by the effectual energy of a single will'.[45]

These ideas could not be more compatible with traditional Chinese writings on strategy. 'The ultimate in disposing one's troops is to conceal them without ascertainable shape', Sun Tzu wrote.[46] Sun Tzu's reasons for making this statement are much the same as Corbett's.

The enemy must not know where I intend to give battle. For if he prepares to his front, his rear will be weak, and if to the rear, his front will be fragile. If he strengthens his left, his right will be vulnerable, and if his right, there will be too few troops on his left. And when he sends troops everywhere, he will be weak everywhere. Numerical weakness comes from having to guard against possible attacks; numerical strength from forcing the enemy to make these preparations against us.[47]

The best defense is said to be a good offense, and not only do these principles allow weaker naval powers to inflict damage, they also help them to protect their own assets from harm. Corbett cites, as an example, Sir Francis Drake's strategy of defeating the Spanish fleet before it could set sail. '[W]ith fifty sail of shipping we shall do more upon their own coast than a great many more will do here at home; and the sooner we are gone, the better we shall be able to impeach them.'[48] Corbett emphasizes that Drake used the term 'impeach', which means not to destroy but to prevent.[49] Such strategies of impeachment are particularly useful as a defense against amphibious invasion, which requires the attacker to achieve such meticulous preparations involving many different kinds of forces.[50]

Callwell makes many of the same points, but reminds readers that stronger navies can still use their strength to crush their weaker opponents.[51] Therefore, even a navy which relies on hit-and-run tactics needs some way to protect its ships from systematic destruction by superior force. Corbett sees this as a job for capital ships, and suggests that the main role of a friendly battle fleet may be to protect one's cruisers from the enemy battle fleet.[52] This division of labor leaves the fleet's cruisers free to range across the oceans, carrying out the navy's more fundamental function of controlling communications.

Callwell suggests that weaker navies can also tie down enemy resources simply by keeping a portion of their fleet in port.[53] Since the stronger naval power cannot discount the possibility that the enemy ships might eventually sail out and attack, it must commit ships to watching the weaker navy's harbors. The more of the strong navy's ships are engaged in this standoff along the coastline, the easier it will be for the weak navy's cruisers to operate elsewhere. Callwell acknowledges that such a strategy gives the stronger navy great freedom of action to strike against its weaker opponent's ships and overseas possessions, but he feels that fleets in harbor have enough military potential to make amphibious operations against port cities indispensable.[54]

When one attempts to apply Corbett and Callwell's ideas on the defense of ports and the protection of raiding ships at sea to the contemporary strategic environment, one must pay particularly close attention to the effects of modern technology. Air power has become critical to both problems. The fact that submarines have replaced cruisers as the vessel of choice for raiders means that the specialized technology of anti-submarine warfare (ASW) and counter-anti-submarine warfare has become more salient than the strength of a country's surface fleet in determining which side will be able to control oceanic communications. Modern command, control and reconnaissance systems have made technological superiority more important than the firepower of individual ships in every other aspect of naval warfare as well, and the fact that much of this technology depends upon satellites makes naval warfare potentially dependent on space warfare. These developments mean that it is more important for a nation to be at the forefront of electronic technology than it was in Corbett's and Callwell's day. They also mean that naval commanders must integrate their plans more closely than ever with their nation's strategy in other dimensions of warfare – a point that both of these theorists would have appreciated.

Both Callwell and Corbett emphasize the point that land power and seapower compliment each other. Callwell notes that a land offensive against a crucial port may serve as the *coup de grâce* to a victorious naval campaign.[55] Japan's capture of Singapore in the Second World War is a classic example of the fact that a successful ground attack may actually serve as a substitute for maritime operations. Corbett, on the other hand, points out the fact that ground commanders must operate with great caution if there is even a remote threat that their enemies may stage an amphibious landing on their flanks. Amphibious troops can hamstring forces much larger than their own.[56]

Likewise, both authors note that one must use land forces and naval forces alike, not to achieve abstract strategic desiderata, but to impose a favorable conclusion to a war. Military commanders must make strategy to match their country's foreign-policy objectives and the enemy's will to resist. These factors determine both the ways in which they will use seapower and the level of force each side must exert to achieve victory. Carl von Clausewitz made the definitive analysis of these principles, noting that war is a mere continuation of political intercourse by other means.[57]

Military commanders often find that the political context of a war keeps them from using all of the resources at their disposal. Therefore, the political factor gives an advantage to the materially weaker side, at least for as long as its diplomats can maintain a situation in which their enemies feel compelled to practice restraint. The side which is willing to risk losing more is likely to be less restrained, and is therefore at an advantage. Callwell notes that one element which may affect the outcome of naval wars is the comparative readiness of the opposing sides to lose the resources that they have invested in expensive warships.[58]

The political factor can also alter the purpose of military operations. This reduces the value of proficiency with well-established tactics and increases the importance of qualities such as flexibility and the ability to assess a situation. As Corbett notes, it is a mistake for a commander to follow maxims without grasping their underlying meaning and knowing how they apply to specific circumstances. No matter what the virtues of 'seeking out the enemy fleet', to use Corbett's example, a commander must not do it if it involves leaving a strategically important point unguarded or a strategically vital land operation without support.

> The vice of the opposite procedure is obvious. If we assume the maxim that the first duty of our fleet is to seek out the enemy wherever he may be, it means in its nakedness that we merely conform to the enemy's dispositions and movements. It is open to him to lead us wherever he likes.[59]

Corbett continues in this Clausewitzian vein. He notes that, depending on the other advantages held, and how much one is willing to gamble, the political and circumstantial factors may be exploited to create situations in which the available military power can be used effectively, without overreaching oneself. Corbett writes:

> The [example] which presents [this principle] in [its] clearest and most simplest form is without doubt the recent war between Russia and Japan. Here we have a particularly striking example of a small Power having forced her will upon a much greater Power without 'overthrowing her – that is, without having crushed her power of resistance ... The case is particularly striking; for every one felt that the real object of the war was in the abstract unlimited, that it was

in fact to decide whether Russia or Japan was to be the predominant power in the Far East. Like the Franco-German War of 1870 it had all the aspect of what Germans call 'a trial of strength'. Such a war is one which above all appears incapable of a decision except by the complete overthrow of the one Power or the other.[60]

As Corbett notes, Japan had little hope of defeating Russia in such an unlimited war:

'[W]ho will contend that, if Japan had tried to make her war with Russia, as Napoleon made his, she could have fared even as well as he did?' … Fortunately for her the circumstances did not call for the employment of such extreme means. The political and geographical conditions were such that she was able to reduce the intangible object of asserting her prestige to the purely concrete form of a territorial objective. The penetration of Russia into Manchuria threatened the absorption of Korea into the Russian Empire, and this Japan regarded as fatal to her own position and future development. Her power to maintain Korean integrity would be the outward and visible sign of her ability to assert herself as a Pacific Power. Her abstract quarrel with Russia could therefore be crystallised into a concrete objective.[61]

Had it not been for the difficulty of land communications across Russia, Japan's strategy of limited war might have proven impossible. This, however, does not diminish the importance of Corbett's observation. There are innumerable examples of ways in which nations have taken advantage of the unique circumstances of particular wars to limit the conflict in ways that favor their own forces. Britain has traditionally used its control of the sea to limit its commitment upon the land.[62] The Communist victory in Vietnam provides a recent example of how nations can prevent even a determined superpower from turning its immense reserves of force into victory.

CONCLUSION

For the Chinese state, the sea can be either a great asset or a great liability. Mahan's principles and historical precedent indicate that China has great maritime potential, but warn that Chinese leaders can never afford to take their position for granted. A threat from the land can undermine China's seapower at any time. Internal divisions between the coast and the inland provinces can cheat the central government of its maritime capabilities as well.

The same principles and precedents indicate that it is dangerous for the central government to lose its grip on the oceans. In periods when China's rulers have managed to exploit the sea, they have reaped great economic and military rewards. These were eras in which China as a whole has prospered, and the regime has been strong. In times when the Chinese state failed to make use of the sea, however, the people of the coastal provinces typically saw their interests in terms of their own trade, and not with the nation as a whole. Since their commerce makes them wealthy, they have often had not only the incentive to defy the central government, but the ability to do so as well.

Thus, one can conclude that, although China will always have to struggle to maintain its maritime strength, it has a great opportunity to achieve seapower and may suffer great penalties if it fails to do so. Beijing's means for harnessing seapower are currently limited, particularly in military terms. Nevertheless, this need not be a permanent handicap. Corbett and Callwell suggest that, even at sea, sound strategy and the indirect approach may often allow the materially weaker side to achieve its ends. Their ideas provide a useful starting point for analyzing Chinese naval strategy.

NOTES

1. Paul Kennedy, *The Rise and Fall of British Naval Mastery* (New York: Charles Scribner's Sons, 1976), p. 9.
2. Jon Tetsuro Sumida, *Inventing Grand Strategy and Teaching Command: The Classic Works of Alfred Thayer Mahan Reconsidered* (Baltimore, MD: Johns Hopkins University Press, 1997), *passim*.
3. Wayne P. Hughes, 'Mahan, Tactics and Principles of Strategy', in John B. Hattendorf (ed.), *The Influence of History On Mahan: The Proceedings of a Conference Marking the Centenary of Alfred Thayer Mahan's The Influence of Sea Power Upon History, 1600–1783* (Newport, RI: Naval War College Press, 1991), p. 36.
4. John H. Mauer, 'Mahan on World Politics and Strategy: The Approach of the First World War, 1904–1914', in Hattendorf (ed.), *The Influence of History on Mahan*, p. 157.
5. J. Michael Robertson, 'Alfred Thayer Mahan and the Geopolitics of Asia', *Comparative Strategy*, Vol. 15, No. 4 (Oct.–Dec. 1996), pp. 353–66.
6. Carl von Clausewitz, *On War*, trans. and ed. Michael Howard and Peter Paret (Princeton, NJ: Princeton University Press, 1976), p. 141.
7. Colin S. Gray, *The Navy in the Post-Cold War World: The Uses and Value of Strategic Sea Power* (University Park, PA: Pennsylvania State University Press, 1994), p. 6.
8. Alfred Thayer Mahan, *The Influence of Sea Power upon History, 1660–1783* (Boston, MA: S.J. Parkhill, 1890), p. 26.
9. Joseph Needham, Wang Ling and Lu Gwei-Djen, *Science and Civilisation in China, Volume 4* (London: Cambridge University Press, 1971), p. 527, note b.
10. Jacques Gernet, *A History of Chinese Civilization*, trans. J.R. Foster (Cambridge: Cambridge University Press, 1972), p. 144.

11. Ibid., pp. 144–5.
12. Jung-Pang Lo, 'The Emergence of China as a Sea Power during the Late Sung and Early Yuan Periods', *Far Eastern Quarterly*, Vol. 14, No. 4, Special Issue on Chinese History and Society (Aug. 1955), p. 489.
13. Needham, Wang and Lu, *Science and Civilization in China*, p. 488.
14. Ibid.
15. Ibid., p. 399.
16. Ibid., p. 488.
17. Mahan, *The Influence of Sea Power*, pp. 87–8.
18. Ibid., p. 88.
19. Lo-Shu Fu, *A Documentary Chronicle of Sino-Western Relations (1644–1820)* (Tuscon, AZ: University of Arizona Press, 1966), pp. 70–80.
20. Ellis Joffe, 'How Much Does the PLA Make Foreign Policy?', in David S.G. Goodman and Gerald Segal (eds), *China Rising: Nationalism and Interdependence* (London: Routledge, 1997) p. 63.
21. Mahan, *The Influence of Sea Power*, pp. 28–9.
22. Jung-Pang Lo, 'The Emergence of China as a Sea Power', p. 489.
23. As early as 1658, Chinese commanders relied on Korean allies for logistical support in their campaigns against Russia. Lo-Shu fu, *A Documentary Chronicle*, p. 22.
24. Ibid., p. 25.
25. Needham, Wang and Lu, *Science and Civilization in China*, pp. 527, 545.
26. Jung-Pang Lo, 'The Emergence of China as a Sea Power', p. 498.
27. Ibid., p. 502.
28. Michael Yahuda, 'How much Has China Learned about Interdependence?', in Goodman and Segal, *China Rising*, p. 11.
29. Jung-Pang Lo, 'The Emergence of China as a Sea Power', p. 495.
30. Mahan, *The Influence of Sea Power*, p. 45.
31. Ibid.
32. Ibid., p. 50.
33. Gernet, *History of Chinese Civilization*, p. 28.
34. Ibid., p. 401.
35. Mahan, *The Influence of Sea Power*, p. 58.
36. Ibid., pp. 58–9.
37. Sumida, *Inventing Grand Strategy*, p. 75. Sumida notes that those who focus too narrowly on quotations of this nature may end up with a simplistic understanding of Mahan's own thought.
38. Eric J. Grove, 'Introduction', in Julian S. Corbett, *Some Principles of Maritime Strategy* (Annapolis, MD: Naval Institute Press, 1988 (originally published 1911)), p. xxxiv.
39. Gray, *The Navy In The Post-Cold War World*, p. 17.
40. Corbett, *Some Principles of Maritime Strategy*, p. 91.
41. Ibid.
42. Ibid., pp. 93–4.
43. Hughes, 'Mahan, Tactics and Principles of Strategy', p. 32.
44. Corbett, *Some Principles of Maritime Strategy*, pp. 168–70.
45. Ibid., p. 131. As Eric J. Grove points out in a footnote to his Introduction in ibid., Corbett is misquoting Mahan, who, in fact, referred to cattle rather than sheep.
46. Sun Tzu, *Sun Tzu's Art of War*, trans. Yuan Shibing, commentary Tao Hanzhang (New York: Sterling, 1987), p. 106.
47. Ibid.
48. Corbett, *Some Principles of Maritime Strategy*, p. 172.
49. Ibid.

50. Ibid., p. 255.
51. Charles E. Callwell, *Military Operations and Maritime Preponderance: Their Relations and Interdependence* (Annapolis, MD: Naval Institute Press, 1996 (originally published 1905)), pp. 52–3.
52. Corbett, *Some Principles of Maritime Strategy*, p. 114.
53. Callwell, *Military Operations and Maritime Preponderance*, p. 60.
54. Ibid., p. 110.
55. Ibid., p. 129.
56. Corbett, *Some Principles of Maritime Strategy*, pp. 66–7.
57. Von Clausewitz, *On War*, p. 87.
58. Callwell, *Military Operations and Maritime Preponderance*, p. 51.
59. Corbett, *Some Principles of Maritime Strategy,* pp. 168–9.
60. Ibid, pp. 78–9.
61. Ibid., p. 79.
62. Ibid., pp. 64–5.

4

Enter the People's Republic of China

When Mao Zedong and his followers founded the People's Republic of China (PRC), they inherited the legacy of their country's decline under the Ming and Ch'ing Dynasties. China's new government also encountered many of the same economic, geographic, demographic and philosophical issues as their predecessors throughout the previous 5,000 years. To understand what this means in practice, one must consider the goals and methods of the Chinese regime. The PRC has experimented with a variety of policies and ideological lines since its birth in 1950, but its most fundamental national aspirations have remained constant, and its leaders have evolved long-term strategies for achieving these ends. From the 1980s onward, these aspirations and strategies have led China to develop itself as a seapower.

The first three sections of this chapter discuss the enduring national ambitions of the communist regime: national sovereignty, central power and political identity. Although the PRC has been infamous for its ideological turmoil and famous for its dramatic shifts in policy, its commitment to these goals has seldom wavered. The remainder of the chapter addresses the strategies which China has applied in pursuit of those goals. This material begins with a discussion of Mao's writings, and goes on to discuss how Chinese strategic thought evolved in the 1980s and 1990s, with an emphasis on how China's leaders have applied these ideas to grand strategy.

MORE SOVEREIGN THAN THOU

The Manchus, the Europeans and the Japanese humiliated China by dictating policy to them in their own country. From Mao Zedong onward, China's leaders have struggled to guarantee that their country will be able to choose its own destiny. As General Li Jijun of the People's Liberation Army (PLA) put it in an address at the US Army War College in 1997:

> Before 1949, when the People's Republic of China was established, more than 1,000 treaties and agreements, most of which were

unequal in their terms, were forced upon China by the Western powers. As many as 1.8 million square kilometres were also taken away from Chinese territory. This was a period of humiliation that the Chinese can never forget. This is why the people of China show such strong emotions in matters concerning our national independence, unity, integrity of territory and sovereignty. This is also why the Chinese are so determined to safeguard them under any circumstances and at all costs.[1]

The Chinese prize national self-determination in its most pure form. Their leaders show little patience for the redefinitions of sovereignty that have intrigued academic political scientists in the West. For examples of Beijing's absolute position on this issue, one need only look at the statements of PRC leaders and editorialists concerning the West's 1998–99 humanitarian intervention in Kosovo.[2] One non-Chinese scholar, apparently in a tone of frustration, recently titled an essay 'How Much has China Learned about Interdependence?'.[3] The answer to judge from the statements of PRC leaders is, enough to take precautions.

'To open to the world is a fundamental policy for China', Deng Xiaoping once noted.[4] Mao Zedong cooperated with outsiders from Chiang Kai-Shek to Richard Nixon in order to further his interests. China's leaders understand that they need to work with foreign powers, both economically and otherwise. The PRC cannot afford isolation, and its leaders know it. Therefore, the Beijing regime also knows that, if it wishes to resist outside influences on China, it must counter them with influences of its own.

Mao Zedong argued that China's independence depended upon a supportive global political environment.[5] In his view, the best environment for his country would have been one of world communism. By the same token, he claimed, a sincere communist should see no contradiction between internationalist political ideals and fervent Chinese patriotism, because the cause of China and the cause of communism were the same.

Later generations of Chinese leaders have followed Mao's example in trying to establish international principles of behavior that support their national aims. Radicals such as Lin Biao famously called for China to 'hold aloft the national banner' in a revolution of global proportions.[6] Other Chinese thinkers criticized classical and Soviet concepts of sovereignty on the grounds that countries such as the PRC needed even stronger legal safeguards for their independence.[7] In the 1990s, writers in China's army newspaper *Jiefangjun bao* ('People's Army Daily') stated that China's armed forces exist, not only to defend the PRC's borders, but to create an international order that supports their country's interests. China must defend itself, they explain, not only against direct attack but against 'fundamental contradictions or interest conflicts, such as opposing social systems and ideologies as well as disputes in economic interests, territorial and ocean rights'.[8]

One should not assume that *Jiefangjun bao* refers to social systems and ideologies lightly. Although outside commentators commonly suggest that the PRC's commercial exploits of the 1980s and 1990s have nullified communism in China, the Beijing regime states otherwise. When the newspaper the *People's Daily* printed an article suggesting that the writings of Marx and Lenin might not be enough to solve China's modern problems, the editors issued a quick correction.[9] To PRC leaders, 'bourgeois liberalisation' remains a threat to be guarded against and building a 'socialist spiritual civilisation' remains the national goal.[10] In 1994, when asked whether China still favoured global communism, the vice-chairman of the Chinese Communist Party replied, 'Yes, of course. That is the reason we exist.'[11]

China's adherence to communism ties into older traditions in Chinese politics. Just as the Chinese define sovereignty in an exceptionally straightforward way, they define the state as a tangible entity as well. Ancient and modern thinkers alike have identified the concept of the state directly with the political organisation that wields power. To Shang Yang, an exponent of the ancient school of political thought known as Legalism, the ruler alone can determine national goals and to Li Si, the thinker who put Legalist ideas into practice under the Ch'in Dynasty, the ideal state is one in which 'the ruler will, by himself, control the state, and will not be controlled by anyone'.[12] Mao Zedong updated this sentiment with his famous statement that, since power grows out of the barrel of a gun, the party – and not, one notes, any more abstract entity such as the state – must keep the gun for itself.[13]

Mao's party continues to rule China, and organizes itself on the basis of communism. Many Chinese leaders, no doubt, hope for the social reforms that communism promises. Even those who doubt communism may see the PRC's distinct political system as a vital tool for maintaining China's independence from Western-dominated global institutions, both formal and informal. 'If China does not uphold socialism', Deng Xiaoping stated, 'it will be turned into an appendage of the capitalist countries.'[14] China's president (as of late 2001), Jiang Zemin, has expressed similar beliefs.[15]

Indeed, PRC leaders suggest that the West has deliberately spread the idea that China is abandoning communism in order to weaken their country. 'The entire imperialist Western world plans to make all socialist countries discard the socialist road and then bring them under control of international monopoly capital', Deng warned. Jiang Zemin has reiterated this principle in more detail.

International hostile forces will never stop using peaceful evolution against us for a single day. Bourgeois liberalisation is an internal matching force which they use to carry out peaceful evolution. These kinds of hostile activities constitute a real threat to China's independence, sovereignty, development and reform. In other words, peaceful evolution and bourgeois liberalisation are aimed not only at overthrowing our socialist system but, fundamentally, at depriving us of our national independence and state sovereignty.[16]

Given these sentiments, no one should be surprised that China's leaders have expressed their determination to make economic reforms work for the communist regime, and not the other way around. 'Reform and opening to the world are means of strengthening the nation', Jiang Zemin stated in an 'agenda-setting' speech shortly after he took power.[17] Reform, in other words, is the means, and national strength is the end. Chairman of China's National People's Congress, Li Peng, has reminded people in China's Special Economic Zones (SEZs) to keep these priorities clear:

The SEZs must uphold the Four Basic Principles and put great effort into developing socialist spiritual civilisation. The special zones engage in foreign intercourse. At the same time that they earnestly study advanced foreign technology and management, in politics they must maintain clear heads. They must strengthen Party building and develop the function of the Party as a protective fortress.[18]

The fact that China's recent reforms seem radical need not imply that China's leaders have changed their mind about fundamental issues. China has a long tradition of social experiments on a grand scale, reaching back to the Great Wall and the Sung-era agricultural reforms and continuing under Mao with the Great Leap Forward and the Cultural Revolution. China's communists accept the principle that one may conduct major social experiments as long as one remains true to communist goals.[19] Although China's leaders are aware that economic reforms might threaten the regime if taken too far, they plan to avert this danger. In 1992, Deng Xiaoping noted:

As long as we keep ourselves sober-minded, there is nothing to be feared. We still hold superiority, because we have large and medium state-owned enterprises and township and town enterprises. More importantly, we hold the state power in our hands.[20]

Whenever necessary, Deng implies, power can still flow from the barrel of a gun.

One must also note that China's new private enterprises are not as private as many commentators seem to assume. During the 1990s, the Chinese government announced that it had privatised 10,000 state-run firms. Of these newly independent firms, however, only 300 have been publicly listed in Shanghai and Shenzen. Banks continue to lend to these firms as if they expected the state to cover their debts. Perhaps most significantly of all, the management of the privatized industries remains unchanged.[21] China's industrialists, China's intelligence officials, China's military officers, and China's political leaders tend to be closely related by birth, when they are not actually the same individuals.[22]

China's political reforms appear designed to strengthen the communist regime as well. Government officials, as well as student demonstrators, have called for more democracy in China.[23] One cannot rule out the possibility that they will achieve some of what they seek. This movement's goals, however, are not to give citizens greater freedom, but to reduce the role of individual (and thus, potentially idiosyncratic) leaders in policymaking and to unite the people more solidly behind government programs. Democracy advocates argue that collective government is more 'scientific' (kexue) than oligarchy, and that 'the process will lead to more correct policy, which all people could be educated to embrace and support'.[24]

Mao Zedong himself supported democracy on much the same grounds. To him, democratic processes were a way to call forth 'activeness', from the people. This, he hoped, would stimulate creativity, inspire people to work with greater energy and provoke useful criticism of party policies. Nevertheless, Mao wished to moderate democratic institutions with centralist ones that would prevent individuals from lapsing into 'licence of action'. In his view, democracy 'is meant to strengthen discipline and raise fighting capacity, not to weaken them'.[25]

Deng Xiaoping expressed similar enthusiasm for democracy, combined with similar qualifications.[26] China's current (as of late 2001) president, Jiang Zemin, has continued this tradition. Jiang has supported 'socialist democracy' and a 'socialist legal system' on the grounds that they promote 'China's long-term order and stability', but has hastened to add, 'we must draw a clear line of demarcation between socialist democracy and capitalist democracy'.

> People's democracy and the dictatorship over hostile elements and antisocialist elements are closely linked and in unity with each other. As long as class struggle remains within a certain scope, the function of this dictatorship cannot be weakened.[27]

Overall, the Chinese regime remains committed to its distinct political identity. Whether or not Mao Zedong would endorse Beijing's current economic policies, China's rulers have no more desire to conform to the liberal international order today (2001) than they have had at any other time since their revolution. Whatever else Beijing chooses to reform, China's determination to shape world politics in the interests of its communist regime appears unlikely to change.

A STARTING POINT FOR CHINESE STRATEGY

The PRC's goals of national sovereignty, state power and ideological independence are bold. Its resources for achieving them, however, are modest, and were even more so in the earlier decades of its existence. For China's national objectives to be anything more than pipe dreams, the Chinese government must use these limited resources to lever itself into a position from which it can change its relationship with the rest of the world at a fundamental level. In other words, China requires an exceptionally well-conceived long-term strategy.

Fortunately for Chinese patriots, the founders of the People's Republic had an affinity for strategic thought. Mao and his colleagues wrote insightfully about the methods their country might use to achieve its national goals. Although their work focused on the problems of insurgent warfare and frequently lapsed into Marxist-Leninist theology, it rested upon fundamental principles that apply equally well to the grand strategy of a state like twenty-first-century China. Although contemporary Chinese strategists have reappraised Mao's writings extensively, they have not wavered from these basic ideas. As future chapters will show, both logic and events seem to vindicate their approach.

As a guerrilla in the 1920s and 1930s, Mao faced the same problems of unlimited goals and limited means that his entire country would face in later years. In order to overcome his stronger opponents, he developed a strategy of protracted war in which his forces built up their strength in stages, using different methods at each stage. First, the guerrilla forces would remain on the defensive, defending positions when advantageous but fighting mainly to preserve themselves. At the end of the first stage, Mao notes, 'owing to the insufficiency in his own troops and our own firm resistance, the enemy will be forced to fix a point as the terminus of his strategic offensive'.[28]

At that point, the enemy would stop pursuing the communist forces. Instead, the enemy would have to defend his own positions, allowing guerrillas to infiltrate his rear areas and strike him wherever he showed weakness. If the enemy lacked the resources to continue his own offensive, he would certainly lack the resources to defend every point throughout his territory against attacks which might fall anywhere.

58

Eventually, the enemy's forces would be spread so thin that the guerrillas would be able to seize positions and keep them. At this point, guerrilla forces might advance to the stage of 'mobile warfare', in which they used large units to capture territory and annihilate enemy forces.[29] At each point, Mao's guerrillas escalated to more decisive modes of warfare by stretching opposing forces to the point where their enemies acknowledged their overcommitment and withdrew.

Mao advised guerrillas to position their forces so as to achieve a war of 'jig-saw pattern', in which friendly units and enemy units lie spread across the map like pieces in a half-assembled puzzle or bits of cloth on a patchwork quilt. Most communist guerrilla units were able to sustain themselves within their own enclaves, meaning that they could both maneuver on interior lines and enjoy the advantages of a secure rear. Nevertheless, they could also coordinate their operations with friendly forces in other enclaves, instantaneously surrounding the enemy forces positioned between them. Mao compared this strategy to *wei chi*, a game in which players take turns placing tiles on a board in an attempt to surround each other's pieces.[30]

Mao also emphasized the concept of initiative, which he defined as a commander's freedom to fight in whatever way he finds most advantageous: 'Freedom of action is the very life of an army and once this freedom is lost, an army faces defeat or annihilation.' For these reasons, commanders must take advantage of enemy blunders and position their own forces so as to maximize the number of options at their disposal. Nevertheless, Mao told us, initiative depends on more than tactical shrewdness. 'The initiative is inseparable from superiority in fighting strength, while passivity is inseparable from inferiority in fighting strength.'[31]

Here, Mao echoes Sun Tzu, who noted, perhaps wryly, that there are times when one may know how to win but be unable to do so.[32] Strategic brilliance is useless unless one equips oneself with the means to put it into practice. To seize the all-important initiative, one must make adequate logistical preparations. No commander, however, can make such preparations unless the army can provide him with the supplies he needs. Therefore, the question of which side will enjoy the initiative in battle ultimately becomes a question of national military potential, involving economics, technological development and political mobilization.[33]

Although Mao's writings on warfare focus on the Communist forces' struggle against Japan, his principles apply to grand strategy as well. In *On the Protracted War*, Mao took pains to emphasize the unity of battlefield tactics, campaign strategy and more overarching national goals such as regenerating China and bringing about international communism.[34] Mao states that his ideas about the advantages of adopting a 'jigsaw pattern' apply as much to grand strategic contests among whole nations as they do to guerrilla operations in the field.[35] The Chinese revolutionary, Lin Biao, extended Mao's theories of guerrilla warfare to international politics by analogy.[36] Other veterans of Mao's campaigns praised the classic strategic writings of Sun Tzu for introducing the concept of 'universal laws of war' that connect warfare with politics, economics, diplomacy and geography.[37]

At the level of diplomatic policy, Mao himself actively sought alliances with outside organizations even when those organizations were ideologically opposed to him. The most notable example of such an alliance was the United Front between the Red Army and Chiang Kai-Shek's Kuomintang, but Mao discussed such policies of mutual 'assistance and concession' in general terms, implying that his followers would be wise to adopt them on a regular basis. Mao paid lip service, at least, to promoting the 'consolidation and expansion' of one's allies in order to direct them against common enemies. In response to the criticism that cooperation with the class enemy compromised communist principles, Mao quoted the ancient Confucian thinker Menicus: 'Refrain from doing certain things and you will be able to do other things.'[38]

Mao might equally well have quoted another traditional proverb, 'Yi-yi-zhi-yi' ('Use barbarians to fight barbarians').[39] Certainly, the Chinese revolutionaries saw such alliances as a step back in order to 'get a better run for a bigger leap forward', and not as a move toward permanent coexistence.[40] United fronts are inherently temporary, and Maoist diplomats reserve the right to realign themselves as soon as 'contradictions' appear within the alliance.[41] This diplomatic policy, one notes, dovetails with Mao's more purely military strategies, giving him additional (and eminently expendable) pieces for his metaphorical *wei chi* board.

Succeeding generations of Chinese diplomats have followed Mao's advice about alliances. In 1977, Chinese premier Hua Goufeng invoked Mao's ideas about united fronts to explain his own government's support of Iran, Chile, Zaire and the Philippines.[42] At that time, all of those countries were ideologically opposed to China. Nevertheless, Hua considered all of them momentarily useful against the United States.[43] For an example of this policy on a grander scale, one might examine the triangular diplomacy of the 1970s and 1980s, when China shifted its allegiance back and forth between the United States and the Soviet Union, attempting to play the two superpowers off against each other for its own advantage.

ENDURING PRINCIPLES, CHANGING TIMES

China's reformers of the 1980s and 1990s honored Mao as the grandfather of their own strategic thought. Not only did they praise his ideological vision, they noted that he, like they, emphasized the point that one must continually update policies to reflect the present circumstances. The principle of evolving with the times, after all, was the essence of Mao's teachings about fighting a guerrilla war by using different methods at different stages. During the revolutionary period, Mao had distinguished himself from other aspiring strategists by promoting the principle of 'active defense', which called on leaders to seize the initiative wherever possible, even when on the defensive. Such defense 'is achieved through readiness to fight'.[44]

Chinese military leaders of the mid-1990s observed that Mao himself had raised these principles to a 'strategic level'.[45] In that spirit, they called for national policies to focus on scientific and industrial modernizations that would allow them to achieve new levels of readiness, and thus, new levels of proficiency at 'active defense'. PLA commanders made modernization the first priority of their military policy, and civilian leaders made economic modernization the first priority of China's national political program.[46]

Deng Xiaoping and his followers noted that the events of the late twentieth century reduced the chances that China could succeed with an overtly aggressive foreign policy while simultaneously being granted an unprecedented opportunity to concentrate upon improving its economy.

> At a time when the international strategic structure is undergoing profound changes and the socialist movement is temporarily at a low ebb, we should calmly observe and cope with the situation, be good at keeping a low profile, and try our best to do our work well in China.[47]

Deng believed that China was in a position where it could postpone major war if it chose. In 1975, he stated that there would be no world war for five years, and by the mid-1980s, he was willing to predict that peace would last 'for a fairly long period of time'.[48] Although Deng repeated the Marxist-Leninist argument that class conflict made war inevitable, he suggested that China's government had the power to prolong the period of peace if it 'did a good job'.[49] At the same time, Deng, along with others throughout China's political and military establishment, was becoming increasingly impressed by the importance of technology and industrial output in modern war, and correspondingly concerned about the relatively primitive state of Chinese forces.[50] Accordingly, Deng made development strategy the 'core' of his strategic thought.[51]

Certainly, the Chinese desire prosperity for its own sake.[52] There is no doubt, however, that China's leaders see development as being strategic in the most robust sense of the word. Deng emphasized that military and economic development should be linked. In practice, this often means that the armed forces must sacrifice their programs to civilian needs, but, at a higher level, China's leaders hope to coordinate both forms of development in order to increase their country's overall capabilities.[53] As one PLA general observed, paraphrasing Deng, 'When our country is developed and more prosperous, we shall have a bigger role to play in the world.'[54] One Chinese official explained the concept in more detail:

> When we say that we shall link defense with commercial industry, during war and peacetime, we mean that during our normal time of national construction we should have a long-term point of view. We should take into consideration future requirements of warfare, and make appropriate arrangements. Military requirements and civilian needs, during war and peace, should be considered and planned in coordination.[55]

In other areas, China's military thinkers have retained Mao's ideas in their original form. For instance, Senior Colonel Shen Kuigan, writing in 1994, reiterated the concept that weak forces can defeat strong forces through a three-phase strategy.[56] Shen has expunged the doctrine of potentially anachronistic references to guerrilla warfare. Nevertheless, he explains that an inferior force can overcome a superior one by first 'resisting the superior', second, progressing to a stage of 'turning the inferior into the superior' and third, taking the offensive against the once-superior forces. Shen adds the following observation: 'Overall, this must be assured by first defeating the superior with the inferior *piecemeal*.'[57]

He explicitly states that these principles of 'superiority' and 'inferiority' apply to grand strategy. The colonel's strategic ideas involve 'political conditions, powerful military forces, abundant material base, full war preparations, correct operational direction, advantageous natural conditions, favorable mass opinion, and international support'. 'It is impossible', Shen adds, for the inferior side to achieve superiority in a short time, especially in 'high-tech war'.[58] Victory comes from long-term maneuvering that changes 'the overall balance of all factors'.[59]

RISING PROMINENCE OF SEAPOWER

In the 1950s, Mao stated that China should develop a strong fleet.[60] For the first three decades of its existence, the PRC had neither the resources nor the time to act on this idea. Furthermore, the more extreme versions of revolutionary ideology were more conducive to a 'people's war' of guerrillas than to complex and technological forces such as navies. Thus, it is no surprise that, throughout this period, China's fleet remained oriented toward coastal defense.[61]

In 1979, however, Deng Xiaoping made a major speech exhorting China to develop a powerful navy, and in 1985 he reiterated this point, calling for a navy with 'real fighting capability'.[62] By this time, China's political thought, strategic philosophy and geopolitical circumstances had come to favor naval expansion. Whereas the ideologues of earlier eras had mistrusted the scientists, industrialists and military professionals who build modern fleets, the supporters of today's orthodoxy, applaud them.[63] Whereas earlier generations had feared that China would find itself in the middle of a world war before its navy was ready to fight, Deng and his successors believe that they can afford to wait. Chinese military commanders do expect to fight limited 'local wars' in the relatively near future, and in these smaller skirmishes, newly developed naval forces may be effective even before they reach maturity.[64]

A strong fleet may be indispensable to China's coordinated program of military and economic development. Certainly, any naval build-up will benefit from general economic and scientific advances. Conversely, without a capable fleet, the overall modernization effort may be doomed. As Colonel Peng Guangqian noted, writing in 1994, China's economic development depends upon a 'favorable international strategic situation'. 'The development of modern China cannot be separated from the outside world, especially at a time when the world is growing smaller each day. In the information age of closer relationships, practicing isolationism is suicidal.'[65] For these reasons, Deng Xiaoping, whom Peng urges all Chinese strategists to emulate, 'always considered China's development in the context of the overall world strategic situation and has adopted an active posture in international society'.[66] To adopt such a posture, China must acquire the ability to act internationally, and this, in practice, will be largely a matter of seapower.

Chinese military writers have paid a great deal of attention to the importance of ocean resources. As a PLAN captain and two Chinese naval lieutenants who served as his co-authors wrote in 1995:

> In the last decade or two, ever-growing numbers of countries have been realizing the importance of the seas as a '21st-century resource for human survival and development. As all countries gain a stronger sense of the values, rights and interests of the seas and oceans, disputes over matters such as maritime economic zones, continental shelves, and sea-area boundaries are likely to intensify, thus making it harder to prevent sharper conflicts and even outbreaks of war.[67]

Indeed, deep-sea resources are becoming increasingly valuable. Advances in ocean platform design and seismic scanners for underwater prospecting continually open larger regions of the sea to oil drilling, while simultaneously making this activity more productive and profitable than ever.[68] Given the importance of fishing to the Chinese food supply and the likelihood that petroleum reserves lie beneath the disputed waters of the South China Sea, such concerns are particularly salient for the PRC. Chinese leaders remain sensitive to the fact that 'imperialists' possessing superior navies exploited their nation ruthlessly during the 1800s, and are determined not to let seapowers shut them out of future industrial revolutions.[69]

Furthermore, until the Chinese have an ocean-going navy, their freedom to trade will depend upon the goodwill of others. China's leaders understand this fact, and are determined to remedy it.[70] As if to remind Chinese leaders just how much is at stake, China became a net importer of petroleum products in 1993 and a net importer of crude oil in 1996.[71] China's highest ranking military officer and Politburo member, General Liu Huaqing, summed up the importance of seapower in an address to the China Military Science Association:

> Since the beginning of the 1970s, the strategic importance of the oceans has increased day by day. Exploitation of the ocean has turned into an important condition for coastal countries in developing their economy and overall strength of national power. It is certain that the ocean will be more and more significant to the long-term development of a country. We must understand the ocean from a strategic level and its importance to the whole nation.[72]

CONCLUSIONS

China's regime hopes not only to take its place among the great powers of the world, but to maintain exceptionally high degrees of autonomy and independent influence within the international system that those nations have created. To achieve this, China's leaders must pursue a proactive foreign policy, shaping events rather than being shaped by them. If China is to achieve its goals and practice this sort of statecraft, it will need the ability to protect its interests in every part of the world, and to threaten potential opponents in every part of the world as well. In other words, its ambitions require an ocean-going navy, and its leaders have become frank about these points.

NOTES

1. Li Jijun, *Traditional Military Thinking and the Defensive Strategy of China* (Carlisle Barracks, PA: Strategic Studies Institute, 1997), p. 4.

2. Joseph Fewsmith, 'Reaction, Resurgence and Succession: Chinese Politics Since Tiananmen', in Roderick MacFarquhar (ed.), *The Politics of China: The Eras of Mao and Deng* (Cambridge: Cambridge University Press, 1993), pp. 484–5.
3. Michael Yahuda, 'How Much Has China Learned about Interdependence?', in David G.G. Goodman and Gerald Segal (eds), *China Rising: Nationalism and Interdependence* (London: Routledge, 1997), pp. 6–26.
4. Richard Baum, 'The Road to Tiananmen: Chinese Politics in the 1980s', in MacFarquhar (ed.), *The Politics of China*, p. 376.
5. Mao Zedong, *Selected Works of Mao Tse-Tung, Volume Two* (London: Lawrence & Wishart, 1954), p. 201.
6. Samuel B. Griffith II, *Peking and People's Wars: An Analysis of Statements by Official Spokesmen of the Chinese Communist Party on the Subject of Revolutionary Strategy* (London: Pall Mall Press, 1966), p. 68.
7. Menno T. Kamminga, 'Building "Railroads on the Sea": China's Attitude towards Maritime Law', *China Quarterly*, No. 59 (Sept. 1974), pp. 544–58; Suzanne Ogden, 'The Approach of the Chinese Communists to the Study of International Law, State Sovereignty and the International System', *China Quarterly*, No. 70 (June 1977), pp. 315–37.
8. Allen S. Whiting, 'The PLA and China's Threat Perceptions', *China Quarterly*, No. 146 (June 1996), p. 599.
9. Baum, 'The Road to Tiananmen', p. 372.
10. 'The Sixth Plenary Session of the 14th CCPCC and Seventh Plenary Session of the CCP CDIC', in 'Quarterly Chronicle and Documentation', *China Quarterly*, No. 150 (June 1997), pp. 230–1; Allen S. Whiting, 'Chinese Nationalism and Foreign Policy After Deng', *China Quarterly*, No. 142 (June 1995), p. 304; 'The Sixth Plenary Session', p. 229.
11. Anatoly Golitsyn, *The Perestroika Deception: The World's Slide Toward the Second October Revolution [Weltoktober]* (London: Edward Halle, 1995), p. xxiv.
12. Wade Baskin (ed.), *Classics in Chinese Philosophy* (New York: Philosophical Library, 1972), p. 142; Wm Theodore de Bary, Wing-tsit Chan and Burton Watson (eds), *Sources of Chinese Tradition, Volume 1* (New York: Columbia University Press, 1960), p. 142.
13. Mao Zedong, *Selected Works*, p. 228.
14. Fewsmith, 'Reaction, Resurgence and Succession', p. 485.
15. Jiang Zemin, 'Report on Behalf of the CPC Central Committee State Council at a Grand Meeting of People of Various Walks of Life in the Capital to Celebrate the 40th Anniversary of the Founding of the PRC', in Peter R. Moody Jr (ed.), *China Documents Annual 1989: The Crisis of Reform* (Gulf Breeze, FL: Academic International Press, 1992), p. 17.
16. Whiting, 'Chinese Nationalism', p. 304.
17. Jiang, 'Report on Behalf of the CPC', p. 22.
18. Li Peng, 'Li Peng Points Out at the National Work Conference on Special Economic Zones: The Special Economic Zones Must Serve as Windows and as Base Areas', in Peter R. Moody Jr (ed.), *China Documents Annual 1990: The Continuing Crisis*, p. 120.
19. Melvin Gurtov and Byong-Moo Hwang, *China under Threat: The Politics of Strategy and Diplomacy* (Baltimore, MD: Johns Hopkins University Press, 1980), p. 10.
20. Michael Yahuda, 'Deng Xiaoping: The Statesman', *China Quarterly*, No. 135 (Sept. 1993), p. 557.
21. Nicholas Lardy and Kevin Nealer, 'China's Economic Prospects', in Hans Binnendijk and Ronald N. Montaperto (eds), *Strategic Trends in China* (Washington, DC: US Government Printing Office, 1998), p. 35.

22. Murray Scot Tanner, 'The Erosion of Communist Party Control over Lawmaking in China', *China Quarterly*, No. 138 (June 1994), p. 386.
23. Ibid.
24. Ibid.
25. Mao, *Selected Works*, pp. 210, 211.
26. David Bonavia, *Deng* (Hong Kong: Longman Group, 1989), p. 193.
27. Jiang, 'Report on Behalf of the CPC', pp. 26, 27.
28. Mao, *Selected Works*, pp. 139–41.
29. Ibid., pp. 143–4.
30. Ibid., p. 151.
31. Ibid.
32. Sun Tzu, *The Art of War*, p. 101.
33. Mao, *Selected Works*, pp. 168–9.
34. Ibid., pp. 153–6, 158–61.
35. Ibid., pp. 151–2.
36. Griffith, *Peking and People's Wars*, p. 95.
37. Sun Tzu, *The Art of War*, p. 8 (Commentary by PLA General Tao Hanzhang.)
38. Mao, *Selected Works*, pp. 218–22.
39. Michael D. Swaine and Ashley J. Tellis, *Interpreting China's Grand Strategy: Past, Present and Future* (Santa Monica, CA: RAND, 2000), pp. 68–9.
40. Mao, *Selected Works*, p. 219.
41. Gurtov, *China Under Threat*, p. 10.
42. Ibid.
43. Peng Guangqian, 'Deng Xiaoping's Strategic Thought', in Michael Pillsbury (ed.), *Chinese Views of Future Warfare* (Washington, DC: National Defense University Press, 1998), p. 3.
44. Wang Naiming, 'Adhere to Active Defense and Modern People's War', in Pillsbury (ed.), *Chinese Views*, p. 37.
45. Ibid.
46. Peng, 'Deng Xiaoping's Strategic Thought', p. 6.
47. Ibid.
48. Zhao Nanqi, 'Deng Xiaoping's Theory of Defense Modernization', in Pillsbury (ed.), *Chinese Views*, p. 12.
49. Hong Baoxiu, 'Deng Xiaoping's Theory of War and Peace', in Pillsbury (ed.), *Chinese Views*, p. 21; Zhao, 'Deng Xiaoping's Theory', p. 12.
50. Hong Baoxiu, 'Deng Xiaoping's Theory of War and Peace', pp. 21–2.
51. Peng, 'Deng Xiaoping's Strategic Thought', p. 5.
52. Ibid., pp. 5–6.
53. Zhao, 'Deng Xiaoping's Theory', p. 12.
54. Ibid., p. 17.
55. Fang Ning, 'Defense Policy in the New Era', in Pillsbury (ed.), *Chinese Views*, p. 21; Zhao, 'Deng Xiaoping's Theory', pp. 51–2.
56. Shen Kuigan, 'Dialectics of Defeating the Superior with the Inferior', in Pillsbury (ed.), *Chinese Views*, p. 21; Zhao, 'Deng Xiaoping's Theory', p. 214.
57. Ibid. (emphasis in original).
58. Ibid., pp. 214–15, 216.
59. Ibid., p. 216.
60. Ibid., p. 218.
61. Anon., *The Communist Bloc and the Western Alliance: The Military Balance 1961–1962* (London: ISS, 1961), p. 7.
62. Barry M. Blechman and Robert P. Berman, *A Guide to Far Eastern Navies* (Annapolis, MD: United States Naval Institute Press, 1978), p. 5; Zhao, 'Deng Xiaoping's Theory', p. 14.

63. Peng, 'Deng Xiaoping's Strategic Thought', p. 6.
64. For a discussion of these issues, see Nan Li, 'The PLA's Evolving Warfighting Doctrine, Strategy and Tactics, 1985–95: A Chinese Perspective', *China Quarterly*, No. 146 (June 1996), pp. 443–63.
65. Peng, 'Deng Xiaoping's Strategic Thought', p. 9.
66. Ibid.
67. Shen Zhongchang, Zhang Haiying and Zhou Xinsheng, '21st-Century Naval Warfare', in Pillsbury (ed.), *Chinese Views*, p. 21; Zhao, 'Deng Xiaoping's Theory', p. 262.
68. Kevin L. Falk, *Why Nations Put to Sea: Technology and the Changing Character of Sea Power in the Twenty-First Century* (New York: Garland Publishing, 2000), pp. 65–6.
69. Liu Huaqing 'Defense Modernization in Historical Perspective', in Pillsbury (ed.), *Chinese Views*, p. 21; Zhao, 'Deng Xiaoping's Theory', p. 118.
70. Swaine, *Interpreting China's Grand Strategy*, p. 144.
71. Eric A. McVadon, 'The Chinese Military and the Peripheral States in the 21st Century: A Security *Tour d'Horizon*', in Larry M. Wortzel (ed.), *The Chinese Armed Forces in the 21st Century* (Carlisle, PA: Strategic Studies Institute, 1999), p. 72.
72. Liu Huaqing, 'Defense Modernization', p. 118.

5

The Twenty-first-Century PLAN

China's maritime ideas are grand, but China's navy is primitive. On examining the current state of the PLAN, one can see the substance to Mahan's warning that a country with China's social, political and geographical characteristics will always be handicapped at sea. Nevertheless, Mahan himself acknowledged that skilled leaders and governments can find more strategic opportunities on the high seas than a narrow reading of his writings on the 'elements of seapower' would indicate.[1] Other strategic thinkers broadened the concepts of maritime power yet further. The expanded concepts of seapower are the ones that explain how contemporary China is developing its fleet.

However, the fact that China's navy remains materially weak does not mean that it is strategically useless. The PLAN serves a purpose in peace and is designed to serve a purpose in war. Beijing has developed both its navy and its naval strategy in accordance with principles that Mao, Corbett and Callwell would have found familiar. When one reflects upon how China's navy measures up to the tasks Beijing is putting it to, and combines those reflections with a consideration of how the Chinese fleet may develop over time, the PLAN begins to seem more adequate.

This chapter begins by discussing what Chinese strategic theorists have written about naval warfare, and goes on to address the extent to which China's fleet can put these theories into practice. The final sections appraise China's attempts to raise the quality of its forces, both through training programs within the military and through national economic development.

USES OF SEAPOWER

Chinese strategists have developed a substantial body of thought about the ways in which a nation can use naval forces, both in general and in their own specific case. As noted in Chapter 4, their thought tends to emphasize the idea that armed forces must proceed through a process of metamorphosis as they evolve from weakness to strength. From the 1950s to the 1970s, Chinese writers tended to discuss naval matters in terms of 'coastal defense'.[2] Since the 1980s, however, China's military thinkers have developed a consensus that maritime strategy must be global, active and long term. To the new way of thinking, seapower is a 'strategic concept', in which even a nation committed to defensive war must, as a tactical matter, seize the initiative by assuming the offensive upon the open ocean.[3] The goal is no longer merely to fend off amphibious invasions, but to achieve 'mastery of the seas'.[4]

China's military writers note that maritime capabilities give state leaders additional options in international disputes.[5] This observation gives a clue about how Beijing might incorporate naval forces – even relatively weak naval forces – into its grand strategy. The idea of coordinating a variety of different techniques in order to achieve a combined effect is an elemental concept in Chinese strategic thought. To quote Sun Tzu, 'use the normal force to engage and use the extraordinary to win'.[6]

By synthesizing various kinds of forces, the commander becomes flexible and unpredictable. 'The musical notes are only five in number, but their combination gives rise to so numerous melodies that one cannot hear them all.'[7] By mastering this range of possible combinations, the commander can apply force in a critical way at a critical moment. 'When torrential water tosses boulders, it is because of its momentum; when the strike of a hawk breaks the body of its prey, it is because of timing.'[8]

In 1974, the PRC seized control of the Paracel island chain in the South China Sea. This gambit provides a dramatic example of Sun Tzu's principle of timing. At the time, the Republic of Vietnam (RVN) governed the islands. The RVN, however, was in the final throes of its war with the Communist Democratic Republic of Vietnam (DRV) to its north. The United States had already committed itself to withdrawing from the war in Southeast Asia, and was unlikely to intervene.

Shortly after China occupied the Paracels, the RVN ceased to exist. The new government of Vietnam was in no position to reclaim the islands by force. Given the fact that China, a communist country, had taken the Paracels from the hated South Vietnamese regime, even Vietnam's moral position was compromised. In the early 1970s, the PLAN had far fewer capabilities than it has today, but China took advantage of a confluence of circumstances to use it, in Sun Tzu's language, 'as a grindstone against eggs'.[9]

The PRC's attempts to intimidate the Republic of China (ROC) government in Taiwan provide another example of how China is already using its limited armed forces at well-chosen times to accomplish grand strategic goals. Throughout the 1990s, Beijing signaled its displeasure with political trends in Taipei by test-firing ballistic missiles, staging fleet maneuvers and rehearsing amphibious landings. In November 1995, for instance, the PRC held a dramatic landing exercise on Dongshan Island – within a month of Taiwan's legislative elections.[10] The following year, shortly after the internationally assertive candidate Le Teng-hui won Taiwan's presidential election, the PRC conducted live-fire military exercises in the Taiwan Straits.[11] America sent two carrier battle groups to the region in response.

The China scholar Andrew Nathan interprets China's Taiwan Straits exercises as part of a long-term operation to escalate military pressure against Taiwan, test the United States' resolve and locate Taiwan's breaking point.[12] Whereas no one in China has confirmed these ideas directly, they are in keeping with Chinese military thought. In 1994, for instance, Lin Yinchao, the commander of the PLA's 65th Group Army published an article in China's military newspaper on the topic of psychological warfare.[13] Lin's version of psychological operations go on in peace as well as war, across the whole spectrum of national activities, including 'strategy, military technology, politics, diplomacy, religion, economics and propaganda'.[14] Lin outlined four objectives of psychological operations.

- To attack and influence the target's policy makers, causing their position to waver and make them choose a policy which is in fact disadvantageous to themselves.
- To instil fear and awe in the minds of enemy soldiers, destroy their mental equilibrium and boost the morale of one's own troops.
- To create panic among the adversary's civilian population by inducing fear of war, war weariness and antiwar feelings.
- To obtain the sympathy and support of neutral states, solidify coalitions among allied states and strengthen the desire for victory in one's own country.[15]

One cannot know the exact degree to which China's Taiwan Straits exercises influenced the governments and peoples involved. Nevertheless, these events highlight the fact that the PRC has developed its armed forces to the point where even the United States takes its military threats seriously. As Lin points out, and other senior Chinese officers have emphasized in other contexts, genuine military capabilities are necessary in order to achieve psychological or political effects.[16] Empty bluffs are not enough.

If US leaders publicly acknowledge the PRC's military significance in the Taiwan Straits, one can only speculate about the degree to which government officials in various Asian countries privately take China's armed might into account as they make policy on less publicized issues. Chapter 6 will discuss this issue in greater detail. However, despite all the uncertainties, China clearly uses its maritime forces to achieve national objectives, not just in isolated incidents such as wars, but continually. The stronger those forces become, the more effective they will be.

STRONG ENEMIES OR WEAK ENEMIES?

Meanwhile, Chinese military thinkers have debated a number of general doctrinal issues which have implications for the times and ways in which they will be able to use their fleet. China's strategists agree that contemporary China faces relatively little threat of invasion by a superior opponent. This means that China's armed forces no longer need to accept the kind of sacrifices they once took for granted, in terms of men, territory or time. Whereas earlier PLA doctrine assumed that China's forces would have to abandon cities, survive early defeats, retreat from contested positions and possibly absorb nuclear blasts, contemporary Chinese thought calls for the armed forces to repulse attacks near the border, win decisive battles early in a war and respond to nuclear threats with nuclear forces of their own.[17] In the same vein, China can afford to take the risk of acting farther from its borders and taking the offensive with relatively modest forces.

China's strategists are divided over the issue of how much has changed. The more optimistic (from a Chinese perspective) among them feel that the days when their country must always expect to fight lengthy wars against more highly developed opponents have passed, and that the time has come for China to adopt a doctrine of capitalizing on its strengths rather than prevailing despite weaknesses. Nearly all Chinese thinkers agree that future struggles are likely to take the form of limited 'local wars' rather than global fights to the finish. China's opponents are likely to be developing nations or small expeditionary detachments, not the fully mobilized forces of global superpowers. Beginning with that premise, a prominent optimist contends:

> In local war, we are not necessarily in a weak position. To suppress the enemy ... and to gain an upper hand in seeking a political solution, in strategic guidance, it must be absolutely necessary not to prolong conflict without a resolution. It is therefore necessary to take all measures to 'fight a quick battle to force a quick resolution,' and achieve the objective.[18]

Another point of view, however, warns that even in local wars China may well confront superior opponents such as the United States. As one of these thinkers noted, 'if we and the enemy all want a quick fight to achieve a quick resolution, we may . . . end up in a quick resolution defeat'.[19] Chinese leaders are not certain how much their power has grown, or what kind of tactics they are currently ready to implement. This debate is reminiscent of the sort of debate orthodox Maoist strategists might have had over the degree to which a protracted war had progressed to its next stage of development.

THE EVOLUTION OF NAVAL OPERATIONS

When Chinese military writers discuss the problems specific to naval warfare, they emphasize the importance of joint operations and technological change.

> For thousands of years, the theory of 'mastery of the seas has always been praised as the infallible law of decisive naval engagement. As aircraft carriers and carrier-based aircraft have appeared, however, the theory 'without mastery of the air, there is no mastery of the seas,' has found favor throughout the world. Since the 1970s, 'electromagnetic dominance' has also been held to be crucial to naval victory.[20]

By the next century, the authors of the above suggest, spacecraft will 'observe and control maritime operations from high altitudes'.[21] Meanwhile, the lines between land and sea combat will begin to blur.

> In joint operations, naval surface ships, submarines, carrier-based aircraft and possible other new service arms will have the capacity to conduct strategic offensive attacks in great depth and even against intercontinental land-based targets. As land-based arms will be sharply improved in reaction capacity, strike precision, and range, they will be able to powerfully strike formations at sea, and even individual warships and cruise missiles.[22]

In all these environments, information warfare, electronic warfare, stealth technology, precision-guided munitions and modern command, control and communications systems will achieve ever-greater significance.[23] After the Coalition victory in Operation Desert Storm, China's strategists wrote passionately about the growing importance of joint warfare.[24] One of the most critical aspects of modern military technology, they believe, is its potential to unite air, sea, land, space, radio-electronic and other forms of warfare into a devastating totality. Not only is the whole greater than the sum of its parts, but with modern C4I (command, control, communications, computers and intelligence) technology, the whole's margin of advantage is growing.[25]

These observations recall Callwell's writings about the relationship between land power and seapower. One can draw off the enemy's strength in one environment by deploying forces in another. To control open water, one must control the adjacent landmasses, and vice versa. Although this has always been true to some extent, the range of aircraft and cruise missiles means that landpower can interact with seapower over ranges of hundreds or even thousands of miles.

For these reasons, PLAN officers have argued that, if they are to defend China's coasts, they must control the 'two island chains'.[26] The first of these chains consists of the Ryukyus, Taiwan, the Philippines and Borneo.[27] The second includes the Marianas, Guam and the Carolines.[28] A review of the Second World War in the Pacific will indicate how vital these island bases were for air, land and sea operations even in that era.

The spread of new technologies has led to new forms of combat, many of which – under the right circumstances – might prove devastating in naval warfare. This holds out the possibility that any one of them could play a role analogous to that once played by so-called 'fleets in being'. As Corbett wrote, capital ships serve a function even if they are kept in reserve. If country A possesses a fleet of capital ships, country B's capital ships cannot take the risk of ignoring them, and while the opposing battle fleet is tied down keeping an eye on country A's battle fleet, country A's raiders are relatively free to do their work. Today, a variety of technologies present at least a notional threat to naval forces, and even if China cannot actually use such weapons to destroy an enemy fleet, it may hope that it can use them to induce caution.

Chinese writers have considered air forces, orbital weapons platforms, electronic warfare and information warfare against enemy command systems as potential 'killer maces' that can trump a battle fleet.[29] Nuclear weapons can serve as a killer mace as well. Although Chinese strategists have been more circumspect about discussing them, Major-General Wu Jianguo of the PLA has published an article reminding his fellow officers that, despite the taboo against using nuclear devices, such weapons have a role to play in local wars.[30] There are parallels between his writings and Corbett's thought concerning battleships, but Wu sees nuclear weapons as being more than a mere deterrent.

First, Wu asserts that Britain, the United States and the Soviet Union either deployed tactical nuclear weapons or threatened to use them in Korea, Vietnam, the period of Sino-Soviet tension, the Falklands War and the Gulf War.

> These countries threatened to use nuclear weapons in conventional wars because they believed that with nuclear weapons in hand, psychologically they would be able to hold a dominant position, which would enhance troop morale and frighten the enemy on the

one hand, and restrict the enemy's use of some conventional means on the other, thus changing the direction of the war.[31]

China, presumably, is capable of doing the same. At the very least, China must be strong enough to resist such intimidation. Furthermore, these threats are not idle. Although Wu appreciates the psychological role of nuclear explosives, he emphasizes that 'deterrence and actual combat are complementary and closely interrelated'.[32] When a country's attempts to achieve its goals through 'deterrence' fail, it will

> strive to win a victory through actual combat, so as to remove obstacles to its political, economic and diplomatic activities. Militarily, the immense effect of nuclear weaponry is that it can serve as a deterrent force and, at the same time, as a means of actual combat.[33]

Wu rejects the idea that nuclear weapons are inherently unusable. Rather, he implies, one must consider what they are physically capable of, and use those capabilities to best effect.

> We are materialists, so when we study an issue, we must proceed from objective reality rather than from a subjective wish, and, through investigation and study of objective reality, we derive our principles, policies and measures.[34]

The general goes on to offer an extended quotation from Mao:

> Investigation and study are very important. When we see someone hold something in his hand, we should look into the matter. What is he holding in his hand? It is a knife. What is the use of a knife? It can kill a person. Whom will he kill with the knife? He will kill the people. After probing into these matters, we should further the investigation. The Chinese people also have hands, and they can hold knives too. They can forge one if they have none.[35]

As later sections will note, the PLAN has 'forged' a variety of nuclear mines and projectiles for use at sea.

LIMITS ON NAVAL WAR

As Chinese thinkers contemplate recent developments in seapower, they note that state-of-the-art navies are becoming prohibitively costly.[36] Not only has the expense of building warships skyrocketed, but the operational challenges of commanding them and supporting them have multiplied as well. Modern C4I systems give naval officers such advantages in coordinating their ships that they have become the 'nerve center' of future naval warfare, and that the race to achieve more effective C4I will continually increase the complexity of the commander's job. Chinese strategists note also that Coalition forces in the Gulf War used 4.6 times as much ammunition per day as US forces did in Vietnam, and 20 times as much as UN forces in Korea. Not only are ammunition requirements becoming greater in volume, they are becoming more diverse in category and level.[37] Moreover, the growing problems of munitions supply are merely one example of a general increase in logistical requirements of all kinds.

These factors limit the scale and duration of naval wars. Chinese strategists note that nations may go on to fight general wars anyway, despite all obstacles, and that there may be future technological developments which make large-scale fleet actions more feasible again. Nevertheless, despite these caveats, it seems probable that 'there will be few naval engagements beyond the scale of battles; instead, there will be ever-growing numbers of medium and small conflicts with high-tech, small forces'.[38] From the Chinese point of view, this state of affairs presents both advantages and disadvantages. On the one hand, China is currently weak in high technology, but on the other, it can only benefit from factors that restrain states such as the United States from committing their full national resources in a war against the PRC. Corbett's points about limited war and the Russo-Japanese conflict come to mind.[39]

The cost and complexity of modern naval war have other implications as well. As fleets become smaller and the number of weapons systems that can potentially determine victory at sea proliferates, a commander's skill to coordinate different kinds of forces will become more critical than ever. Meanwhile, armed forces of all kinds will become dramatically more vulnerable to attacks on their support networks. These attacks may take the form of 'soft' electronic or information-technology attacks on C3I systems, or they may be more traditional raids on logistical systems. Even as forces become more susceptible to these methods, the spread of long-range precision-guided weapons makes such attacks increasingly effective and easier to carry out.[40]

GUERRILLA WARFARE AT SEA

To summarize, the Chinese believe that larger strategic factors will set the parameters for maritime warfare. This environment rewards navies that can reduce their own vulnerability to such outside threats while increasing their ability to prey on enemy weaknesses. As budgets and national resources play a growing role in determining the scale of military effort that even the industrialized countries can mount, it becomes increasingly important for navies to do their job economically, maximizing the ratio of losses inflicted to losses suffered. As Corbett might have observed, one must measure these losses, not merely in terms of ships sunk, but in terms of how effectively maritime forces hamper each other's ability to use the sea.

Naval expert Kevin Falk has described China's fleet as a 'naval guerrilla' force.[41] Although this term is misleading in a strategic sense, it sums up China's approach to maritime tactics. During the 1950s and early 1960s, as China fought Taiwan over the 'offshore islands', the Chinese proved adept at the art of naval ambush, concealing their torpedo craft behind reefs or fishing vessels.[42] Today, Chinese strategists advocate more technological means of hit-and-run combat at sea.

Chinese maritime strategists echo Corbett regarding the relationship of mass and dispersion in naval tactics. These writers feel that contemporary technological trends give such ideas more salience than ever:

> In naval combat, vessels are usually organized in task forces or battle groups to fulfil tasks. Concentration is conveniently used for organizing effective command, using massive firepower and forming the most favorable defense system in order to reduce enemy threats. However, in the informationized battlefield, vessels can have direct communication with the command post. Vessels can have access to each other's location and situation and have information about enemy vessels and aircraft. In addition, the capacity for long-range precision attack is also improved. Information enables dispersal of platforms. Under such circumstances, the firepower needed to attack targets can be allocated through precise information transfer and long-range attack instead of concentration of platforms. Concentrations of battle groups in future warfare will probably be replaced by small formations and single vessels. Vessels will be dispersed 'evenly' at sea.[43]

In this environment, 'remote attack will be the major combat concept'. Long-range missiles will play an ever-increasing role. Satellites will guide these missiles to targets. Missiles will also become increasingly proficient at guiding themselves. These weapons and the ships that fire them 'will survive better' and maximize the ability of naval forces to use 'stealth and sudden strikes'.[44]

Chinese maritime strategists reflect that just as the archetypal Maoist guerrilla movement needs one method of fighting to survive in the face of overwhelming counterrevolutionary forces but another to shift from defense to offense and overthrow the enemy, navies will evolve as countries grow stronger. Weaker nations will focus on destroyers, corvettes, minesweepers and minelayers, whereas emerging powers will move on to develop aircraft carriers and amphibious ships. Some kinds of vessels, however, will be vital to all navies, regardless of their stage of development: 'In future global wars, the most powerful weapon will be the submarine.'[45]

Submarines suffer the least from current trends in technological development, while benefiting the most. Satellite reconnaissance, for instance, can locate targets for submarine raids, but is considerably less effective at detecting the submarines themselves, at least while they are under the water. Meanwhile, Chinese officers suggest, nuclear propulsion will become more common, and although all ships will benefit from this development, submarines have the most to gain. Nuclear engines, after all, allow submarines to remain in the relative safety of the ocean depths for extended periods of time, and to range over long distances in order to attack enemy shipping wherever it appears. Future-generation submarines will be able to dive deeper, and will carry missiles that can engage land targets more effectively.[46] Western naval strategists confirm that even obsolete submarines retain considerable advantages of concealment over anti-submarine warfare.[47]

CHINA'S NAVAL ASSETS

The PLAN is gradually acquiring the equipment it needs to put its theorists' ideas into effect. At the dawn of the twenty-first century, the areas in which Chinese strategists have expressed the most far-reaching ambitions have also been those in which the armed forces have realized the most dramatic material improvements. As recently as 1978, Western analysts could describe the PLAN as a force 'without apparent interest or significant capabilities for open-ocean operations', and conclude that 'China's Navy is not used as an instrument of diplomacy'.[48] As Chinese thinkers began to emphasize the role of seapower in global strategy, the PLAN reversed this situation.

In 1985, the Chinese fleet began making visits to foreign ports, sending flotillas to Sri Lanka, Bangladesh and Pakistan.[49] Since then, Chinese ships have ranged throughout the region, with noteworthy visits to Hawaii, Thailand and Bombay.[50] The Chinese navy expects to start escorting military-related trade in northern European waters as early as 2001.[51] Chinese sources report that 'hundreds' of China's naval vessels have proved themselves on long-range expeditions.[52] Such voyages express China's diplomatic commitment to distant regions, demonstrate the reach of the Chinese fleet and help the PLAN to improve its operational methods.

Nearly all China's naval officers have training in long-range voyages.[53] Nevertheless, the PLAN's transition to global operations has not been completely smooth. Like many other navies in the process of extending their reach, it has had some difficulty with the most low-tech of its command and control assets – the stamina of individual officers. At present, the internal command structure on board Chinese vessels depends excessively upon the ship's captain and his heads of departments.[54] Observers at PLAN exercises have noted that ship performance declines as captains become weary. The Chinese fleet, like other modern navies, will eventually have to train more of its junior officers to act independently, so that its ships can remain fully functional 24 hours a day.[55]

The Chinese have steadily built up their ability to support long-range operations. China's ships now carry the necessary apparatus to take on fuel and other supplies while at sea.[56] Since the late 1980s, China has more than quadrupled its tonnage of supply ships. As of the year 2000, the PLAN contained a force of at least six submarine support ships, three salvage and repair ships, three replenishment ships and 29 supply ships. Richard Sharpe suggests that the actual numbers may be higher.[57]

More logistical vessels are under construction in China's shipyards. When complete, they will double the PLAN's complement of fleet replenishment ships from three to six. China's navy will also add two salvage and repair ships to its existing fleet of three, and three supply ships to its fleet of 29.[58] Furthermore, many of the ships in China's merchant marine contain features which make them highly suitable for use as naval auxiliaries.[59]

This support fleet gives China a global reach on a par with mid-sized European navies. Table 1 compares China's naval logistical forces to those of France. Note that China also has six submarine support ships and at least 29 smaller supply ships of varying types, whereas France has no such resource.[60] French logistical ships do, however, carry considerably better developed countermeasures against air, submarine and missile attack.

The United Kingdom (UK), by way of comparison, has four replenishment vessels and one repair ship, somewhat superior in performance to the French vessels. The UK also boasts nine tankers, two of which have a range and capacity on a par with the other nations' replenishment ships.[61] It also has 14 smaller logistical vessels of assorted types in its Royal Maritime Auxiliary Service, and can mobilize others from private industry. The US Navy, unsurprisingly, dwarfs all others: it has four oilers, four salvage ships, two submarine tenders and eight fast combat support ships on active service, in addition to the seven

TABLE 1
COMPARATIVE LOGISTICAL ESTABLISHMENTS: FRANCE, PRC

	Speed (knots)	Range (miles)	Cargo Capacity (tons)
France			
4 x Replenishment Vessels*			
4 x Durance Class	19/15	9,000	10,500
1 x Repair Ship			
1 x *Jules Verne*	18/18	9,500	–
PRC			
3 x Replenishment Vessels			
2 x Fuqing Class	18/14	18,000	11,950
1 x Nanyun Class	16/n.a.	n.a.	9,630
3 x Salvage and Repair Ships			
1 x Dadong Class	18/n.a.	n.a.	–
1 x Dadao Class	18/n.a.	n.a.	–
1 x Achelous Class	12/n.a.	n.a.	–

Notes: * One more ship in reserve; n.a. = not available.

Source: Compiled from Richard Sharpe, *Jane's Fighting Ships 1999–2000* (Coulsdon, Surrey: Jane's Information Group, 1999), pp. 238–9 and 136–8.

ammunition ships, six combat stores ships, 14 oilers and four ocean tugs in its Military Sealift Command.[62]

China's navy is also working to increase the range of its air arm. The PLAN has started to modify some of its Xi'an B-6D bombers/maritime patrol aircraft to serve as aerial refuelling tankers.[63] These land-based planes have a range of 2,600 miles without refuelling.[64] China appears to have imported technology from both Israel and Iran for use in this project.[65]

A GLASS HALF EMPTY: THE 'KILLER MACES' OF HIGH TECHNOLOGY

As noted above, Chinese military thinkers have emphasized the ways in which joint operations using advanced technology can turn the tables in naval combat. From a Western perspective, such discussions only highlight one of China's greatest weaknesses. Analysts for the US Department of Defense estimate that, as a rule of thumb, China's more advanced weapons systems are ten years behind their Russian counterparts.[66] Nevertheless, saying that China's tools for fighting advanced-technology warfare are currently backward is another way of saying that China is developing tools for fighting high-technology warfare.

In this area, the doctrine that China's next wars will remain limited and local becomes critical. Western navies can perform feats of technology that the Chinese cannot hope to match. Other Asian countries, however, have no such superiority. Analysts using the US Department of Defense (DoD) report on *Militarily Critical Technologies* conclude that, '[f]or conflicts not likely to involve the United States, Beijing will not hesitate to employ a force-on-force strategy'.[67] In such a war, China would be equipped to use the technologies which Western strategic thinkers have identified with the so-called 'Revolution in Military Affairs' (RMA), notably 'battle-space transparency, command and control, long-range precision strike and information warfare'.[68]

China's most valuable RMA resource is its space program. Chinese writings on the role of modern technology in naval warfare emphasize the ability of spacecraft to 'observe and control' maritime battles, the ability of space-based navigation systems to guide long-range weapons to precise targets and the ability of modern communication networks, which depend on satellites, to coordinate joint operations.[69] At a more speculative level, Chinese military commanders have also shown enthusiasm for orbiting weapons platforms that can attack targets directly from space.[70] With the exception of orbiting weapons platforms, China has functional capabilities in all of these areas. Since China's achievements in other RMA technologies such as high-performance computing, intelligence systems, signal processing and transmission systems and software design remain limited, its space assets are doubly important to its aspirations of fielding a twenty-first-century military.[71]

Beijing still defines its reconnaissance satellites as 'experimental', but it has been developing them since the mid-1960s.[72] In other words, China had plans for spy satellites even before it had the rockets to launch them. As of the late 1990s, China continues to use its Fanhui Shi Weixing (FSW) series of satellites for intelligence purposes.[73] These spacecraft take photographs on chemical-based film, and must drop the pictures back to earth in recoverable canisters before anyone can look at them.[74] This method makes it impossible for Beijing's intelligence analysts to watch events from space in so-called real-time as they occur, and limits the operational lifespan of an FSW satellite to a maximum of 18 days.[75]

The PRC's putatively civilian ground imaging resources are considerably more advanced. *Beijing Review* notes that China routinely uses satellite imagery for: 'meteorological research, the planning and evaluation of agricultural resources, forest surveillance, development, utilization and protection, environmental monitoring, marine and sea wave meteorology, marine pollution monitoring and earth surveying and mapping'.[76] It must be noted that the Chinese have achieved this level of proficiency by collaborating with foreign countries and private corporations, although it may also be observed that China's armed forces have been notoriously successful at forging links with overseas organizations themselves.[77] China's civilian satellites have been radioing electronic images to ground stations without the need for recoverable film canisters since 1981.[78]

China's armed forces can expect to gain more regular access to satellite imagery in the near future. China and Brazil plan to launch a pair of earth observation satellites known as the Ziyuan-1 series.[79] These spacecraft will be able to transmit images by radio in real time, and Western analysts expect that the Chinese armed forces will have full access to them.[80] Although the Chinese and Brazilians failed to carry out their planned launch of the first Ziyuan-1 in 1998, there is no reason to assume that they will not deploy these spacecraft within the next few years.

The Ziyuan satellites have a ground resolution power of only 19.5 meters.[81] In other words, their cameras cannot make out details which are less than 19.5 meters across. This is poorer than most commercial systems, and much worse than the US KH-12 satellite, which can resolve details as small as 1.5 meters.[82] China has announced its ambition to build a satellite with similar powers of resolution, but this project remains at the planning stage.[83]

Beijing claims that civilian broadcasts from Chinese communication satellites reach 83 per cent of the Chinese people. The Dong Fang Hong-3 satellite, which became operational in 1997, can relay six television channels and 8,000 telephone calls at a time. Meanwhile, China has rushed ahead in expanding its use of satellite communications technology on the ground. In 1996, China routinely routed 33,000 phone calls per day through space.[84] Four years later, an article in the *Beijing Review* boasted that 38 Chinese television stations and 30 voice-only radio stations were broadcasting by satellite.[85]

China's use of satellite broadcasting has outstripped its ability to put vehicles in orbit. Native Chinese spacecraft handle approximately 20 per cent of China's communication needs.[86] Chinese agencies hope to dramatically reduce their reliance on foreign systems as they deploy a new generation of Dong Fang Hong spacecraft in the early twenty-first century.[87] Nevertheless, one may assume that, with a satellite network that already encompasses 20 per cent of its voluminous civilian traffic, China is free to devote a substantial amount of communications bandwidth to military purposes.

China relies on the American Navstar and the Russian Glonass spacecraft for satellite navigation.[88] The Chinese, however, have made full use of these resources for civilian purposes, and one can presume that the armed forces exploit them as well. One may note that the Chinese have paid particular attention to the maritime use of this technology. *Beijing Review* states that 30,000 fishing vessels use Navstar Global Positioning System (GPS) systems, and that this accounts for 11 per cent of the GPS receivers in the country.[89] China has repeatedly hinted that it hopes to develop its own constellation of navigational satellites, which would be known as TwinStar.[90]

China has a well-developed system of earth-based stations for tracking and controlling satellites. This network employs 20,000 people, including 5,000 trained engineers.[91] During the 1970s, China's ground-control network used outdated optical systems to track spacecraft, but it has now adopted laser devices which meet high standards of accuracy. Since the Chinese do not have ground control stations in other countries, they depend on three tracking ships to observe satellites in positions which are invisible from mainland China. Like most space agencies, the Chinese ground-control network monitors satellites from all countries, not only its own.[92]

To summarize, China has applied space-based technology avidly. The Chinese take full advantage of internationally accessible satellites. Beijing's own space program remains in its infancy but appears to be growing steadily. China has suffered a number of well-publicized space accidents, which appear to have set back its program of developing spy and communications satellites.[93] Nevertheless, the overall failure rate of its commercial launches is only 13.7 per cent, which compares favorably with the 14 per cent failure rate of launches on the US Atlas booster and the 12 per cent rate of failure on Russia's Proton.[94] There is no reason to doubt that China's space program could give the PLAN a considerable boost in wars against enemies at a similar level of technological development, or that it will grow increasingly robust as time goes on.

Where space and the RMA fail, China can fall back on its nuclear capability. Nuclear weapons are, perhaps, Beijing's most effective tool for convincing other countries to respect its need to keep wars limited. As noted above, Chinese strategists have avowed their willingness to use such weapons to even the odds in actual combat. For these reasons, China's intercontinental nuclear forces are a crucial part of its maritime strength. The Chinese also deploy tactical nuclear weapons specifically intended for use at sea.

The size and composition of China's nuclear stockpile is notoriously difficult to determine.[95] Analysts at Jane's believe that, as of 1989, China deployed 25 nuclear torpedoes and depth charges, along with 25 more HY-2 ship-to-ship missiles carrying nuclear warheads.[96] Chinese aircraft carried an additional 75 nuclear weapons mounted on cruise missiles of types designed for naval warfare, along with 225 gravity-propelled nuclear bombs.[97] Some observers, however, feel that Western analysts have greatly underestimated China's holdings.[98]

TOOLS FOR GUERRILLA WARFARE

Chinese strategic thinkers emphasize the importance of economical hit-and-run tactics in naval warfare, and the PLAN has fielded the kind of weapons systems that such a doctrine requires. For a navy which wishes to strike suddenly and viciously, missiles, torpedoes and mines would seem to be the ideal weapons. The PLAN appears to appreciate this point. Even before China's modernization drives of the 1980s, the ships of the Chinese fleet carried a cumulative 596 anti-ship missile launchers, as opposed to 27 for Taiwan, 28 for South Korea and 12 for the US Seventh Fleet.[99] During this same period, China also deployed 1,190 torpedo tubes, along with 508 more on submarines, which dwarfed the other Asian navies by similar margins.[100]

The PLAN's newer ships are as heavily armed with missiles and torpedoes as its older ones. China's potential opponents, however, have increased their own arsenals of such weapons. This shift in the correlation of forces presents Chinese seamen with new threats to worry about, but does not change the fact that the PLAN is well equipped to attack with missiles at long range and torpedoes at close quarters. China has reportedly purchased an underwater missile akin to the Russian Squall and may also be attempting to build a similar weapon of its own.[101]

Western analysts describe China's missiles as a technological 'pocket of excellence' within the PRC's armed forces.[102] The same writers believe that the Chinese HY-2A cruise missile would be 'potentially effective' against US ships. This weapon carries a 1,129-pound warhead, travels at Mach 0.9, uses an infrared homing system and has a 59-mile range. An air-launched version can travel 68 miles, and an extended-range version can carry a 1,100-pound warhead 84 miles. The PLAN deploys these missiles on its Luda-class destroyers, Jianghu-class frigates and H-6D maritime bombers.[103]

The PLAN is introducing more advanced anti-ship missiles as well. The C-101 and HY-3/C-301 are supersonic, and can travel 31 miles and 81 miles respectively. China's YJ-1 series is based on the French Exocet and, while limited to a 25-mile range, is small enough to be fired from Han-class submarines. Currently, the submarines must surface to fire these missiles. Other models in the YJ series have ranges of up to 80 miles and use active radar guidance.[104] US analysts believe that Beijing is 'almost certainly' capable of rigging any of its missiles for satellite guidance.[105]

In the near future, China expects to acquire two Russian Sovremenny-class destroyers. These ships carry the SS-N-22 Sunburn anti-ship missile. The US Defense Department's study rates this weapon at the top of its scale of technological development.[106] Sunburn missiles have both active and passive radar homing systems, an 87-mile range, a 300 kg warhead and a cruising speed of Mach 2.5.[107] On the attack, these weapons can accelerate to speeds of Mach 4.5. The Sunburn may also have the ability to evade anti-missile defenses with rapid maneuvers.[108]

China is also well equipped for mine warfare. As of the year 2000, almost 90 per cent of the major ships in China's fleet could carry mines as part of their standard armament.[109] China's most-publicized new ships, including the Kilo-class submarines, the Luhai-class destroyers, and the promised Sovremenny-class destroyers all have integral minelaying capabilities.[110] For counter-mine operations, the PLAN has a fleet of 27 ocean-going minesweepers, with 13 more in reserve.[111] In 1988, China fielded an indigenously built minelaying vessel capable of deploying 300 mines, which took advantage of advanced minelaying technology.[112]

China's navy has a large counter-mine service, although it uses minesweepers rather than more modern minehunters. Ever since the 1970s, the PLAN also has had a force of unmanned mine warfare drones. This fleet currently includes four vehicles on active service and 42 on reserve.[113] The PLAN recently upgraded some of these craft with Italian Pluto mine countermeasures systems.[114]

China's approach to high-technology warfare has also reflected a guerrilla philosophy. Many of China's efforts to develop RMA forces focus on ways to blind, paralyze and disrupt enemy equipment, particularly the advanced sensor and communication systems that might enable opposing forces to use RMA tactics of their own. One can surmise that the Chinese hope to counter the technological advantage of the United States, or, better yet, develop the ability to deliver a knock-out blow – even a temporary one – against a US task force. US analysts respond that the United States has designed its technology to resist any countermeasures the Chinese might hope to develop, and that China's chances of successfully inconveniencing Western-style armed forces are remote.[115]

The same analysts, however, note that China's efforts to develop anti-technology countermeasures introduce a new element of uncertainty into US war plans.[116] This might force US military commanders to adopt more cautious strategies. Furthermore, if China could threaten to neutralize key American weapon systems, American political leaders would almost certainly become more reluctant to confront China.[117] Therefore, China's attempts to develop anti-technology may buy the PRC greater levels of freedom to carry out its policies without risk of US intervention.

Against less advanced powers, China's anti-technology devices could play a far greater role. Countermeasures which would fail against US weapons systems might prove far more effective against India or even Japan. By neutralizing the reconnaissance and communication assets of another emerging power, China would put itself in a position to use its own RMA technology to full advantage.

Chinese researchers have made progress with the following high-technology weapons systems:

- Microwave beams and non-nuclear electromagnetic pulse devices capable of destroying enemy electronic systems.[118]
- An anti-radiation missile (already developed) designed to home in on targets emitting the radio frequencies used by the US E-3 AWAC aircraft.[119]
- Stealthy radar-resistant cruise missiles, capable of using satellite navigation.[120]
- Jammers specifically designed to overpower signals from enemy navigational satellites, intended to deprive opposing forces of access to the GPS.[121]
- Anti-satellite weapons. A 1998 US Department of Defense (DoD) report to Congress stated that China may already have the ability to blind optical sensors on satellites that are vulnerable to lasers.[122]
- Computer viruses capable of infecting military command and control systems.[123]
- High-energy lasers capable of attacking satellites, optical sensors and, perhaps in the more distant future, missiles and aircraft. US DoD analysts are skeptical of China's ability to master this complicated technology, but acknowledge that the Chinese are making progress.[124]
- Chinese-made command, control, communications, computers and intelligence equipment, including an army-wide on-line communications network, advanced command automation, remote-display systems that use the GPS, an artificial intelligence system designed to aid commanders, rugged microcomputers for field use and real-time remote sensing image processors.[125]
- Drones and unmanned reconnaissance aircraft.[126] Chinese firms have built operational prototypes of such devices, and the armed forces have tested them in large-scale exercises.[127]
- Airborne and satellite synthetic aperture radar systems.[128]
- Computer attack methods that would allow Chinese hackers to wreak havoc on Western civilian information networks. US DoD reports leave analysts uncertain how much damage Chinese hackers could cause.[129]
- Obscurants to foil guidance systems in an enemy's 'smart' munitions. The US DoD estimates that China's has the resources to field fully modern obscuring systems.[130]
- Anti-radar technology for ships. The PLAN has tested a vessel which could pave the way to a class of 'stealth' destroyers.[131] This ship uses both special materials and a special hull design to reduce its radar profile. China already deploys what *Jane's Fighting Ships* describes as 'large numbers' of stealth boats, most of which have paramilitary

roles. These vessels range from 30 to 60 meters in length and many are capable of speeds in excess of 30 knots.[132]

Chinese strategists extol submarine warfare, and the PLAN has historically lavished resources on its underwater forces. China's development of nuclear-powered submarines ranks as one of the great success stories of the PRC's quest to develop modern technology.[133] The fact that China opted to develop this branch of its navy at this stage of its national development rather than acquiring more prestigious vessels such as aircraft carriers indicates a high level of realism among its strategists. Although airpower is essential for securing absolute control of an ocean, carrier warfare entails elaborate logistical support, along with complex operational procedures to ensure cooperation between air and sea units. Submarines, on the other hand, can act independently, striking with maximum stealth and minimum hazard to themselves.

Simply the size of China's submarine force (65 attack and patrol vessels, plus 31 in reserve) might intimidate any country that lacks confidence in its anti-submarine warfare (ASW) capabilities.[134] In purely quantitative terms, the PLAN's holdings are comparable to the US fleet of 56 attack submarines or the Russian establishment of 47 anti-shipping subs[135] Although US and Russian vessels are spectacularly more effective than their Chinese counterparts, this is a case in which sheer numbers have some significance, because the size of China's fleet increases the amount of ocean area its submarines can patrol. This, in turn, means that China's enemies must watch for them virtually everywhere. As a team of Chinese naval officers put it, 'Even without attacking targets, submarines are menaces existing anywhere at any time'.[136]

China's submarine force has considerable reach as well. Even the PLAN's most obsolete submarines have ranges of between 7,000 and 8,000 miles, which is more than enough, for instance, for them to fan out into the waters around Taiwan or Japan.[137] China's five Han-class attack submarines are nuclear-powered and capable of considerably longer voyages.[138] Thirty-seven of China's patrol submarines, however, come from the obsolete Romeo class, as do all the reserve boats. A shortage of trained crews appears to limit the number of Romeos China can put to sea at any given time.[139]

Against these advantages, one must consider the fact that China's indigenously built submarines are noisy by modern standards, and thus vulnerable to ASW.[140] China is, however, making progress toward quieting its submarine fleet. The Kilo-class submarines which China has acquired from Russia have a coating of anechoic tiles that muffle the noise of their engines.[141] Meanwhile, although Chinese shipyards have not yet begun to produce quiet submarines of their own, Chinese scientists have acquired the theoretical knowledge they need to do so.[142]

Despite their backwardness, China's underwater forces are a potent weapon. Even if only a fraction of the PLAN's submarines prove effective, one might note that Nazi Germany began its anti-shipping campaigns of the Second World War with only 20 operational U-boats.[143] Although detection technology has improved since the 1940s, the submarine remains 'the master of its element'.[144] A variety of circumstances make China particularly well equipped to capitalize on that fact.

ASW is dramatically more difficult in shallow waters, and near land. Noise from surface ships and oil-drilling platforms can mask the sound of undersea vessels. Submarines have added advantages in exceptionally cold and hot regions as well.[145] Along the long Asian littoral, in the crowded waters of the Indonesian archipelago and among the islands of the South China Sea, China's submarines may be able to compensate for much of their technological obsolescence.

Furthermore, ASW remains as much an art as a science. Even with the most advanced technology, it requires exceptionally high levels of training and experience. Without continual practice, sailors lose their ASW skills rapidly.[146] Second-class fleets are unlikely to have anything approaching the anti-submarine capabilities of major naval powers, even if they field modern equipment. Even Britain and the United States have difficulty keeping their seamen at peak performance for ASW and the fact that ASW training is expensive means that this is an area in which both countries are continually tempted to cut corners.[147]

THE PLAN'S VULNERABILITIES

In addition to its general problems of technological underdevelopment, China's maritime forces have several specific vulnerabilities. The Chinese are, to their credit, attempting to address them. As with other areas in which the PRC's armed forces are seeking to modernize, these efforts appear inadequate for battles against major Western navies, but should help the PLAN overshadow other Asian fleets. The PLAN's chief vulnerabilities lie in air defenses, air forces and electronic systems.

The PLAN's most dangerous weakness may be its lack of defenses against air attack. Although all Chinese ships have ample gunnery for close air defense, certain observers in the mid-1990s claimed that only four of them carry surface-to-air missiles (SAMs).[148] If this is true, then aircraft armed with anti-ship missiles could sink China's unprotected vessels while remaining safely out of gun range. The Chinese have attempted to modernize their anti-air defenses, in part by importing weapons systems from the West.[149] As of the year 2000, *Jane's* reports SAM systems on 23 of China's 55 major surface combatants.[150] Ships without mounted anti-aircraft missiles may still carry shoulder-fired SAMs such as the SA-7.[151]

Although Chinese naval officers recognize the importance of airpower in maritime warfare, the PRC's air forces suffer from obsolete equipment, haphazard logistics and limited training abilities.[152] Furthermore, although China is developing an aerial refuelling capability, the bulk of its air forces remain tied to bases in mainland China.[153] China's leaders may have decided that extensive air force modernizations are a luxury they cannot afford at this stage of their development. Prasun K. Sengupta, writing for the *Asian Defence Journal*, suggests that the People's Liberation Army Air Force (PLAAF) may actually decline in overall quality during the first decade of the twenty-first century.[154]

Others, however, suggest the opposite. *Flight International* has published a digest of a US Department of Defense study which indicates that the PLAAF may manage to 'change the balance of power' by 2005.[155] This report noted that China expects to have at least 150 fourth-generation fighters by then, and that it will be able to equip them with an air-to-air missile using active radar guidance systems comparable to the US advanced medium-range air-to-air missile (AMRAAM). The same report noted that although China has yet to build a stealth aircraft, its theoretical knowledge of anti-radar technology is 'excellent', and the Chinese are known to be developing effective anti-ballistic missiles for tactical use.[156]

The areas in which China is modernizing its air forces are those of greatest relevance to maritime strategy. The Chinese have assigned some of their most modern new planes, the 73 Su-27 fighters they have acquired from Russia, to the navy.[157] The PLAN has been upgrading the radar systems on many of its maritime aircraft to Western standards, and intends to improve the guidance systems on its aerial anti-ship missiles as well. Meanwhile, the PLAAF has acquired 10 IL-76TD heavy transport aircraft from Russia and has begun to train crews for long-range transport operations.[158] This should help the PRC's ground and air forces support the navy in joint operations removed from China's shores.

Despite its aspirations to conduct RMA warfare, the PLA suffers from technological backwardness. China's information systems, information warfare, command and control systems, sound-based sensor systems and optical sensor systems are uniformly obsolete.[159] This limits the PRC's ability to field precision-guided weapons of the sort that have become so critical to the US version of the RMA. Worse, from a Chinese perspective, these weaknesses hamper the PLAN in the game of hide-and-seek which has characterized naval warfare since the invention of ships, and has grown only more lethal since the advent of the submarine.

China has attempted to improve its naval reconnaissance capabilities, largely by acquiring foreign radar technology. By 1999, the PLAN had outfitted some of its Luda-class destroyers with the 'Rice Screen' system, which provides 3-D coverage.[160] China is working to develop more advanced phased-array systems similar to those used in the West.[161] The PRC reportedly obtained much of the technology for the Rice Screen system through commercial contacts with American companies.[162]

The airborne early warning (AEW) radars China had hoped to acquire from Israel would also have been valuable in maritime operations.[163] Although the United States has restrained Israel from transferring these craft, at least for the moment, Moscow has offered to fill the gap. Russia is training Chinese crews in the use of airborne early warning aircraft.[164] The Russians have offered to lease China three A-50 AEW planes. These aircraft can stay aloft for seven hours without refuelling, tracking fighter aircraft at a range of 138 miles and missiles at a range of 480 miles.[165] The A-50 can guide 12 friendly fighter aircraft to targets.[166]

Since the process of modernization is slow, the Chinese hope to overcome some of their shortfalls through tactics that allow them to use the equipment they have to better effect. Chinese strategic thinkers remind officers not to forget the kinds of difficulties they face. 'We should never evade our shortcomings', one writer in the Chinese army newspaper reminds readers, 'the result of evasion can only be a widening of the gap.'[167] This author goes on to emphasize the importance of the military art, both in surmounting disadvantages and using new weapons systems more effectively.[168]

Major-General Wang Pufeng, a former director of the Strategy Department in Beijing's Academy of Military Science, provides more specific ideas about how China's navy might compensate for its weaknesses. In some areas, he notes, such as missiles and submarines, China can still 'shock' the enemy.[169] China can develop its forces to raid enemy 'operations platforms' and 'foil the enemy offensive', using sabotage, mobility and special operations where possible.[170] In other words, even if China cannot sustain a high-technology campaign, it can still seize the initiative. In so doing, China can hope to cripple its weaker opponents, and give even its stronger ones pause. There may be an element of bluster to Wang's statements, but this approach fits into the larger body of Chinese doctrine, which this chapter has characterized as guerrilla warfare at sea.

FUTURE STAGES OF DEVELOPMENT: CARRIERS AND AMPHIBIOUS FORCES

Chinese military writers have noted that, as nations evolve from emerging seapowers into established seapowers, they will acquire aircraft carriers and amphibious forces.[171] The fact that Chinese strategists place such emphasis on joint operations indicates that they would find many uses for such assets. Beijing has, however, pursued a cautious policy in these areas, particularly regarding carriers. Beijing's interest in advanced forces indicate that China's leaders believe that their nation is on the verge of becoming a seapower. The Chinese government's restraint, however, indicates that those leaders do not believe that their country has yet become one.

The Chinese have shown great interest in aircraft carriers. Rumors that China is about to acquire such a vessel have circulated for more than a decade. The Chinese have already acquired the hulls of two carriers, one from Australia and another from Russia.[172] Although they eventually converted the Russian vessel into a restaurant, it is safe to assume that maritime engineers have studied both of them with an eye toward learning militarily useful information. In 1999, Hong Kong's *Mingpao News* reported that China would have a 48,000 ton carrier operating by 2005.[173] The 1999/2000 edition of *Jane's Fighting Ships* notes a report that China has given the Russian Nevskoye Design Bureau a contract to design a carrier based on the PLAN's requirements, but states that there has been no evidence of progress on this project.[174]

The Chinese appear to have based their restraint on strategic forethought. In the words of an anonymous Chinese 'naval expert', whether or not China develops an aircraft carrier must depend 'on the country's naval strategy, which should be in compliance with the country's overall military and economic development strategy'. China News Services has found a variety of other authorities to point out the expense of carriers. Many of these experts also suggest that China can get aircraft to likely war zones without them.[175]

Readers may speculate on the issue of whether these statements are sincere, or, if not, what they signify. The China News Services report could be an attempt to paper over embarrassing difficulties in China's carrier program or it could equally well be an attempt to lull China's rivals into a false sense of security – there is no way for an outsider to know. The PLAN, however, is preparing for the day when higher authorities acquire the long-awaited carrier. The Chinese navy has built carrier bases in Dalian, Shanghai and Zhanjiang. Chinese pilots have been training for carrier operations since the mid-1990s.[176]

China has made more tangible progress in acquiring amphibious capabilities. The Chinese navy has 16 landing ship, tanks (LST), 43 landing ship, mediums (LSM) and 44 vessels designated LCM or LCU (landing craft, mechanical or landing craft, utility). The Chinese also have 248 LCM/LCU type vessels in reserve.[177] In addition to carrying ground forces, the six Yuting-class LSTs have helicopter decks, and can support two aircraft each. China also has approximately 500 smaller landing craft designed for ferrying supplies and personnel.[178]

A study by the US Army War College suggests that, if China actually attempted to mount an amphibious invasion, it would be able to attack a hostile beach with a force of one division (10,000–14,000 men).[179] Analyst Larry Wortzel estimates that, if China mobilized its merchant marine, it could move 40,000 more men onto the beachhead in a follow-up operation.[180] The Chinese could supplement such an attack with airborne and airmobile forces. Throughout the 1990s, PLA units have been training at coordinating air and amphibious assaults.[181] In all likelihood, a first wave of attackers would land by sea and parachute in an attempt to seize an airfield, so that the PLAAF could fly in other troops by more conventional methods.

China has numerous troops available for such operations. The 15th Airborne Army, based in Heinan China, is China's best-trained and equipped assault force. This unit initially consisted of three brigades, but is expanding to include three whole divisions. The PLA has designated approximately 15 more divisions as Rapid Reaction Forces (RRF). In total, the RRFs have a strength of 200,000 to 300,000 men.[182]

The Chinese have prepared these units for large-scale combat on short notice. Although RRFs use the same equipment as the rest of the Chinese army, they receive intensive training, maintain themselves at full strength, and can reputedly be ready for combat within 24 hours. Although the Chinese have yet to rehearse a major aerial troop movement, the RRFs train to take place in large-unit operations. The PLA has encouraged the People's Armed Police (PAP) to develop its own paramilitary rapid-reaction forces, so that regular army RRFs need not concern themselves with internal security.[183]

China maintains other potential assault forces as well. The PLAN has a marine brigade of 5,000 troops based in Zhanjiang, Guangdong Province and the 31st Group Army in Fujian Province has three divisions capable of conducting amphibious landings. An additional three or four of the PLA's 24 group armies provide heavier support for the RRFs. Analysts have identified the 38th, 39th and 54th Group Armies as being among these units. The Chinese have dedicated reconnaissance and electronic-warfare units to support the RRFs as well. Western analysts believe that China will expand these forces as it continues to modernize its military.[184]

Currently, however, China's lack of transport aircraft limits its ability to deploy forces by air. The PLAAF has approximately 10 IL-76 heavy transports and 50 lighter Yun-7 and Yun-8 aircraft, capable of transporting a total of 3,000 to 4,000 troops at a time.[185] Some reports indicate that China has as many as 14 IL-76s.[186] Some have speculated that the PLAAF may press civilian airliners into service as well.[187] For shorter-range operations, the Chinese are developing helicopter-borne airmobile forces.[188] China also has a number of experimental programs involving hovercraft, ekranoplans and other high-speed water-skimming assault craft.[189]

The significance of China's assault forces depends on how Beijing intends to use them. American analysts speak derisively of the PRC's ability to invade Taiwan.[190] There is, however, no doubt that the PLA could carry out air and amphibious descents in support of a campaign on mainland Asia. The PLA's assault forces could also prove overwhelming in battles for islands in the South China Sea, and perhaps for attacks on more distant islands as well. China, in other words, is well equipped to use land forces as part of a joint maritime strategy.

PROSPECTS FOR EXPANSION

For those interested in China's prospects for fighting a war with the United States or other great naval powers, the most important question is not what the PLAN is, but what it can become. Given China's population, geographical size, pockets of commercial success and history of empire, some see no limits to what Beijing can accomplish. Skeptics, however, might respond that China is a country which will always have great potential. China's people are capable of greatness. The PRC's main challenge lies in developing the means to make use of them.

China has no shortage of scientific ability. Over the past few decades, Chinese scientists and engineers have proven their abilities by building a modern nuclear arsenal. Having mastered this technology, the PRC has gone on to develop the industrial base it needs to produce both warheads and reactors.[191] Chinese researchers continue to advance in critical military areas. Some of these are discussed elsewhere in this chapter. Others include materials technology (vital, among other things, for high-technology munitions and high-technology armor), power systems technology and chemical/biological warfare.[192]

The advanced industrial countries, however, have been making progress in a much wider variety of fields.[193] China cannot afford to keep up with all of these areas of study. Chinese leaders are realistic about their country's limitations, and have tried to concentrate their efforts on the most promising areas of inquiry. The PRC's government coordinates basic research with explicitly military planning.[194] The fact that Chinese military/industrial planners have called for reforms to strengthen such coordination indicates that the system remains imperfect, but also indicates their commitment to improving it.[195] In this fashion, China's leaders hope to squeeze as much military use out of their scientific programs as possible, and to achieve the closest possible match between new weapons and strategies for using them.

China's armed forces are also working to maximize the capabilities of their personnel. During the 1990s, the Chinese military carried out a comprehensive training program throughout all services. Asia specialists from the US DoD note several failings in this program. Many of the most publicized training exercises appear to have been heavily scripted, so that they served more to provide a spectacle than to hone military skills. Although small units have practiced dramatic helicopter assaults, China's armed forces have not attempted the massive aerial troop movements that their RRF doctrine appears to demand. Nevertheless, the DoD experts conclude that 'a comprehensive, orderly programme of training reform is well under way'.[196]

In 1995, China's armed forces carried out a particularly dramatic training exercise on Dongshan Island. This operation involved airborne landings, naval gunfire, SU-27 airstrikes and regimental-size amphibious assaults. Although Beijing clearly staged the Dongshan Island maneuvers to intimidate Taiwan, the event was more than just a good show. Among other things, Dongshan Island tested the Chinese armed forces' ability to command and control large-scale joint operations. The PLA, PLAN and PLAAF passed this test.[197]

Although a few selected maneuvers have attracted an inordinate amount of fanfare, China has carried out dozens of large-scale exercises every year. Between 1990 and 1995, the PLAN conducted at least 19 fleet-level maneuvers simulating purely naval warfare, along with at least 14 that involved amphibious operations. The Chinese military carried out at least seven more exercises which entailed joint operations among all forces. Various maneuvers have covered chemical warfare, long-range ocean transport, helicopter assaults, long-range air transport and high-technology warfare.[198] Meanwhile, China's armed forces have also conducted hundreds of smaller training operations annually.[199]

The PRC's training program seems designed, not only to drill military personnel in traditional skills, but to educate them in new ways of fighting. The Chinese recognize that if their forces are to win modern battles against technologically superior opponents, commanders must think imaginatively and their subordinates must be able to exercise independent initiative. China's new training system emphasizes simulated battles against 'blue forces' who attempt to fight like a real enemy. Chinese officers testify that these realistic, unstructured exercises have helped their units shake off outdated habits and tactical rigidity.[200] The Chinese are also reforming their use of non-commissioned officers in an attempt to encourage greater levels of independence at lower levels of command.[201]

Although China's researchers and military personnel have not met first-world standards, they are making progress. This raises the question of whether China's defense industry can actually produce the equipment that its researchers design and its fighting men need. The Chinese military-industrial complex (CMIC) consists of thousands of firms and hundreds of thousands of workers, including 300,000 trained engineers and technicians.[202] These firms manage to equip millions of soldiers and to maintain air forces of several thousand planes. China's ability to manufacture technologically advanced weapons systems, however, remains problematic.

From the mid-1980s onward, China's leaders have attempted to modernize their defense industrial establishment. Not only have they sought to develop production lines which can build high-technology equipment, they have sought to make the CMIC profitable. In this fashion, they hope to create a defense industry which can fuel its own development with revenue from commercial sales. Deng Xiaoping articulated this concept in his so-called '16-character' slogan: 'Combine the military and the civil, combine peace and war, give priority to military products, let the civil support the military.'[203] There is a noteworthy parallel between their ideas about creating a self-expanding defense economy and Mahan's observation that long-term naval power is a function of trade.

The 16-character slogan is ubiquitous in contemporary Chinese leadership circles.[204] Attempts to 'let the civil support the military', however, have uncovered weaknesses in the CMIC. In the early 1980s, the Chinese government began reforms designed to encourage its defense companies to seek profits. Owing to the shrinking market for munitions and the expanding commercial opportunities in other sectors, China's semi-privatized arms industry diverted as much as 80 per cent of its production capacity to civilian production. Nevertheless, China's State Statistical Bureau reported in 1994 that 81 per cent of the 'weapons ammunition' (*wuqi danyao*) producers were still losing money.[205]

Chinese defense firms have suffered from many of the problems typically associated with transitions from state-protected enterprise to competition on the open market. These include hostility to innovation, lack of horizontal integration within organizations and ideological insistence on 'self-reliance'.[206] The CMIC has had some success at manufacturing products that are not yet widely produced in China, such as motorcycles and color televisions. In markets where there is competition, however, defense industries have done poorly.[207] These circumstances, combined with the fact that China has been reducing the size of its armed forces, have made it nearly impossible for the CMIC to make money.[208]

Perhaps for these reasons, China's defense firms have failed to introduce modern industrial technology as rapidly as PRC commercial enterprises. Shun Zhenhuan of China's State Planning Commission estimates that advanced equipment makes up only 3 per cent of the machinery in China's defense industry, compared with 12.9 per cent in civilian factories. Perhaps 40 per cent of China's defense industry equipment is more than 20 years old, and some dates back to the Second World War.[209] The State Planning Commission has resolved to redress this deficiency. If the PRC succeeds in modernizing its factories, its overall output of modern weapons may rise.

The commercial side of China's defense industry has also suffered from the legacy of Mao-era strategic policy. During the 1960s and 1970s, the PRC relocated much of its defense industry to remote areas of central and southern China in order to shield them from attack in the event of a major war. The relocated industries, however, suffer from transportation problems which curtail their ability to manufacture and sell their goods at a profit. These corporations have also found that, in an era when people can choose their jobs, trained managers and engineers are unwilling to work in the hinterlands.[210]

China's defense industry has, however, showed signs of progress. The PRC has experimented successfully with having corporations bid for military contracts, rather than simply determining prices by fiat.[211] This should open the way for Beijing to acquire its weapons at lower prices, while simultaneously encouraging greater efficiency in the CMIC. The Chinese press reports that defense industry profits have begun to rise, at least in certain areas. These reports, one should note, contradict other data, and officials in certain Chinese corporations have accused them of containing less than the whole truth.[212]

In April 1998, the PRC instituted major new reforms to boost competition among defense firms. Before then, the government's Commission for Science, Technology and Industry for National Defense (COSTIND) had both overseen defense corporations and procured equipment for the armed forces.[213] In other words, it had represented both producers and consumers – hardly a way to ensure market efficiency. The contradictions between these two functions had led to considerable bureaucratic infighting within COSTIND as well. In 1998, Beijing separated the procurement department from COSTIND, placed them directly under the control of the military, and renamed them the General Equipment Department (GED).[214]

'More development less production,' urges a slogan which circulates throughout the Chinese defense industry.[215] In other words, the CMIC is trying to cut back on its investment in aging weapons systems while acquiring the capacity to produce more modern ones. According to one source, Chinese defense firms follow the rule of thumb that if a military production line does not receive a contract for three straight years, plant managers must shut it down.[216] The CMIC shed large numbers of workers throughout the 1990s, and analysts expect it to lay off at least 4,000 more in the first years of the twenty-first century.[217]

Chinese firms have indeed reduced their production of older weapons systems. The most dramatic drop-off appeared in aircraft production. By the mid-1990s, the CMIC was producing roughly half as many aircraft as it had in the early 1980s.[218] China's aerospace industry appears to have cancelled production of the H-5 and H-6 bombers entirely.[219] Meanwhile, China's defense firms have developed new-generation products in a variety of areas. These include the Type 093 nuclear attack submarine, the Type 094 nuclear ballistic-missile submarine, the F-10 fighter and a variety of new ballistic missiles.[220]

One of the GED's top priorities is to get new weapons systems into general production.[221] China's State Planning Commission reports that this effort is proceeding well. Of the more than 20 types of aircraft on Chinese assembly lines, 75 per cent are new models. China's ordinance factories have been, in one commission official's words, 'fruitful' in turning out modern infantry weapons and armored fighting vehicles.[222] China also introduced newly designed naval vessels throughout the 1990s, notably the Yuting class of amphibious assault ship (capable of carrying helicopters), the Song class of submarines, the Luhu class of destroyers, the Luhai class of destroyers, an assortment of survey and research ships and updated versions of several other models.[223]

China's defense firms have begun preliminary work on many of their more advanced systems as well. Chinese firms began to prefabricate materials for the Type 093 submarine as early as 1994 and analysts expect the Huludao Shipyard to launch the first operational model by 2002.[224] The PRC has set its industry the goal of moving new weapons systems from theoretical evaluation to production and deployment within five years, but in practice, the process can still take more than twice that long. PLAAF units report that it can also take them as much as three years to integrate new technology into service.[225]

The PRC augments its native defense industry by buying military technology from abroad. Key purchases made or planned in the 1990s include:

- Four Kilo-class submarines from Russia. Beijing has confirmed orders for 10 more, and may buy an additional 12 after that.[226]
- 73 Su-27 maritime strike aircraft, equipped with AA-10 and AA-11 air-to-air missiles.[227] China plans to buy 60 of the more advanced Su-30 model as well.[228]
- 220 SA-10 surface-to-air missile systems.[229]
- 12-14 IL-76 transport aircraft.[230]
- Two Sovremenny-class destroyers with SSN-22 anti-ship missiles.[231]
- Advanced engines for 100 of its native-built Super-7 and F8-3 fighter aircraft.[232]
- Both Iran and Israel have assisted China's efforts to develop the ability to refuel aircraft in flight.[233]
- China plans to purchase 12 Kamov ASW helicopters.[234]

These acquisitions shore up China's maritime assets in precisely the areas that the CMIC's production capabilities fall short of China's strategic concepts.

Beijing uses these purchases, not only to bolster its armed forces, but to acquire the knowledge it needs to produce similar equipment in China. PRC researchers routinely attempt to reverse-engineer new technology.[235] The Chinese have developed the means to produce Kilo-class submarines, for instance, in their own yards and appear to have incorporated technology from the Kilo into their own Song class of submarines.[236] PRC firms also plan to produce 200 SU-27 maritime strike aircraft, along with 300 copies of the MiG-31 interceptor.[237]

China is also notorious for using its business connections to facilitate outright espionage. COSTIND has its own clandestine information-gathering department, and is integrated into China's larger intelligence establishment.[238] There is no evidence that the recent reorganization of COSTIND has changed this.

ECONOMIC BASE

Whatever difficulties China has faced in making its arms industry profitable, it has enjoyed healthy expansion in certain commercial fields, many of which have military applications. Chinese industry's areas of strength include space, electronics, automobiles and shipping. Although China has not achieved Western levels of sophistication in the more technological fields, its equipment is widespread and functional. Here also, China has benefitted greatly from trade with foreign countries. China is noted for its use of reverse engineering in civilian areas as well.[239]

China's space program remains modest compared to its American and Russian counterparts, but it has fuelled a great deal of technological development. Beijing launched satellites steadily throughout the 1980s and 1990s. Although the launch rate has not accelerated rapidly, it has, nevertheless, been increasing, from highs of three per year in 1975 and 1984 to four in 1989, five in 1990 and 1994 and six in 1997.[240] The Chinese estimate that their space program has led to measurable technological improvements in over 1,800 industrially important areas, including optics, sensors, chemicals, cryogenics, telecommunications, nuclear technology, fiber-reinforced plastics, production line systems, machinery control systems, high-strength alloys, laser welding and plasma beam welding. The demands of space technology have led to general increases in standards throughout Chinese industry as well.[241]

The growth of China's electronics industry surprised even Chinese analysts. In 1996 alone, Chinese firms produced 1.3 million personal computers (PCs), doubling the previous year's output. That same year,

China's market for PCs increased by 40 per cent. In the first half of the 1990s, China's revenue from computer parts exports increased from US $200 million per year to 3.78 billion. Although the quality of Chinese products varies, China's best programmers and engineers appear to be among the best by world standards as well.[242]

China's government has identified supercomputer technology as a high-priority area for development. In 1997, China's University of Science and Technology for the National Defense (USTND) built a supercomputer known as the Yinhe (Galaxy) III, which can perform at least 10 billion and perhaps as many as 13 billion calculations per second. Although the most advanced American supercomputers are almost twice this fast, the Galaxy III exceeds US government export restrictions for computer exports to China.[243] This project represents a triumph, not only for China's researchers, but for the Chinese government's program of fostering research in areas of military importance.

The Chinese telecommunications industry has expanded at a similar rate. China is already the third largest telecommunications market in the world. Beijing has also launched a national project to create a thoroughly modern communications infrastructure known as Golden Bridge. According to one report issued in 1999, China's communications grid is expanding at the rate of 'a Bell-Canada sized network' every year.[244]

China has identified automobile production as a 'pillar industry' of key strategic importance. The reasons for this include the economic importance of the automobile business and the general level of industrial technology needed in modern automobile production. For these reasons, Beijing imposes high tariffs on imported cars. The Chinese government also subsidizes enterprises that appear to benefit its automotive industry.[245]

China's policies have produced spectacular results. In 1986, 80 per cent of the autos in China were imports, but by 1999, 90 per cent of the cars on Chinese roads were locally made. From 1992 to 1997, China more than tripled its revenues from exporting auto-parts to the United States. China achieved these successes, one might note, largely through skilfully managed collaboration with foreign firms. Chinese auto-companies have successfully used overseas partners as sources of capital and technology.[246]

Although Beijing has not identified aerospace as a pillar industry, China's aircraft industry pursues a more modest version of these policies. The Chinese expect their country's requirement for civilian air travel to increase significantly in the early twenty-first century, and they are relying on joint ventures with Boeing, Pratt and Whitney and other foreign firms to meet much of this demand. In the process, Chinese industry will gain assembly-line technology that could improve their ability to produce military aircraft as well. China is also importing navigation, communication and air-traffic control systems which could improve the PLAAF's command and control capabilities – one of its most significant weaknesses. Meanwhile, China has announced plans to spend the equivalent of over US $1 billion building airports and upgrading technology at existing ones, a program with potential military benefit.[247]

The PRC has expanded its commercial shipping industry dramatically. Both the tonnage and the number of ships in China's merchant marine increased by a factor of over 100 per cent between the mid-1980s and mid-1990s.[248] By 1997, PRC owners controlled 1,815 civilian ships, making China's merchant fleet the third largest in the world in terms of numbers of vessels.[249] China's merchant marine weighed in at a total of 35,904,212 dead weight tons (DWT), making it the world's fifth largest fleet by that standard of measurement. The United States, by way of comparison, had 1,061 vessels and 52,010,508 DWT, while Greece, the world's leader in both departments, had 2,849 ships and 119,712,440 DWT.[250]

China has also developed its shore facilities for servicing this fleet. In the mid-1990s, China had 1,000 berths and 300 deep-water docks, capable of handling a total of 600,000,000 tons of cargo per year. By early in the twenty-first century, China hopes to have a full 2,000 ports operating. At that point, it will have an annual handling capacity of over one billion tons.[251]

Although China has not yet mastered the technology it needs to build advanced warship propulsion systems, its commercial shipbuilding industry is relatively modern.[252] In the early 1990s, China's State Planning Commission estimated that 47.7 per cent of the PRC's shipbuilding industry had reached 'advanced world standards'. This placed Chinese dockyards ahead of the rest of China's industries. At that time, only 38.6 per cent of the PRC's overall manufacturing output reached similar technological levels.[253]

The strategic significance of China's merchant marine goes beyond the fact that China is developing an economically robust shipping and ship-building industry. Not only might this industry provide ships and sailors for the PLAN at some future point, but it also helps the Chinese government ensure that China's foreign trade serves national purposes even in the present. The fact that 72 per cent of all Chinese-owned ships are actually registered under the Chinese flag increases Beijing's control over its commercial fleet. Only 53 per cent of US-owned freighters, by way of comparison, fly the Stars and Stripes, and only 34 per cent of the huge Greek fleet is registered in Greece.[254]

Kevin Falk compares national control over merchant fleets in the twenty-first century to national control over armed forces in the fifteenth. The mercenary soldiers of the 1400s, as Machiavelli famously noted, 'are only too ready to serve in your army when you are not at war;

but when war comes they either desert or disperse'.[255] By maintaining direct control over its merchant fleet, the Chinese government both insulates itself against the danger that changing market conditions will induce shipping firms to defect from its economic strategies and enhances its ability to keep trade flowing in the event of an actual war. The fact that Chinese naval strategists, like Falk, expect struggles over ocean territory to become increasingly prevalent in the twenty-first century helps to explain why both of them are concerned with these issues.[256]

In general, China's civilian industry has expanded in the areas its armed forces need most. The 16-character policy implies that this is more than a coincidence. In the cases of automobiles, supercomputers and telecommunications, China's armed forces have directly sponsored commercial expansion.[257] If China can sustain its general economic growth, its strength in these sectors bodes well for its prospects of eventually acquiring a robust defense industry and a first-rate fleet.

CONCLUSION

The PLAN remains modest, but China's maritime capabilities correspond to China's maritime thought. The Chinese appear to have built a fleet that suits their current state of industrial development, and they appear to be working toward a time when they will be able to aspire to more. Given their technological limitations, they appear to have fielded exactly the kinds of equipment their naval thinkers have called for. One can debate the extent to which these correspondences represent deliberate planning and the extent to which they merely represent an unspoken and unexamined consensus among China's elite. This debate, however, is of secondary importance, since the outcome in both cases remains the same – the PRC has both the material and the intellectual instruments it needs to continue expanding its influence at sea.

NOTES

1.   It must however be admitted, and will be seen, that the wise or unwise action of individual men has at certain periods had a great modifying influence on the growth of seapower in the broad sense, which includes not only the military strength afloat, that rules the sea or any part of it by force of arms, but also the peaceful commerce and shipping from which alone a military fleet naturally and healthfuly springs, and on which it securely rests.

       (Alfred Thayer Mahan, *The Influence of Sea Power Upon History 1660–1783* (Boston, MA: S.J. Parkhill, 1890), p. 28.)
2.   Barry M. Blechman and Robert P. Berman, *A Guide to Far Eastern Navies* (Annapolis, MD: United States Naval Institute, 1978), p. 107.

3. Anon., 'Largest-Scale' Military Naval Exercises Held Off Zhejiang', *BBC Summary of World Broadcasts* (as reported on LEXIS-NEXIS) (21 Sept. 1994).
4. Tseng Hui-Yeh, 'Shandong Faction Reportedly Controls Military', *FBIS-CHI-94-204* (21 Oct. 1994), p. 34.
5. Ibid.
6. Sun Tzu, *Sun Tzu's Art of War: The Modern Chinese Interpretation*, trans. Yuan Shibing (New York: Sterling Publishing, 1987), p. 107.
7. Ibid.
8. Ibid.
9. Ibid.
10. Dennis J. Blasko, Philip T. Klapakis and John F. Corbett Jr, 'Training Tomorrow's PLA: A Mixed Bag of Tricks', *China Quarterly*, No. 146 (June 1996), pp. 520–1.
11. Nathan is cited in Laura K. Murray, 'China's Psychological Warfare', *Military Review*, Vol. 79, No. 5 (Sept.–Oct. 1999), p. 20.
12. Cited in ibid.
13. Ibid., p. 19.
14. Ibid.
15. Ibid.
16. Ibid.; General Tao Hanzhang, in Sun Tzu, *The Art of War*, pp. 44–9.
17. Nan Li, 'The PLA's Evolving Warfighting Doctrine, Strategy and Tactics, 1985–95: A Chinese Perspective', *China Quarterly*, No. 146 (June 1996), p. 443.
18. Ibid., p. 453.
19. Ibid.
20. Shen Zhongchang, Zhang Haiying and Zhou Xinsheng, '21st-Century Naval Warfare', in Michael Pillsbury (ed.), *Chinese Views of Future Warfare* (Washington, DC: National Defense University Press, 1998), p. 263.
21. Ibid.
22. Ibid., p. 262.
23. Ibid., pp. 271–2.
24. Bernard D. Cole and Paul H.B. Godwin, 'Advanced Military Technology and the PLA: Priorities and Capabilities for the 21st Century', in Larry M. Wortzel (ed.), *The Chinese Armed Forces in the 21st Century* (Carlisle, PA: Strategic Studies Institute, 1999), p. 163.
25. Ibid.
26. Blechman and Berman, *A Guide to Far Eastern Navies*, p. 107.
27. Ibid.
28. Ibid.
29. Zhongchang, Haiying and Xinsheng, '21st-Century Naval Warfare', in Pillsbury (ed.), *Chinese Views*, p. 263. (A mace is an iron club used to smash through armor in medieval warfare.)
30. Wu Jianguo, 'Nuclear Shadows on High-Tech Warfare', in Pillsbury (ed.), *Chinese Views*, p. 142.
31. Ibid., pp. 142–3.
32. Ibid., p. 144.
33. Ibid.
34. Ibid., p. 145.
35. Ibid.
36. Zhongchang, Haiying and Xinsheng, '21st-Century Naval Warfare', in Pillsbury (ed.), *Chinese Views*, p. 267.
37. Ibid., pp. 268, 271–3.
38. Ibid., pp. 268, 269, 270–3.

39. Corbett, *Some Principles of Maritime Strategy*, pp. 78–9.
40. Ibid., p. 273.
41. Kevin L. Falk, *Why Nations Put to Sea: Technology and the Changing Character of Sea Power in the Twenty-first Century* (New York: Garland Publishing, 2000), p. 63.
42. John W. Lewis and Litai Xue, *China's Strategic Seapower* (Stanford, CA: Stanford University Press, 1994), p. 222.
43. Zhongchang, Haiying and Xinsheng, '21st-Century Naval Warfare', in Pillsbury (ed.), *Chinese Views*, pp. 276–7.
44. Ibid, p. 277.
45. Ibid, p. 283.
46. Ibid., pp. 262–3, 277.
47. Keith W. Edmunds, 'ASW – Current and Future Trends', *Defense Analysis*, Vol. 16, No. 1 (Apr. 2000), pp. 73–88.
48. Blechman and Berman, *A Guide to Far Eastern Navies*, p. 107.
49. Tai Ming Cheung, *Growth of Chinese Naval Power* (Singapore: Institute of Southeast Asian Studies, 1990), p. 14.
50. Ibid., p. 13; Kyodo News Service, 'Chinese Naval Vessel Arrives at Bombay Port', *Japan Economic Newswire* (as reported on LEXIS-NEXIS) (15 Nov. 1993).
51. Richard Sharpe, *Jane's Fighting Ships 1999–2000* (Coulsdon, Surrey: Jane's Information Group, 1999), p. 83.
52. Anon., 'Naval Modernization', *BBC Summary of World Broadcasts* (as reported on LEXIS-NEXIS) (12 Jan. 1993).
53. Cheung, *Growth of Chinese Naval Power*, p. 36.
54. Sharpe, *Jane's Fighting Ships 1999–2000*, p. 83.
55. Ibid.
56. Sharpe, *Jane's Fighting Ships 1999–2000*, pp. 114, 136.
57. Ibid.
58. Ibid.
59. Blechman and Berman, *A Guide to Far Eastern Navies*, p. 108
60. Sharpe, *Jane's Fighting Ships 1999–2000*, pp. 136–8.
61. Ibid., pp. 779–80.
62. Ibid., p. 789.
63. Prasun K. Sengupta, 'PLA Force Modernisation Activities and Future Plans', *Asian Defence Journal*, Vol. 6, No. 5 (Apr. 1999), p. 23.
64. Sharpe, *Jane's Fighting Ships 1999–2000*, p. 129.
65. Sengupta, 'PLA Force Modernisation', p. 23.
66. Cole and Godwin, 'Advanced Military Technology and the PLA', in Wortzel (ed.), *Chinese Armed Forces*, p. 168.
67. Ibid., p. 201.
68. Ibid.
69. Ibid., pp. 262–3.
70. Zhongchang, Haiying and Xinsheng, '21st-Century Naval Warfare', in Pillsbury (ed.), *Chinese Views*, p. 263.
71. Cole and Godwin, 'Advanced Military Technology and the PLA', in Wortzel (ed.), *Chinese Armed Forces*, pp. 181–4.
72. Ibid., p. 178.
73. Brian Harvey, *The Chinese Space Program: From Conception to Future Capabilities* (Chichester: John Wiley, 1998), p. 90.
74. Ibid.
75. Cole and Godwin, 'Advanced Military Technology and the PLA', in Wortzel (ed.), *Chinese Armed Forces*, p. 178.

76. Li Ning, '30 Years of Development in Space Technology', *Beijing Review*, Vol. 43, No. 25 (19 June 2000), p. 14.
77. Ibid.
78. Harvey, *The Chinese Space Program*, pp. 43–4.
79. Ibid., p. 84.
80. Cole and Godwin, 'Advanced Military Technology and the PLA', in Wortzel (ed.), *Chinese Armed Forces*, p. 178.
81. Ibid.
82. Ibid.
83. Harvey, *The Chinese Space Program*, p. 152.
84. Ibid., p. 69.
85. Ning, '30 Years of Development', p. 14.
86. Harvey, *The Chinese Space Program*, p. 70.
87. Ibid., pp. 68–70.
88. Ning, '30 Years of Development', p. 14.
89. Ibid.
90. Harvey, *The Chinese Space Program*, p. 153.
91. Ibid., p. 108.
92. Ibid., p. 109.
93. Ibid., p. 66.
94. Ibid., p. 143.
95. International Institute for Strategic Studies, *The Military Balance 1994–1995* (London: Brassey's, 1994), p. 147.
96. Anon., *China In Crisis* (Coulsdon, Surrey: Jane's Information Group, 1989), p. 112.
97. Ibid.
98. International Institute for Strategic Studies, *The Military Balance 1994–1995*, p. 147.
99. Blechman and Berman, *A Guide to Far Eastern Navies*, p. 52.
100. International Institute for Strategic Studies, *The Military Balance 1994–1995*, p. 147.
101. Charles Smith, 'China's Newest Secret Weapon', *World Net Daily*, http://www.worldnetdaily.com (30 Nov. 1999).
102. Cole and Godwin, 'Advanced Military Technology and the PLA', in Wortzel (ed.), *Chinese Armed Forces*, p. 195–6.
103. Ibid., p. 126.
104. Ibid.
105. Ibid., p. 199.
106. Ibid., p. 197.
107. Sharpe, *Jane's Fighting Ships 1999–2000*, p. 119.
108. Cole and Godwin, 'Advanced Military Technology and the PLA', in Wortzel (ed.), *Chinese Armed Forces*, p. 191.
109. Sharpe, *Jane's Fighting Ships 1999–2000*, pp. 114–46.
110. Ibid., pp. 117–20.
111. Ibid., p. 114.
112. Ibid., p. 133.
113. Ibid.
114. Sengupta, 'PLA Force Modernisation', p. 23.
115. Cole and Godwin, 'Advanced Military Technology and the PLA', in Wortzel (ed.), *Chinese Armed Forces*, pp. 203–6.
116. Ibid., p. 203.
117. Ibid.
118. Barbara Opall-Rome, 'DoD Rings Alarm on Chinese Antisatellite Plans', *Defense*

News (2–8 Nov. 1998), p. 6.

119. Robert Wall, 'China Seen Building Conventional Might', *Aviation Week and Space Technology* (3 July 2000), p. 32.
120. Opall-Rome, 'DoD Rings Alarm', p. 6.
121. Ibid.
122. Ibid.
123. Ivo Dawnay, 'China Plots to Bug West's Defences', *Sunday Telegraph* (17 June 1997), p. 33.
124. Cole and Godwin, 'Advanced Military Technology and the PLA', in Wortzel (ed.), *Chinese Armed Forces*, p. 182.
125. John Frankenstein and Bates Gill, 'Current and Future Challenges Facing Chinese Defence Industries', *China Quarterly*, No. 146 (June 1996), p. 422.
126. Ibid.
127. Blasko, Klapakis and Corbett, 'Training Tomorrow's PLA', p. 507.
128. Frankenstein and Gill, 'Current and Future Challenges', p. 422.
129. Cole and Godwin, 'Advanced Military Technology and the PLA', in Wortzel (ed.), *Chinese Armed Forces*, p. 183.
130. Ibid., p. 179.
131. Anon.,'PLA Tests Invisible Destroyer', *Asian Defence Journal*, Vol. 6, No. 9 (Aug. 1999), p. 56.
132. Sharpe, *Jane's Fighting Ships 1999–2000*, p. 145.
133. Lewis and Xue, *China's Strategic Seapower*, *passim*.
134. Sharpe, *Jane's Fighting Ships 1999–2000*, pp. 116–18.
135. Ibid., pp. 556, 789.
136. Zhongchang, Haiying and Xinsheng, '21st-Century Naval Warfare', in Pillsbury, *Chinese Views*, p. 277.
137. Sharpe, *Jane's Fighting Ships 1999–2000*, p. 118.
138. Ibid., p. 116.
139. Ibid., p. 118.
140. Cole and Godwin, 'Advanced Military Technology and the PLA', in Wortzel (ed.), *Chinese Armed Forces*, p. 188.
141. Ibid., p. 88.
142. Ibid., p. 173.
143. Harold J. Kearsley, 'An Analysis of the Military Threats Across the Taiwan Strait: Fact or Fiction', *Comparative Strategy*, Vol. 19, No. 2 (Apr.–June 2000), p. 108.
144. Edmunds, 'ASW', p. 74.
145. Ibid., pp. 80–1.
146. Ibid.
147. Ibid., *passim*.
148. Michael G. Gallagher, 'China's Illusory Threat to the South China Sea', *International Security*, Vol. 19, No. 1 (Summer 1994), p. 178.
149. Sengupta, 'PLA Force Modernisation', p. 23.
150. Sharpe, *Jane's Fighting Ships 1999–2000*, pp. 119–28.
151. Larry M. Wortzel, 'China Pursues Traditional Great-Power Status', *Orbis*, Vol. 38, No. 2 (Spring 1994), p. 163.
152. Sengupta, 'PLA Force Modernisation', p. 24.
153. International Institute for Strategic Studies, *The Military Balance 1994–1995*, p. 166.
154. Sengupta, 'PLA Force Modernisation', p. 24.
155. Anon., 'PLA Air Growth "Set to Change Balance of Power"', *Flight International*, Vol. 4, No. 10 (July 2000), p. 16.
156. Ibid.
157. Sharpe, *Jane's Fighting Ships 1999–2000*, p. 129.

158. Sengupta, 'PLA Force Modernisation', p. 24.
159. Cole and Godwin, 'Advanced Military Technology and the PLA', in Wortzel (ed.), *Chinese Armed Forces*, pp. 174–5.
160. Sengupta, 'PLA Force Modernisation', p. 23.
161. Ibid.
162. Ibid.
163. Anon., 'China to Acquire Israeli Radar System', *Asian Defence Journal*, Vol. 7, No. 1 (Dec. 1999), p. 84.
164. Nikolai Novichkov and Yihong Zhang, 'Russia Discusses AWE&C Lease to China and India', *Jane's Defence Weekly* (28 June 2000), p. 5.
165. Ibid.
166. Ibid.
167. Yang Wei, 'Tactical Studies', in Pillsbury (ed.), *Chinese Views*, p. 384.
168. Ibid., *passim*.
169. Wang Pufeng, 'The Challenge of Information Warfare', in Pillsbury (ed.), *Chinese Views*, p. 324.
170. Ibid.
171. Zhongchang, Haiying and Xinsheng, '21st-Century Naval Warfare', in Pillsbury (ed.), *Chinese Views*, p. 283.
172. Lester J. Gesteland, 'China: China Naval Experts Ponder Need for Aircraft Carrier', *ChinaOnline News*, http://www.chinaonline.com (12 Feb. 1999).
173. Ibid.
174. Sharpe, *Jane's Fighting Ships 1999–2000*, p. 119.
175. Gesteland, 'China Naval Experts'.
176. Nayan Chanda, 'Aiming High', *Far Eastern Economic Review*, Vol. 157, No. 2 (20 Oct. 1994), p. 15.
177. Sharpe, *Jane's Fighting Ships 1999–2000*, p. 114.
178. Ibid., p. 133.
179. Kearsley, 'An Analysis of the Military Threats Across the Taiwan Strait', p. 107; Michael D. Swaine, 'The Modernization of the Chinese People's Liberation Army: Prospects and Implications for Northeast Asia', *National Bureau of Asian Research Analysis*, Vol. 5, No. 3 (Oct. 1994), p. 11, n. 10.
180. Swaine, 'The Modernization of the Chinese People's Liberation Army', p. 11.
181. Kearsley, 'An Analysis of the Military Threats Across the Taiwan Strait', p. 107.
182. Anon., 'Rapid Deployment Key to PLA Modernisation', *Jane's Defence Weekly*, Vol. 29, No. 15 (15 Apr. 1998), p. 31.
183. Ibid., p. 30.
184. Ibid., p. 31.
185. Ibid.
186. R.P. Khanua, 'Impact of China's Ambition to be a Regional Superpower', *Asian Defence Journal*, Vol. 6, No. 9 (Aug. 1999), p. 8.
187. Kearsley, 'An Analysis of the Military Threats Across the Taiwan Strait', p. 107.
188. Sengupta, 'PLA Force Modernisation', p. 23.
189. Sharpe, *Jane's Fighting Ships 1999–2000*, p. 133; Anon., 'China's Hubei Develops Passenger Ekranoplan', *Flight International* (25 Nov.–1 Dec. 1998), p. 8.
190. Kearsley, 'An Analysis of the Military Threats Across the Taiwan Strait', p. 107.
191. Cole and Godwin, 'Advanced Military Technology and the PLA', in Wortzel (ed.), *Chinese Armed Forces*, p. 173.
192. Ibid.
193. Ibid., pp. 173–6. The DoD study identified 14 general areas of militarily critical technology in which China was notably weak, as opposed to seven in which China was notably strong.

194. Ibid., p. 162.
195. Shun Zhenhuan, 'Reform of China's Defense Industry', in Pillsbury (ed.), *Chinese Views*, p. 203.
196. Blasko, Klapakis and Corbett, 'Training Tomorrow's PLA', pp. 497, 518, 520.
197. Ibid., pp. 520, 521.
198. Ibid., pp. 500–15.
199. Ibid., p. 516.
200. Ibid., p. 498.
201. Ibid., p. 494.
202. Cole and Godwin, 'Advanced Military Technology and the PLA', in Wortzel (ed.), *Chinese Armed Forces*, p. 166.
203. Frankenstein and Gill, 'Current and Future Challenges', p. 417.
204. Cox report, http://www.house.gov/coxreport/chapfs/ch1.html.
205. Frankenstein and Gill, 'Current and Future Challenges', p. 396.
206. Ibid., p. 407.
207. Ibid., p. 419.
208. Ibid., p. 401.
209. Zhenhuan, 'Reform of China's Defense Industry', in Pillsbury (ed.), *Chinese Views*, p. 202.
210. Frankenstein and Gill, 'Current and Future Challenges', p. 403.
211. Ibid., p. 409.
212. Ibid., p. 419–20.
213. Anon., 'Industry Embraces Market Forces', *Jane's Defence Weekly* (16 Dec. 1998), p. 28.
214. Ibid.
215. Frankenstein and Gill, 'Current and Future Challenges', p. 411.
216. Ibid., pp. 411–12.
217. Anon., 'Industry Embraces Market Forces', p. 28.
218. Frankenstein and Gill, 'Current and Future Challenges', p. 413.
219. Ibid.
220. Anon., 'Industry Embraces Market Forces', p. 28.
221. Ibid.
222. Zhenhuan, 'Reform of China's Defense Industry', in Pillsbury (ed.), *Chinese Views*, p. 190.
223. Ibid., p. 190; Sharpe, *Jane's Fighting Ships 1999–2000*, pp. 117–33.
224. Sharpe, *Jane's Fighting Ships 1999–2000*, p. 116.
225. Frankenstein and Gill, 'Current and Future Challenges', p. 409.
226. Khanua, 'Impact of China's Ambition', p. 8.
227. Sharpe, *Jane's Fighting Ships 1999–2000*, p. 129.
228. Anon., 'China to Acquire 60 SU-30 Fighter-Bombers', *Asian Defence Journal*, Vol. 6, No. 11 (Oct. 1999), p. 70.
229. Dennis J. Blasko, 'Evaluating Chinese Military Procurement from Russia', *Joint Forces Quarterly*, No. 17 (Autumn–Winter 1997–98), p. 93.
230. Ibid.
231. Sharpe, *Jane's Fighting Ships 1999–2000*, p. 119.
232. Blasko, 'Evaluating Chinese Military Procurement', p. 92.
233. Khanua, 'Impact of China's Ambition', p. 8.
234. Blasko, 'Evaluating Chinese Military Procurement', p. 92.
235. Frankenstein and Gill, 'Current and Future Challenges', p. 423.
236. Richard Sharpe, *Jane's Fighting Ships, 1994–1995* (Coulsdon, Surrey: Jane's Information Group, 1994), p. 541; Sharpe, *Jane's Fighting Ships 1999–2000*, p. 117.
237. Thomas W. Zarzeck, 'Weaponry and War: Are Arms Transfers From the Former

Soviet Union a Security Threat? The Case of Combat Aircraft', *Journal of Slavic Military Studies*, Vol. 12, No. 1 (Mar. 1999), p. 142; Swaine, 'The Modernization of the Chinese People's Liberation Army', p. 13.
238. Nicholas Eftimiades, *Chinese Intelligence Operations* (Annapolis, MD: Naval Institute Press, 1994), pp. 104–7.
239. Kathleen A. Walsh, *US Commercial Technology Transfers to the People's Republic of China* (Washington, DC: US Department of Commerce, 1999), pp. iv–v.
240. Harvey, *The Chinese Space Program*, p. 96.
241. Ibid., pp. 111–12.
242. Walsh, *US Commercial Technology Transfers*, p. 72.
243. Ibid., p. 73.
244. Ibid.
245. Ibid.
246. Ibid., p. 53.
247. Ibid., p. 55.
248. Sharpe, *Jane's Fighting Ships 1994–1995*, p. 113.
249. Falk, *Why Nations Put To Sea*, p. 98.
250. Ibid., p. 125.
251. Anon., 'Beijing to Build more Ports with Foreign Capital', *FBIS-CHI-94-236* (7 Dec. 1994), p. 27.
252. Cole and Godwin, 'Advanced Military Technology and the PLA', in Wortzel (ed.), *Chinese Armed Forces*, p. 186.
253. Zhenhuan, 'Reform of China's Defense Industry', in Pillsbury (ed.), *Chinese Views*, p. 190.
254. Calculated from data found in Falk, *Why Nations Put To Sea*, pp. 94–5.
255. Cited in ibid., p. 95.
256. Ibid., pp. 105–9; Zhongchang, Haiying and Xinsheng, '21st-Century Naval Warfare', p. 261.
257. Walsh, *US Commercial Technology Transfers*, pp. 73–4.

6

The Diplomacy of Chinese Seapower

Whatever the state of its fleet, the PRC has begun to act like a seapower in international affairs. The coastal nations of Southeast Asia defer to China as one expects weaker maritime countries to defer to a stronger. China's equals on land and sea have become increasingly willing to accommodate its interests. Many states have elected to cooperate actively with China, and this has allowed the PRC to forge the political links it will need to expand its maritime influence yet further. These facts indicate the success of Beijing's current policies, and suggest the directions Chinese strategy will take in the future.

This chapter discusses developments in China's foreign relations that appear to improve the PRC's position upon the seas. Maritime power is, however, only one of China's foreign policy objectives. Beijing has many other reasons for pursuing the policies described in this chapter. One should conclude not that China is engaged in a single-minded bid for oceanic supremacy, but that China's overall diplomatic interests tally with the interests of its admirals. For this reason, the success of China's larger policies has allowed it, among other things, to develop its power at sea.

One cannot know how many of China's successes reflect deliberate plans. The worldly will observe that chance plays a greater role than cunning in international affairs. Nevertheless, one can identify unmistakable patterns in China's foreign relations. These patterns mesh with both Western and Chinese strategic thought. This thought, therefore, helps us to determine the significance of what has already happened, and to guess at how competent Chinese leaders might choose to proceed.

Mao's writings on protracted war (and the updated versions of the 1990s) suggest that China may try to improve its position on the seas by proceeding through a series of discrete phases. When China's opponents find themselves overstretched and begin to reduce their commitments, Mao's thought calls for China to take advantage of their withdrawal by adopting more active policies. During the early 1990s, China saw both of its most powerful rivals pull back from East Asia. Not only did the PRC go on to adopt a considerably more assertive maritime policy, but

Chinese leaders have declared that they hope to continue this process through further stages of development.

There are key differences between revolutionary warfare and international relations. Revolutionaries have a clear end in mind – the overthrow of the state – whereas diplomatic affairs can grind on indefinitely. One can suppose that the Chinese hope to raise their maritime power to new heights, but one need not assume that they intend to destroy their rivals in the literal sense that Mao's Red Army destroyed Chiang Kai-Shek's mainland Republic. Also, state leaders have a wider range of options at their disposal than have soldiers. When the Soviet Union and its successors declined in power, China seized the initiative, not by attacking them, but by forming what appears to have become a mutually beneficial alliance.

Mahan's writings on the elements of seapower summarize China's handicaps and advantages as a maritime nation. One can assume that, as China gains more freedom of action, Chinese strategists will seek to compensate for the former and build upon the latter. China's political and economic initiatives suggest that the Beijing regime is aware – if, perhaps, insufficiently aware – of the factors Mahan encapsulated as – number of (technically proficient) population, character of the people and character of the government. Mahan's observations about geography, physical conformation and extent of territory provide a guide to China's objectives in other geographical regions – that is, other countries. Chapter 7 will discuss how China has attempted to seize the initiative in the areas of greatest importance to its maritime potential.

THE LANDWARD FLANK

Historically, the greatest obstacle to China's seapower has been the threat of invasion by land. As the rulers of the Han Dynasty discovered, China's maritime capabilities are strongest when its landward trade and security are robust as well. China's contemporary regime has acted on these principles as dramatically as the Han emperors. The defining event of the early 1990s was the collapse of the Soviet Union, and China took advantage of this development to establish relations that support its initiatives at sea.

Russia and China have ongoing disputes over their land border and a cloudy political history, but, barring cataclysm, they must regard each other as permanent neighbors. At this point in history, they must both come to grips with the fact that if they wish to act freely in the rest of the world, they cannot waste their energy against one another. The two of them happen to be peculiarly well suited for a maritime alliance. Neither of them has much to gain by pursuing their land dispute, and both of them have much to lose from a continued arms race there. There are no direct rivals at sea for either of them, or for their strongest potential opponents in the Pacific Ocean, the United States and Japan. Russia and China have every logical reason to seek a condominium, and all indications show that they have done precisely that.

Not only do Russia and China seem to have drawn closer since the break-up of the Soviet Union, but the substance of these new Sino-Russian relations seems to be overwhelmingly naval. In May 1994, for the first time since the founding of the Peoples' Republic, Chinese warships visited a Russian port.[1] Shortly afterward, Feliks Gromov, the commander in chief of the Russian fleet, toured several Chinese naval bases.[2] Following this visit, Gromov announced that China had accepted his offer to train Chinese naval officers in Russian academies.[3] By 1999, the Chinese and Russians had begun to hold joint naval maneuvers.[4] Most of the arms Russia has sold to China have had some maritime orientation.

In July 2000, Jiang Zemin and Russian President Vladimir Putin met in Beijing. Following this meeting, Putin publicly affirmed that China and Russia share a common position on security issues.[5] In addition to their formal talks, the two reportedly held a two-hour private meeting on strategic matters.[6] At this meeting, Putin and Jiang reputedly agreed that 'both Russia and China are faced with military threat and blackmail from US hegemonism'.[7] Putin also pledged to support the PRC 'unreservedly' in cracking down on 'pro-Taiwan independence forces'.[8]

After Putin left Beijing, Zhu Bangzao of the Chinese Foreign Ministry noted that Russia and China had agreed, not only to oppose 'hegemonism', but to 'promote the multipolarization process'. These terms are significant. Chinese spokespeople of the early twenty-first century frequently condemn hegemonism and praise multipolarity. Not only does this indicate China's hostility to the dominance of the West in general and the United States in particular, but it recalls fundamental principles of strategic thought in contemporary China. A multipolar world is one in which Mao's *wei chi* approach to international politics becomes eminently practicable.

China has also achieved a rapprochement with the smaller states of the former Soviet Union. In 1996, the PRC started a program of annual summits involving the leaders of the so-called 'Shanghai Five' nations (Takikistan, Kyrgyzstan, Kazakhstan, Russia and China).[9] Not only have these countries sought to develop economic, scientific, technical and cultural ties, but they also support each other on strategic issues as well. At their July 2000 summit, the Shanghai Five issued joint statements backing the PRC's stand against Taiwanese independence and supporting the 1972 Anti-Ballistic Missile Treaty.[10]

Jiang Zemin proposed that Shanghai Five armed forces conduct joint actions against 'extremist forces, separatist forces and terrorist forces' in Central Asia: 'We cannot overlook the disrupting and sabotaging factors coming from within and outside of the five-nation region that are threatening peace and stability within the region.' Jiang went on to propose that the five nations should cooperate to form an economic bloc that could generate enough internal prosperity to resist the forces of 'globalization'. The Chinese leader suggested that, for this economic program to succeed, the countries would have to suppress 'disrupting and sabotaging factors' with force.[11]

The Central Asian countries have proved receptive to the idea of military cooperation with China. Within weeks of the July 2000 Shanghai Five Summit, Kazakhstan, Kyrgyzstan and Tajikstan all hosted visits by a delegation of PLA officers. President Emomali Rahmonov of Tajikstan took advantage of the occasion to speak warmly about his satisfaction with the 'steadfast expansion of mutually beneficial cooperation' between his country and China. The head of the Chinese delegation, Area Commander Li Qianyuan, modestly said that he hoped to learn from the experiences of the Tajik armed forces.[12]

Other Central Asian countries have proved interested in cooperating with China as well. Uzbekistan sends observers to Shanghai Five summits.[13] Jiang Zemin visited Turkmenistan in the summer of 2000. On that occasion, Saparmyrat Niyazov, the president of Turkmenistan, spoke enthusiastically about economic, cultural and military cooperation with China.[14]

Jiang Zemin used his trip to Turkmenistan to make a speech on global policy. In the words of the Xinhua news service, the Chinese leader pledged that his country would 'make unremitting efforts to work for the setting up of a new world political and economic order', which would encourage pluralism and discourage 'hegemonism'. Niyazov declared his support for key principles of that order, notably a strict definition of sovereignty and opposition to ethnic separatism. The Turkmen president pledged his support for the PRC's position on Taiwan. Niyazov also joined with Jiang in condemning the principle that countries may violate each other's sovereignty to correct human-rights abuses.[15]

Azerbaijan's leaders have expressed their support for China's new world order as well. In 2000, Chairman of China's National People's Congress Li Peng met with Azerbaijani Prime Minister Rasizade. Li Peng expressed his sympathy for Azerbaijan's problems with Armenian separatists in the province of Nagorno-Karabakh. Rasizade, in turn, endorsed the principle of 'multipolarity'.[16]

Azerbaijan's leaders claim to have launched a project to create a 'new Silk Road' of commerce and industrial development from the Caucasus to China.[17] The Chinese have warmly endorsed this idea. Other Caucasian states such as Georgia are enthusiastic about economic ties with China as well.[18] The fact that many of these countries have oil reserves makes such cooperation particularly valuable to the PRC. As the 16-character policy indicates, Beijing will use any economic expansion to strengthen its armed forces, including its fleet.

Moving further west, China has developed ties with Belarus. At a meeting with Chinese Vice-President Hu Jintao in July, 2000, Belarussian President Alyaksandr Lukashenka stated that 'Belarus and China have always been supporting each other and cooperating in the international arena, and share identical views on upholding strategic stability and safety in the world.' Lukashenka offered China his full support on the Taiwan issue.[19] The PRC also buys military equipment from Belarus, notably optics, navigation technology, information systems and equipment for constructing field pipelines.[20] China is the Belarussian defense industry's second-biggest customer, after Russia.[21]

THE DAGGER AND THE BRIDGE

China has traditionally seen Korea as 'the dagger and the bridge' between mainland Asia and Japan.[21] As noted in Chapter 3, Korea's alignment in world politics has a marked effect on China's freedom of action at sea. This raises the question of what the Chinese regime would like to see happen in Korea today. As the twenty-first century begins, North and South Korea have begun to take steps to end the hostile deadlock which has prevailed between their countries. These developments give the question of Korea's future particular immediacy.

Some have suggested that China actually benefits from the presence of the US military on the peninsula. US troops, this argument goes, reassure Japan. This keeps Tokyo from feeling sufficiently threatened to develop its own armed forces.[22] Such logic is in keeping with China's tradition of balance-of-power politics.

The Chinese themselves, however, condemn the US presence in ringing terms. Bi Yurong, writing in the PLA newspaper, *Jiefangjun bao*, accuses the United States of maintaining forces in Korea in order to 'hold sway over the whole world'. Bi analyzes the United States' strategic position as follows:

> First, the United States wants to keep a firm grip on its domination of the situation in northeast Asia. The Korean Peninsula is located in the heart of northeast Asia, so its strategic position is extremely important. To dominate the Korean Peninsula is also to have a tight grip on northeast Asia. However, the issue of stationing troops on the Korean Peninsula is also the key to locking or unlocking the easing of tensions on the Korean Peninsula, and as soon as the issue

of stationing troops is touched on, dealing with the United States becomes unavoidable. Thus, as long as the United States does not withdraw its troops, it can continue to have a say in the critical issues in northeast Asia.

Second, [the presence of US troops] is to deal with the so-called 'North Korean threat.' The 'North Korean threat theory' is one reason the United States has used to replace the Soviet Union threat in northeast Asia following the Cold War. For a long time, the United States has always treated North Korea as the 'major threat' to security in northeast Asia, as well as viewing them as a so-called 'rogue state,' bringing the Western nations together to impose comprehensive sanctions on them for a long time. In recent years, based on the strategic goal of the peaceful evolution of the Korean Peninsula, the United States has begun a dialogue with South Korea, hoping to achieve a 'soft landing,' but in their heart of hearts they have not gotten rid of their hostility to North Korea at all, nor have they relaxed their safeguards against North Korea, and in particular they have never renounced the option of using military means to deal with North Korea. Therefore, the United States inevitably must continue to stress keeping US troops in South Korea.

Third [the presence of US troops] is to strengthen their control of South Korea ... [23]

These statements not only indicate the depth of Chinese hostility toward the US presence, but also elucidate the reasons why PRC strategists want the US forces to withdraw. The *Jiefangjun bao* article indicates an acute awareness of Korea's geographical significance. Although the author does not put it in these terms, one can assume that PRC strategists would like to have a 'tight grip on northeast Asia'. Later in the article, the author accuses the United States of trying to dominate Asia through its 'system of bilateral military alliances'.[24] As later sections will discuss, the PRC routinely uses bilateral negotiations to maximize its diplomatic influence throughout Southeast Asia, and if US forces did withdraw from the peninsula, there would be nothing to stop Beijing from using this approach in Northeast Asia as well.

'South Korea really wants to develop its own military power', Bi tells us, 'and is not content to remain under the "protection" of the United States for a long time.' Bi suggests that many South Koreans feel that the US presence implicates them in potential conflict rather than protecting them from it, and that the US forces are hampering South Korea's development as an independent economic power.[25] From a cynical point of view, it is easy to see why a Chinese strategist might wish to encourage rifts between South Korea and its ally across the Pacific. No matter how freely South Korea develops its own military power, it is unlikely to become as immovable an obstacle to Chinese policy as the United States.

Nevertheless, one must also consider the possibility that Bi's sympathy for Korean self-determination is sincere. Some Chinese leaders may view an independent Korea as a potential ally. Even a strong but neutral Korea could serve as a shield on China's borders. The fact that South Korea has pursued an aggressively capital-oriented economic model need not hinder such an alliance. China's political theorists of the early twenty-first century continue to stress the concept of the United Front.[26]

These possibilities make Bi's treatment of ideological issues noteworthy. Although Bi does not explicitly endorse the North Korean regime, he protests US attempts to undermine it. This is consistent with much of Beijing's foreign policy. Jiang Zemin has emphasized that China stands for 'equality of sovereignty' and 'independent choice of ways of development'.[27] The Chinese have frequently sought to make common cause with governments which Western states have stigmatized as 'rogues' or human rights violators.

PRC leaders seem to feel that anti-Western countries are naturally inclined to support China in international politics. For this reason alone, they are likely to remain sympathetic to the North Korean system of government. If the two Koreas elect to reunite, the PRC will support those who seek to give Pyongyang's old rulers some role in the new regime. Bi implies that even the South Korean polity would prefer to be more independent from the US world order.[28] Beijing will attempt to promote this trend as well.

In the summer of 2000, the leaders of North and South Korea held a historic summit meeting. Not only did the leaders agree on the desirability of closer relations, but the countries also have taken material steps to achieve such ties. In the first half of 2000 alone, the two Koreas increased their trade by over 20 per cent.[29] This increase gave their commerce a total value of US $202.8 million. North and South Korea have also begun preparations for a trans-Korean railway. This project will take an estimated five years to complete, and will increase the value of inter-Korean commerce by an expected US $100 million.[30]

PRC leaders have supported this process enthusiastically. After the summit, the Chinese arranged follow-up meetings between North and South Korean ambassadors in Beijing.[31] The Chinese see this rapprochement between North and South Korea as a key step in getting the US forces out of Korea. Bi's article directly linked these events to the issue of the US presence.

[T]he fact that the summit conference between the North and South went smoothly shows that things are starting to thaw on the Korean Peninsula, which is the only place in the world which maintains a

Cold War situation, and that the trend of the age of peace and development is irreversible. How much longer can the US troops in South Korea, which are a stumbling block to peace on the Korean peninsula, remain?[32]

Korea is critical to Russia's Pacific aspirations as well. Moscow actively supported the Summer 2000 exchanges between North and South Korea.[33] In July 2000, Putin commented on the US presence in Korea. His comments were far more guarded than those of Bi Yurong. Although Putin acknowledged South Korea's right to 'individual and collective self defense', he concluded that the 'exercise of these rights must fully correspond to the common interests of easing military-political confrontation'.[34]

Russia and China have coordinated their Korea policy. After Putin visited Korea in July 2000, he discussed his trip with Jiang Zemin in person, by telephone.[35] Jiang reputedly praised Putin highly for his efforts. China's cooperation with Russia on the Korea issue indicates that their alliance is strong at many levels.

JAPAN: PAST AND FUTURE

Many PRC strategists see Japan as China's most serious military threat.[36] As the Chinese academic Gao Heng explains, 'After the Cold War ... Japan was not satisfied with the situation of being a "big economic country, small political country and tiny military country".' This scholar goes on to cite documents which Japanese officials presented to back up their request for a permanent seat on the United Nations Security Council. According to Gao, these papers claimed that Japan could start producing nuclear weapons in a matter of months, has the materials it would need to make 1,000–2,000 nuclear bombs, has the technology to build intercontinental ballistic missiles and has a powerful navy. 'Japan has trampled on its Peace Constitution', Gao warns. 'The Japanese government advocates a "new nationalism" and is preparing to become a military superpower.'[37]

Japan and China both claim sovereignty over the Senkaku islands, known in China as the Diaoyus. As of the year 2000, Japan controls these islands. During the Ming Dynasty, however, Chinese warships used the Diaoyus as outposts in their anti-pirate campaigns.[38] The fact that possession of these islands grant the owner exclusive economic rights to over 42,600 square miles of ocean territory in an area known to have rich fish, oil and gas reserves gives the dispute special significance in the twenty-first century.[39]

China must take Japan's armed forces seriously. Japan's Maritime

Self-Defense Force (MSDF) has more modern equipment than the PLAN.[40] In terms of destroyers and frigates, Japanese forces rival China's in terms of numbers as well, with combined totals of 55 each.[41] Neither China nor Japan appears to be in a position to launch a direct attack on the other with any assurance of success.

To the extent that the PRC's relationship with Japan consists of rivalry, China's leaders appear determined to maintain the initiative. The Chinese continually seek to maintain and improve their position versus Japan in both psychological and military terms. '[P]ast experience, if not forgotten, is a guide to the future', Li Peng told the Japanese Prime Minister in 1995, and the Chinese take advantage of every opportunity to remind the world of Asia's 'past experiences' with Japan in the 1930s and 1940s.[42] The Chinese zealously expose both actual and potential suggestions of renewed Japanese militarism.

Reminders of Sino-Japanese history presumably help keep China's people from becoming, in one Chinese journalist's words, 'muddleheaded'.[43] The Chinese seem determined to prevent what they call 'muddleheadedness' abroad as well as at home. The rhetoric of Chinese declarations typically emphasizes Japan's aggression against all Asian countries, not only their own.[44] Such rhetoric strikes a chord even in Japan itself, where many regret their nation's role in the Second World War and are determined not to support any kind of military interventionism again.[45] China's strategy of emphasizing 'past experiences' almost certainly increases both Japanese and international political difficulties for advocates of Japan's armed forces.

The PRC's opposition to Japanese resurgence consists of more than rhetoric. China's navy holds frequent exercises to prepare for a hypothetical war against Japan.[46] Chinese ships also probe Japanese waters. PLAN vessels violated Japan's exclusive economic zone 17 times in the first half of 2000 alone.[47] Most of these incursions were probably intelligence-gathering missions, and some may even have been accidental, but the fact that Beijing trespasses in Tokyo's waters so often and so openly indicates that China's leaders wish to demonstrate their willingness to stand up to Japan for all the world to see.

Sumihiko Kawamura, formerly a Rear Admiral in the MSDF, suggests that the Chinese may have displayed their determination to project influence into Japanese waters more aggressively, by encouraging pirates to attack Japan's shipping. These attacks reached maximum intensity in the early 1990s, and took place in the East China Sea.[48] British scholars have noted that China seems to pursue a more general policy of 'piracy as low-intensity conflict' to achieve its political aims throughout Asian waters.[49] Such covert attacks may not be damaging enough to influence Japanese national policy directly, but they surely intimidate sailors and shipowners, thus contributing to a climate of caution and appeasement.

China's prospects in an open war with Japan would depend greatly on how that war was fought. Although PLAN commanders might hesitate to meet the MSDF in a fleet battle on the open sea, Japan is exceptionally dependent on its merchant shipping. Over 70 per cent of Japan's oil, for instance, comes from the Middle East through the Straits of Malacca.[50] The MSDF currently limits itself to operations within a 1,000-mile radius of the Japanese home islands, but even if it freed itself from that restriction, it would have great difficulty patrolling routes of such length.[51]

If China chose to harass Japan's shipping, it would be able to take full advantage of its submarine fleet. Such a campaign would also allow the PRC to exploit its influence in Southeast Asia. The US Navy, and not the MSDF, is Japan's surest guarantee of immunity to such threats. One should not be surprised to learn that the Chinese are sharply critical of Japan's alliance with the United States.

The Chinese see their attempts to get US forces out of Korea as a prelude to getting them out of Japan as well. '[I]f the United States were to withdraw its conventional forces from South Korea', one Chinese strategist writes, 'it would then be harder for them to find a reason to have US troops stationed in Japan. Thus, one flank in their so-called "Eurasian strategy" would be lost.'[52] Meanwhile, China's military demonstrations appear to have convinced many Japanese that, even with the US commitment, they are vulnerable. One of Japan's former prime ministers has argued that Japan should ask the United States to close its military bases in Japan on the grounds that the presence of US forces on Japanese territory might make Japan a target in a future war with China.[53]

Despite the PRC's military exertions against Japan, China's leaders do not seem committed to the idea that their relations with Tokyo have to be hostile. Younger members of the PRC hierarchy tend to depict Japan as potentially friendly.[54] There appears to be a genuine difference of opinion between them and older, warier Chinese officials, but the PRC leadership has found a place for both points of view. Jiang Zemin has called for closer relations between the two countries.[55] Overall, Beijing appears to be demonstrating its readiness to confront Japan with one hand while offering the proverbial olive branch with the other.

Japan seems to be responding to this technique. In the words of the US Asia scholar Chalmers Johnson, 'Japan's policy is to do everything in its power to adjust to the reemergence of China on the world stage.' Tokyo has reaffirmed its position that Taiwan belongs to mainland China and it tried, with limited success, to block the United States from using Japanese bases in support of the Taiwan regime.[56] Japan also gave China over 2.6 trillion yen in economic aid during the 1980s and 1990s.[57]

TAIWAN

The PRC's policies toward the Republic of China (ROC) on Taiwan can seem confusing, if not merely confused. Mainland Chinese leaders hint that they would go to war – even nuclear war – to prevent the ROC (Taiwan) from declaring permanent independence.[58] The PLA and PLAN have conducted spectacular missile tests and amphibious exercises in the Taiwan Straits. Nevertheless, not only does Beijing lack the military means to invade Taiwan with any assurance of success, but studies of the PLA's training exercises do not even indicate that the PRC is seeking to develop such capabilities.[59] Meanwhile, other mainland officials have adopted a conciliatory tone toward the breakaway republic.[60]

Although the PRC's Taiwan policy seems contradictory when examined in isolation, it is consistent with Beijing's approach to other countries with similar strategic characteristics. One can, for instance, draw numerous parallels between Taiwan and Japan. Both are islands which dominate important sections in the fragmented waters of the western Pacific. Both have fleets that rival Beijing's own, and both have close relationships with the United States. Both could serve, in the words of Douglas MacArthur, as 'unsinkable aircraft carriers' off China's coast.

There are differences between Taiwan and Japan as well. For reasons of cultural pride and national prestige, Beijing has committed itself to re-absorbing the ROC at the earliest possible date. The PRC has no such psychological need to subjugate Japan. On the other hand, the presence of US military bases in Japan makes that country a greater immediate hindrance to Beijing's freedom of action in the Pacific. Japan's economic performance indicates that it has more potential to be a future military opponent for the PRC as well.

Beijing's policies toward Taiwan and Japan reflect these parallels and differences. PRC armed forces conduct frequent demonstrations against both countries. These operations accomplish minor military purposes of training, intelligence-gathering and testing potential opponents' reactions, but they also accomplish the more significant diplomatic purpose of establishing limits to acceptable behavior within China's sphere of influence. The facts that the ROC has refrained from declaring independence and that US policymakers have urged its government to behave prudently indicates that those countries have accepted Beijing's implicit ultimatum. As noted above, Japan also seems to have responded favorably (from a Chinese perspective) to subtle military pressure.

Mainland China's historical relationship with Taiwan virtually guarantees that Beijing's threats against the ROC will be explicit. Nevertheless, the fact that the PRC's military modernization program has not involved a concerted effort to prepare for an invasion of the ROC indicates that PLA leaders recognize their limitations and do not wish to risk their larger strategic goals by pouring their resources into the Taiwan problem. Beijing needs to prevent Taiwan and Japan from improving their native armed forces too dramatically, and it needs to limit their military ties to the United States, but it has no short-term imperative to conquer them. If Mainland China can achieve these goals through military pressure, it can indeed achieve mutually beneficial trade with both countries, while continuing to advance its strategic ambitions unhindered elsewhere. Trade and friendly relations in the present can only improve the PRC's long-term prospects for unification with Taiwan and cooperation with Japan as well.

MARITIME STRATEGY IN SOUTHEAST ASIA

China's fate as a maritime nation depends upon its ability to operate in the Indonesian Straits and the South China Sea. These waters are Beijing's route to Eurasia. China's rivals and China's allies both depend on them as well. A full 25 per cent of the world's shipping goes through the South China Sea.[61] The fact that the South China Sea is rich in fish and, potentially, oil is a bonus for whatever nation can act as the arbiter of this region.

The waters of Southeast Asia are shallow and dotted with islands. Most of the main shipping routes pass through long, narrow straits. These facts make shipping peculiarly vulnerable to any kind of attack. During the Second World War, the US Navy conducted a lethally effective campaign against Japanese shipping in this region. Contemporary pirates lack aircraft and submarines, but still operate in these waters with great ease.[62]

Even minor threats to Southeast Asian commerce can have profound economic consequences. The cost of re-routing shipping even slightly can be phenomenal. Simply switching vessels from the Malacca Strait to the nearby Strait of Lombok would cost $200,000–300,000 per ship. These costs become all the more significant when one considers the fact that the Malacca Straits handle over 270 ships per day.[63]

At a minimum, China needs to be able to provide its own shipping with safe passage through this region. If the PRC can threaten to harass other countries' commerce off Southeast Asia, it gains leverage over a staggering number of potential rivals. Japan is exceptionally vulnerable to such pressure, but even the United States would probably go to considerable lengths to avoid a situation in which it would have to choose between acquiescing to a Chinese power play in the Indonesian Straits and going to war. Chinese strategists may also see the South China Sea as a stepping-stone between their coastal waters and the Pacific.

Not only are Southeast Asia's waters highly valuable, they are hotly contested. Taiwan, Vietnam, Malaysia, Indonesia, mainland China and the Philippines all have overlapping claims within the region. This creates a situation in which any country which has the power to improve its position has a pretext for doing so. China has such power, and it has systematically expanded its maritime influence at every level.

Analyzing the PRC's policies toward Japan and Taiwan, one finds evidence that Beijing is using the proverbial 'carrot-and-stick' method of diplomacy. In both cases, China makes shows of force while simultaneously holding out the hope of improved relations, and in both cases, Beijing appears to have had some success at shaping those countries' policies. China uses these tactics more blatantly in Southeast Asia. The PRC's southern neighbors find themselves caught between two views of China, hoping that they can maintain a benign trading relationship with the Chinese, while terrified of the consequences if they do not.

John Lilley, the former US Ambassador to China, summed up the mood in Malaysia as follows: 'One official will say, "I don't see anything wrong with China. They are the wave of the future". Then, quietly, another official comes to you and says, "We know where the threat is, believe me".'[64] What Lilley says about Malaysia could easily apply to the rest of Southeast Asia.

These conditions allow China to apply pressure against the Southeast Asian countries, isolating them and individually compelling each of them to obey its will. For instance, China claims the entire South China Sea as an 'exclusive economic zone' (EEZ),[65] to the detriment of the other nations in the region. Admiral Prachet Siridej of the Royal Thai Navy, for instance, notes that the imposition of the exclusion zone has reduced his nation to a net importer of seafood. In working out the details of the EEZ, China insists on negotiating with the other Asian countries one at a time, thereby, in the words of a Thai commentator, using its 'massive geopolitical weight' to 'bring great pressure to bear' on each of its 'dialogue partners'.[86]

In April 1994, Indonesia proposed a new way of dividing economic rights in the South China Sea, called the 'doughnut formula'. Under this plan, each nation would receive a 320-kilometer economic zone extending from its coastline. Indonesia raised this idea in the Association of South-East Asian Nations (ASEAN) forum, calling upon all the other countries of Southeast Asia to give the plan their general support. Despite the fact that the 'doughnut' plan clearly benefits all of the nations concerned except China, no country was willing either to support Indonesia or to criticize China's position. One ASEAN official, speaking under conditions of anonymity, noted 'Let's face it. China is simply too big and powerful.'[67]

From the mid-1990s onward, China has sought to regularize relations in the South China Sea. Beijing has frequently offered to set disputes aside and engage in so-called 'joint development' of ocean resources with Southeast Asian countries. Many within the region mistrust China's motives. These skeptics believe that China hopes to use joint development to pacify its potential opponents while it consolidates its gains and prepares to expand its claims even further.[68] Shared economic ventures would also give the PRC access to foreign capital and technological expertise.

In summer of 2000, China initiated a series of negotiations with individual Southeast Asian states concerning the South China Sea. Zhu Bangzao, a spokesman for the PRC Foreign Ministry, said that these talks were intended to 'formulate certain agreements of principle to avoid military clashes'.[69] In particular, Zhu stressed the point that it would be dangerous to rush attempts to solve the South China Sea dispute.[70] Zhu also warned other states that attempts to 'complicate' the dispute, presumably by involving multilateral organizations or extraneous issues, would 'be harmful to regional stability'.[71] The PRC spokesman summed up the negotiations as follows:

> China's stance on South China Sea issues has been consistent. China proposes to resolve disputes with countries concerned through friendly bilateral consultations and peaceful means ... the bilateral consultations have proceeded smoothly and attained positive progress.[72]

Southeast Asian countries have indeed continued to respond warmly to China's overtures. Khamtai Siphandon, President of Laos, met with Jiang Zemin and agreed in principle to strengthen his country's ties to China in a wide variety of areas.[73] Laotian and Malaysian leaders each affirmed their own commitment to the principle of bilateralism.[74] Tran Du Luong, the President of Vietnam, spoke publicly of his country's friendship with China, enacted a treaty formalizing Vietnam's land border with the PRC and called for negotiations to settle the sea border as well.[75]

Meanwhile, China has not hesitated to seize islands in the South China Sea by force. In 1974, the Chinese drove South Vietnamese troops from the Paracel archipelago. Fourteen years later, China fought a naval battle with Vietnam and seized six more islands in the Spratly chain.[76] On 8 February 1995, China made a bloodless landing upon Mischief Reef, which formerly belonged to the Philippines.

China's invasion of Mischief Reef is its most distant conquest, and its first attack on a non-communist country. Furthermore, the landing on Mischief Reef appears designed as an implicit threat to the other countries of Southeast Asia. In 1995, the Philippines took the lead in proposing an international conference to decide which countries should control the islands of the South China Sea, thereby flagrantly opposing China's desire to resolve such questions through individual negotiations with each of the nations concerned.[77] As commentators in the *Far Eastern Economic Review* noted, China had sent the message, 'Negotiate with us on our terms or we will take possession of the territory.'[78]

The Philippines have found no more international support than Indonesia found for its 'doughnut formula'. Indeed, the Indonesians themselves refused to take a stand against China's invasion.[79] In 1998, the Philippines published photographs showing that China was building large military structures on Mischief, transforming the reef into an artificial island. China claims that these buildings are merely huts for fishermen, but that appears highly unlikely. On this occasion, the other nations of Southeast Asia offered almost no reaction at all.[80]

Although the islands of the South China Sea tend to be small, they have genuine military value. Island bases can potentially extend the range of China's radar, sonar, aircraft and missiles. The Chinese currently maintain a substantial military base on Woody Island in the Paracels.[81] In October 1994, on the twentieth anniversary of China's invasion of the Paracels, Chinese radio announced programs to build up the garrison on the islands.[82]

Many of the South China Sea islands require artificial superstructures simply to make them inhabitable. Sea platforms, however, have played a role in warfare before, and could again. The British used such 'sea forts' quite successfully during the Second World War. Those structures served the following purposes:

> 1. to break up enemy aircraft formations approaching a target such as London or Liverpool from the sea; 2. to prevent the laying of mines by enemy aircraft in the navigable channels serving the great ports; 3. to prevent enemy E-boats carrying out raids on shipping and coastal targets in the estuaries; 4. to obtain early warning of the approach of hostile air or sea forces by means of radio location and direct telephonic communications with the shore; and by fulfilling 1, 2, 3, 4, to release for other duties the 'flak' ships which had hitherto patrolled the estuaries, and to provide the missing links in the chain of land defenses on either side.[83]

Fortified positions at sea, like fortified positions on land, free maneuver elements such as actual warships from defensive duties, allowing them to maximize their potential.

Japanese use of islands in their defensive perimeter during the Second World War can be understood as utilizing natural sea forts. However, the Japanese maneuver fleet was incapable of maintaining communications with these islands. Isolated from the fleet, these island forts were defeated piece-meal or even left to wither in irrelevance as the US Navy advanced in other regions. Recollection of the last years of the Pacific War, when the Japanese Navy had already been broken, should not be allowed to cloud the strategic and operational problems that these island forts caused the US Navy while the Japanese Navy remained a viable power.[84]

China has more subtle ways to influence Southeast Asian countries as well. Just as some speculate that China uses pirates to put political pressure on Japan, others speculate that the PRC uses similar methods in the South China Sea. Pirates often sail stolen ships to Chinese ports. There have also been notorious cases in which Chinese port authorities arrested known pirates and subsequently released them without trial.[85]

In 1994, 20 ships reported attacks by pirates who flew Chinese flags, wore Chinese militia uniforms, and had Chinese markings on their vessels. The same year, the government of Hong Kong reported 42 pirate attacks involving Chinese military or para-military forces. These incidents led the director of the International Maritime Bureau to state that, 'there is no doubt that these moves against ships operating in international waters were government-inspired'.[86] The fact that China's Public Security Minister, Tao Siju has publicly applauded the patriotism of China's notoriously piratical Triad organized crime rings lends credence to such accusations.[87]

Many countries in Southeast Asia have large ethnic Chinese minority groups, known as the overseas Chinese. The PRC has attempted to mobilize these populations for political purposes in the past, and may do so again. As an editorial in a 1978 issue of *People's Daily* put it, the Overseas Chinese are 'an important belt for tightening up the friendship of China with the nations of their residence'.[88] Friendship was less in evidence in 1960, when Beijing openly incited the overseas Chinese in Indonesia to riot against government decrees, or during the Cultural Revolution, when radicals used the PRC diplomatic service to agitate for insurrections in Burma, Hong Kong and Macao.[89] Western analysts have identified a long-term pattern in which the PRC promotes unrest among overseas Chinese in Indonesia when its relations with Jakarta are poor, and urges ethnic harmony when the Indonesian government cooperates with its wishes.[90]

The United States remains the ultimate check on China's ambitions in the South China Sea and elsewhere. Beijing, however, has reason to hope that it has found limits to Washington's willingness to intervene. According to news sources, United States intelligence services failed to detect the Chinese move against Mischief Reef for several months, despite the fact that Chinese forces spent that time openly engaged in construction projects on the island.[91] US defense officials explained that their intelligence services do not have the resources to keep reconnaissance satellites focused upon the South China Sea on a regular basis, or to fly aircraft over the region. RAND studies indicate that the US naval presence in the Far East in the early twenty-first century will have fallen to approximately half its 1990 level.[92]

As the United States reduces its military readiness, Southeast Asian countries have become increasingly reluctant to rely upon it for protection, or to cooperate with the United States in any ventures which might draw them into US disputes. In the short run, these attitudes indicate that the United States has lost some of its political influence. In the long run, these attitudes must undercut the United States' material strength as well, because they will deprive it of bases, allies, and pretexts upon which to act. The United States received graphic evidence of these facts in 1994, when the US armed forces sought permission to establish a floating supply depot off the coast of Thailand.

Immediately after Thailand turned down the United States request, a chorus of other Southeast Asian countries scrambled to refuse the depot as well. General Feisal Tanjung of Indonesia declared that his country would reject any such request.[93] Malaysian Defense Minister Datuk Sri Najib stated that 'there is no need for a base anywhere in this region', explaining that 'ASEAN countries should not depend too heavily on the US', because of Washington's budgetary constraints.[94] Datuk added, in perhaps unintentionally revealing language, that his nation had refused the bases because 'Malaysia ... did not want to mention the possibility of being attacked by others'.[95] After these strong rejections, Washington judged that Singapore would not wish to defy its neighbors by accepting the base either.[96]

Thai commentary on the base provides further insight into the state of American prestige. An editorial in the Bangkok paper *Athit* observed that although the United States had been willing to pay a 'high price for friendship' during the Cold War, the 'attitude of the United States' had changed.[97] The author noted the willingness with which the United States abandoned the Philippines, implying that it might abandon Thailand just as precipitately in time of trouble. Furthermore, this article mentioned that 'America's military importance in this region has declined. New problems have arisen.'

Events in Indonesia also illustrate the diplomatic decline of the United States. In 1995, Indonesia decided to invoke rights under the Law of the Sea Treaty to restrict the passage of foreign warships between its islands. Although this policy ostensibly applies to the fleets of all foreign nations, only the United States regularly sends naval vessels through this region, and writers in the *Far Eastern Economic Review* characterized Indonesia's decision as an 'anti-US move'.[98]

US policymakers are aware of the effects their perceived withdrawal might have, and they have proven themselves willing to remind the world of their interest in this region when necessary. During the Asian currency crisis of the late 1990s, for instance, the United States made a point of stepping up its use of Southeast Asian military bases in order to announce its commitment to that part of the world.[99] These efforts undoubtedly increase local confidence in the United States. Nevertheless, they hardly reverse the overall trend.

Although the United States has reduced its military profile in Southeast Asia throughout the 1990s, most countries in the region have been attempting to build up their forces. The Southeast Asian nations focused on developing their air and naval assets. From the late 1980s to the mid-1990s, Southeast Asian defense budgets increased by an average of 40 per cent.[100]

China must have seen the expansion of these navies as a two-edged sword. Obviously, these new forces make their owners less vulnerable to Chinese intimidation. Nevertheless, as the PLA commentator observed regarding Korea, countries which build up their own military establishments are less likely to offer their territory as outposts for the United States. Washington, in turn, is less likely to look on them as candidates for its protection.

China certainly has not behaved as if it felt threatened by the Southeast Asian build-up. Rather, the Chinese have played their part in fueling the arms race by selling four Jianghu-class frigates to Thailand.[101] Thailand, of course, was once a close ally of the United States. Indeed, the Thais organized their armed forces around the US model in order to make maximum use of US aid.[102] The fact that Thailand has been questioning its ties to the United States at the same time as it has been receiving arms from China is probably due to larger diplomatic trends, and is not a direct cause-and-effect relationship. However, the pattern of relationships between Thailand, the United States and China may indicate how the Chinese hope to develop their relations with Indonesia, Malaysia and Singapore as well.

The Malaysians seem willing to follow Thailand's path. Malaysia and China have exchanged defense attachés, and the Malaysian foreign minister commented that 'there is no reason why we cannot cooperate [with China] in the military field'.[103] Despite Singapore's occasional tensions with Malaysia, its position at the end of the Malaysian peninsula means that it cannot escape involvement in its neighbor's strategic alignments. Singapore routinely sends troops to train in Malaysia, and the two nations have established a joint forum between their defense ministries.[104] In the first half of 2000, Malaysia and Indonesia both affirmed an interest in broad naval cooperation with the PLAN.[105]

One might note also that Southeast Asia's military build-up draws attention to tensions between the nations of the region. General Feisal

Tanjung of Indonesia has stated that his nation is building up its fleet so that it will be 'ready to face and anticipate various threats that may arise from *expanding* Indonesia's territorial waters'.[106] When one considers the fact that Indonesia, Malaysia and the Philippines all have contesting maritime claims, this statement begins to sound ominous. Meanwhile, General Chalm Phunsanong of Thailand has noted the growing strength of the Malaysian air force with dismay.[107] Whether or not these disputes develop beyond their present stage, China is in an excellent position to serve as a broker between these nations, and thereby to govern the future of the region.

The Southeast Asian arms build-up allows China to practice its traditional strategic principles of forming alliances of convenience with useful partners, playing outsiders off against one another and using checkerboard tactics to dominate geographical regions. China's leaders may also assume that, over the long term, mainland China's economic potential will always allow it to overshadow the relatively tiny nations to its south. The currency crisis of the late 1990s indicates the advantages a large and diverse country like China holds over smaller states, even when those states have enjoyed economic booms like those of the so-called 'tiger economies'. Although many Southeast Asian states had to curtail their planned naval build-ups, China's own military development proceeded more or less uninterrupted. Indeed, the PRC's cash reserves allowed Beijing to play an important role in stabilizing the crisis, thus reminding the Southeast Asian states that they are economically, as well as militarily, in China's shadow.[108]

NOT JUST FOR THE INDIANS

The pattern of China's diplomatic relations in South Asia conforms almost perfectly to Mao's concept of checkerboard strategy. From a geopolitical perspective, India is clearly China's most serious maritime rival in the region. The fact that India deploys a fleet comparable with the PLAN and shares many of China's economic strengths and weaknesses means that this rivalry is likely to be permanent. China and India also have a history of antagonism, which led to actual warfare in 1962.

Chinese military writings of the 1990s frequently portrayed India as a likely enemy. General Zhao Nanqi, Director of China's Academy of Military Sciences has affirmed China's determination to deploy warships in the Indian Ocean in order to keep India from dominating those waters. 'We are not prepared to let the Indian Ocean become India's ocean.'[109] Just as Mao might have advised, Beijing has systematically cultivated alliances which hem India in.

The PRC's annexation of Tibet brings China to India's eastern border, albeit in the world's most impenetrable mountains. China's alliance with Pakistan is one of the oldest and warmest of its diplomatic relationships.[110] Not only does Pakistan extend China's geographical reach around India's northern flank, it is a significant military power with a deep-seated grudge against the Delhi regime. Pakistan also endorses China's point of view on more general issues of international relations, such as opposing US 'hegemony'.[111]

In the words of Pakistan's ambassador to China, 'Pakistan has always extended unconditional, consistent and strong support for China on the issues of Taiwan, Tibet, human rights and the WTO (World Trade Organization). In return, Pakistan has received invaluable principled support from China on various issues at the international level.'[112] This support consists, not only of words, but of military hardware. Chinese military instructors appear to have helped direct Pakistani operations in the Indo-Pakistani war of 1965.[113] In 2000, after many years of rumors, Pakistan's foreign minister acknowledged that his country receives missile technology from the PRC.[114] The Foreign Minister maintains that China has conformed to international guidelines for the control of such technology, which would forbid the PRC from helping Pakistan to develop missiles with ranges over 300 km. There is evidence, however, that China has assisted Pakistan to develop other types of missiles as well, notably the Ghauri, with its estimated 1,500 km range.[115]

To India's south, China has cultivated military ties with Burma (Myanmar). In 1988, Burma's armed forces took control of the country in order to suppress internal dissent, killing thousands of their political opponents.[116] Since then, Burma has been a pariah in international relations. Nevertheless, Burma's government requires both capital to support its economy and military assistance to combat the assortment of revolutionary, separatist and criminal movements that seek to overthrow it. China has provided both.

China has supplied Burma with more than US $1.5 billion American dollars worth of aircraft, radar systems, patrol boats, heavy artillery, tanks, surface-to-air missiles, small arms and ammunition. The Burmese regime has deployed most of these weapons along its border with India. High-ranking Burmese and Chinese military officers confer regularly. Pakistani military instructors train Burmese troops how to use Chinese equipment.[117]

The PRC is also developing infrastructure in Burma that could extend the reach of its own armed forces. Up until the 1990s, one of China's chief difficulties in deploying warships around the Straits of Malacca was its lack of supply and maintenance facilities on the western side of the straits. The Burmese regime has allowed China to develop military port facilities on islands off its coast. Burma has also given China permission to construct radar and signals intelligence facilities on other islands.[118]

The fact that these installations are near India's own naval bases on the Andaman and Nicobar islands adds to their value against the Indian fleet.

The Chinese have also announced plans to reopen the Burma Road of Second World War fame.[119] Although this project is supposedly intended to get Chinese goods to Burmese markets, one must recall that the Allied forces built the original Burma Road to support military operations based in India and directed at China. A future road could serve the same purpose in the opposite direction. The Chinese also plan to build a railway from China through Laos and Burma to Thailand, giving them an overland route through the center of Southeast Asia.

Not only do such transportation arteries facilitate military operations directly, they give China an overland alternative to the Straits of Malacca and the South China Sea. As Chinese defense planners routinely observe, this reduces China's vulnerability to opponents there.[120] With a land transportation network in Burma, China can use the port of Rangoon as if it were its own. The existence of land routes also reduces the economic cost China would pay if it initiated hostilities in Southeast Asian waters itself. China's attempts to develop overland routes through Burma recall analogous projects in the Han Dynasty, when Chinese emperors discovered that they could maximize their land and seapower by developing both to the point where there was a synergy between the two.

Moving west along India's coastline, China has cultivated ties with the government of Sri Lanka. Like Burma, Sri Lanka needs outside help to suppress insurgents. Once again, China has provided such aid lavishly.[121] Again, this recalls other eras in which China has established itself as a seapower. In the Ming Dynasty junks routinely visited this island, and Cheng Ho famously kidnapped the Ceylonese king. More recently, Mahan identified Ceylon as a critical outpost for controlling the Indian Ocean in general and peninsular India's coastlines in particular.[122]

AFRICA, THE MIDDLE EAST AND THE SEA

Mahan also identified South Africa, the Suez region and the Persian Gulf as pivotal points between East and West in Eurasia.[123] The growing importance of Middle Eastern oil to Asian economies would only seem to increase the value of these maritime bottlenecks. China has been active in all these areas. Not only has China cultivated diplomatic ties in the region, it has demonstrated its ability to mount military expeditions to the most strategically valuable points of East Africa.

Africa borders the western side of the Indian Ocean, and African countries straddle the routes to Europe. Since establishing diplomatic relations with Egypt in 1956, China has conducted an intense campaign to form ties with African regimes. The PRC has actively supported

African insurgent movements, presumably hoping the rebels would found new regimes friendly to Chinese policies. During the 1960s, China targeted foreign aid to African countries in an attempt to increase its profile *vis-à-vis* the United States and the USSR.[124]

In August 2000, for the first time in history, a PLAN task force rounded the Cape of Good Hope and sailed into the Atlantic. This flotilla, headed by the destroyer *Shenzhen*, made goodwill visits to Malaysia, Tanzania and South Africa. The South Africa visit was the diplomatic highlight of the trip, signifying that the Cape is friendly territory for the Chinese military. South African admirals, representatives of Chinese-funded institutions, South African nationals of Chinese descent and overseas Chinese greeted the task force at the docks. China's ambassador to South Africa alluded to the PRC's history of friendship with the South African people and spoke of future naval cooperation between the two countries.[125]

China has had cordial relations with Egypt since 1956. The PRC has supplied the Egyptian armed forces with both ships and missiles.[126] Meanwhile, to Egypt's south, China has formed close ties to the government of Sudan. China's National Petroleum Corporation has taken the lead in developing Sudan's oil resources. When, in the summer of 2000, anti-government forces known as the Sudan People's Liberation Army (SPLA) advanced to within ten miles of the oilfields, China sent troops to intervene.[127]

China's forces arrived by aircraft and ship. In addition to sending army troops, the Chinese reportedly deployed convicts who had been drafted into service as security guards. Sudanese government documents state that China sent 700,000 men to Sudan. Western journalists estimate the size of China's expeditionary force more conservatively, but still believe that it numbers in the tens of thousands. By August 2000, the SPLA had already taken Chinese prisoners, indicating that China's troops have not hesitated to engage rebel forces in combat.[128]

China's intervention in Sudan represents a milestone in the PRC's development as a global power. Even if the PRC's force turns out to be less capable than initial reports have indicated, this action announces China's commitment to East Africa in a way that neither China's potential allies nor China's potential enemies can ignore. If China can intervene in Sudan, it can also do so in Somalia, Ethiopia and other key points along the African coast. The operation also provides China's forces with a valuable training opportunity, allowing them to hone their ability to deploy over great distances.

To Egypt's north, China has sought the role of honest broker in the Arab–Israeli dispute. Beijing buys arms from Israel, and has sought Israeli help in improving its military technology.[129] Meanwhile, China has endorsed the proposition that Israel should trade 'land for peace' in its dispute with the Palestinians.[130] During the summer 2000 Camp David negotiations on the Arab–Israeli dispute, Palestinian leader Yassir Arafat flew to Beijing to report on the talks to Jiang Zemin. Israeli Minister of Regional Cooperation Shimon Peres visited the PRC to brief Chinese leaders on the Israeli perspective.[131]

China maintains a special relationship with Jordan as well. The Chinese National Peoples' Congress has exchanged envoys with Jordan's House of Representatives. Li Peng has described this form of inter-parliamentary diplomacy as unique, and suggested that it may serve as a valuable model for China's relations with other friendly countries. China and Jordan have used their parliamentary exchanges to condemn United Nations sanctions against Iraq and to negotiate greater levels of economic cooperation.[132]

China has also made overtures to Syria. In August 2000, the Deputy Chief of the PLA met with a Syrian army delegation. The Syrians affirmed their support for China in the Taiwan dispute. China, in turn, assured them of its support for the Arab position in the Arab–Israeli dispute.[133] The PRC also shares missile technology with Syria.[134]

Chinese and Iranian leaders speak hopefully of a new 'Silk Road' of friendship between their civilizations.[135] The PRC sold the Iranian navy 10 missile-armed fast-attack craft in the mid-1990s, and appear to have assisted Iran's program to develop ballistic missile technology.[136] China and Iran agree on key issues of international politics as well. In summer of 2000, Jiang Zemin, Premier Zhu Ronji of China's State Council and Chairman Li Ruihuan of the National Committee of the Chinese People's Political Consultative Conference met with President Seyyed Mohammad Khatami of Iran. The Chinese and Iranian leaders issued a joint statement supporting 'world multipolarization', opposing 'hegemonism', opposing the concept of humanitarian intervention, and indicating their 'readiness to work together for the establishment of such a new order'.[137]

The Chinese and Iranian leaders also declared their agreement on more specific issues. Both China and Iran support the idea of a Palestinian homeland, with a right of return for Palestinians abroad. The Chinese and Iranians stressed that 'the security and stability of the Persian Gulf should be safeguarded by the countries in the region free from outside interference'. Zhu Ronji spoke enthusiastically about the prospect of greater economic ties between China and Iran, describing Khatami's visit as a 'new chapter' in Chinese–Iranian relations.[138] Chinese and Iranian defence ministers held a conference of their own to coincide with the summit, paving the way for closer military cooperation.[139]

THE PACIFIC

China's future naval interests may also lead it into the Pacific. The range of modern weapons has given China fresh incentives for such expansion. PLAN officers feel that the defense of the Chinese coast must encompass the 'first chain' of islands, which includes the Ryukyus, Taiwan, the Philippines and Borneo. As these thinkers have considered the range of sea-launched cruise missiles, they have proposed extending China's defenses to a 'second chain' including the Marianas, Guam and the Carolines.[140]

In the Pacific as elsewhere, China must avoid direct confrontation with the United States. The Pacific, however, is another area in which the United States has reduced its presence. Indeed, the United States initially sought to place its supply depot in Thailand to compensate for the fact that it had recently given up a similar base in the Marianas.

China may also be able to gain influence in the Pacific through covert means. The island nations of the Pacific are new, small and peculiarly vulnerable to subversion. Owing to these countries' small populations and smaller cadres of trained government officials, an outside nation could gain an unusually large degree of influence simply by persuading, corrupting or threatening a few key individuals. As an extreme example of this condition, on the island of West Samoa, a single man serves as Prime Minister, Minister of Foreign Affairs, Minister of Broadcasting, Minister of Police and Prisons, Attorney General, Public Services Commissioner, Minister of Public Relations and Minister of Official Information.[141]

The PRC may also acquire outposts in the Pacific simply by offering its support to beleaguered governments there. The first year of the twenty-first century saw coup attempts and insurgencies in Fiji, Papua New Guinea and the Solomon islands. Most of these clashes concerned ethnic disputes. After the government of Papua New Guinea (PNG) suppressed an uprising, China stepped in to offer the PNG Defence Force logistical support. PNG Defence Secretary Vari Fore and PLA General Wu Quanxu committed their countries to work together on military issues in the future.[142] The day after Fore and Wu signed their initial agreement, PNG's Prime Minister announced his support for Beijing in the Taiwan dispute.[143]

LATIN AMERICA

From the 1950s onward, communist Chinese officials have described Latin America as 'the backyard [hou-yuan] of American imperialism' and sought to undermine the United States there.[144] If the PLAN should ever grow strong enough to challenge the US Navy, it will profit from bases in the Western Hemisphere, particularly if those bases are well suited for attacks on the Panama Canal. Although these developments may lie far in the future, the Chinese may be interested in preparing for them now.

On a less belligerent note, the PRC profits from trade and technological cooperation with South American nations.

China and Cuba share an open rivalry with the United States. The current entente between Beijing and Moscow further encourages Sino-Cuban cooperation. The PRC has established electronic-intelligence facilities at Jaruco, Cuba.[145] China is also helping the Cuban government to upgrade its satellite tracking facilities, and to develop its telecommunications network. Although there is no evidence that Beijing and Havana have collaborated on anything more directly offensive, Soviet submarines formerly received support in Cuban ports, and Chinese vessels might someday do the same.[146]

In 1997, the Hutchison Whampoa company of Hong Kong purchased the rights to operate shipping terminals at both ends of the Panama Canal. Whampoa's largest shareholder, Li Ka-Shing, has ties to the PRC government.[147] One must be careful not to overestimate the strategic significance of this purchase. If, for instance, China attempted to block the canal to US shipping, the US armed forces could reopen the waterway in short order. The shipping terminals might, however, allow the Chinese intelligence services to monitor shipping in the region. On a more speculative note, Chinese special forces might someday use Whampoa operations as cover for bringing in explosives and other equipment for use in sabotaging the canal.

Returning to less cinematic aspects of international relations, Beijing routinely participates in Latin American regional organizations. Foreign ministers from the Rio Group of nations (Colombia, Mexico and Chile) recently met with Jiang Zemin in Beijing. These countries expressed their enthusiastic support for the principle of multipolarization.[148] Chile's Foreign Minister stressed that her country had especially close ties with China, and that Chile was the first nation to support the PRC's entry into the World Trade Organization.[149]

CONCLUSION

The range of China's diplomatic advances has been awe-inspiring. Some of Beijing's gains, however, are more concrete than others. Countries from Chile to Iran have agreed in principle with China's views on international relations, but this does not guarantee that they will side with China on substantive issues. China's position is stronger in countries such as Sudan and Burma, which have actually accepted a Chinese military presence. Even there, however, a change of regime or a change in international circumstances might challenge the PRC's influence.

The Chinese themselves place great emphasis on getting foreign diplomats to accept their viewpoints on seemingly intangible issues. PRC negotiators traditionally view questions of principle as vital to progress in any discussion. An American diplomat who took part in the Laos conference of 1961–62 noted how closely his Chinese counterparts adhered to Mao's admonition that 'the right and wrong sides over a controversial issue should be clearly established without compromise or equivocation'.[150] Chris Patten, the last British governor of Hong Kong, observed the same fact in the 1990s.

> At the outset of talks, commercial or political, the Chinese (who learn these tactics when they are taught to negotiate) will try to get you to agree to some principles that appear relatively innocuous. Look at these very carefully. They are probably framed to help shape the outcome and the endgame. At very least, they will be played back against you during the negotiations, when you will be accused of departing from the 'spirit' – a largely meaningless concept designed to shame you on to the back foot.[151]

Patten emphasized that Chinese negotiators consciously study and practice these methods. This negotiating style is a conscious technique, not a racial stereotype. The former governor also allows that French diplomats undoubtedly find their British counterparts equally irritating.[152] With those caveats, however, one can see some of the reasons why China has pressed so many countries to endorse concepts such a multipolarity and opposing hegemonism. To take this logic further, one might observe that nations establish diplomatic principles, not only through words, but through actions, and that arms purchases, pledges of military cooperation and port visits by warships all set precedents for future relations between China and other countries.

One must view China's diplomatic exchanges with a critical eye, particularly those that involve an excessive ratio of words to deeds. Nevertheless, one must also take the expansion of China's foreign ties seriously. Even if agreements in principle occasionally prove less binding than PRC negotiators might hope, the fact that so many countries are willing to endorse China's 'new order' in open defiance of the richer and more powerful West indicates that their leaders believe that they share common interests with the People's Republic. Those common interests may become the basis for more substantive alliances later. The PRC has laid the diplomatic foundations to become a force to be reckoned with at sea.

NOTES

1. Lincoln Kaye, 'Courtship Dance', *Far Eastern Economic Review*, Vol. 157, No. 21 (26 May 1994), p. 24.
2. Anon., 'Russian Navy Chief Reveals Cooperation Pact', *FBIS-CHI-94-216* (8 Nov. 1994), p. 11.

3. Ibid.
4. Anon., 'Russia, China Hold First Ever Joint Naval Maneuvers', WorldTribune.com (1 Oct. 1999).
5. Anon., 'China, Russia Share "Common Position" on Security – Putin', *BBC Summary of World Broadcasts*, FE/3896 (19 July 2000), p. G/4.
6. Anon., 'Chinese, Russian Leaders Reportedly Held Secret Talks on Opposing US Hegemonism', *BBC Summary of World Broadcasts*, FE/3902 (26 July 2000), p. G/11.
7. Ibid.
8. Ibid.
9. Anon., 'Spokesman on Central Asian Summit, Russian Ties', *BBC Summary of World Broadcasts*, FE/3885 (6 July 2000), p. G/1.
10. Anon., 'Shanghai Five Sign Declaration in Tajik Capital', *BBC Summary of World Broadcasts*, FE/3885 (6 July 2000), p. G/2.
11. Anon., 'President Puts Forward Proposal to Improve Shanghai Five Cooperation', *BBC Summary of World Broadcasts*, FE/3885 (6 July 2000), p. G/1.
12. Anon., 'Tajik President to Extend Further Military Cooperation with China', *BBC Summary of World Broadcasts*, FE/3893 (15 July 2000), p. G/5.
13. Ibid.
14. Anon., 'Chinese, Turkmen Presidents Agree to Expand Economic, Trade Cooperation', *BBC Summary of World Broadcasts*, FE/3887 (8 July 2000), p. G/1.
15. Anon., 'President Has Talks with Turkmen Counterpart, Stresses "New World Order"', *BBC Summary of World Broadcasts*, FE/3887 (8 July 2000), p. G/1.
16. Anon., 'Congress Leader Li Peng Meets Azerbaijan Premier', *BBC Summary of World Broadcasts*, FE/3876 (26 June 2000), p. G/5.
17. Ibid.
18. Anon., 'Li Peng Discusses Ties with Georgian Speaker', *BBC Summary of World Broadcasts*, FE/3917 (12 Aug. 2000), p. G/1.
19. Anon., 'Vice-President, Belarussian President Discuss Deepening Bilateral Ties', *BBC Summary of World Broadcasts*, FE/3904 (28 July 2000), p. G/2.
20. Anon., 'China and Belarus Boost Defense Industry Cooperation', *BBC Summary of World Broadcasts*, FE/3909 (3 Aug. 2000), p. G/1.
21. Robert H. Scales Jr and Larry M. Wortzel, *The Future US Military Presence in Asia: Landpower and the Geostrategy of American Commitment* (Carlisle, PA: Strategic Studies Institute, 1999), p. 7.
22. Ibid., p. 4.
23. Anon., 'China Says US Presence Hinders Korean Unification', *BBC Summary of World Broadcasts*, FE/3890 (12 July 2000), pp. G3–G/4.
24. Ibid., p. G/4.
25. Ibid.
26. Anon., 'Consultative Council Official Urges Adherence to United Front Policy', *BBC Summary of World Broadcasts*, FE/3906 (31 July 2000), p. G/3.
27. Anon., 'President Has Talks with Turkmen Counterpart', pp. G/1-G/2.
28. Anon., 'China Says US Presence', p. G/4.
29. Anon., 'Inter-Korean Trade in First Half Year up by Over 20 per cent', *BBC Summary of World Broadcasts*, FEW/0652 (9 Aug. 2000), p. WD/1.
30. Anon., 'Good Prospects for Reconnecting Korean Railway to Trans-Siberian Railroad', *BBC Summary of World Broadcasts*, FEW/0652 (9 Aug. 2000), p. WD/1.
31. Anon., 'Envoys of Two Koreas Hold First Official Meeting in Beijing', *BBC Summary of World Broadcasts*, FE/3903 (27 July 2000), p. D/1.
32. Anon., 'China says US Presence', p. G/4.

33. Anon., 'Russia Taking Positive Measures to Enhance Inter-Korean Dialogue', *BBC Summary of World Broadcasts*, FE/3895 (18 July 2000), p. G/3.
34. Anon., 'Russian President Comments on US Presence on Peninsula', *BBC Summary of World Broadcasts*, FE/3896 (19 July 2000), p. D11.
35. Anon., 'Chinese, Russian Presidents Discuss Ties, North Korea Trip Over Hotline', *BBC Summary of World Broadcasts*, FE/3904 (28 July 2000), p. G/2.
36. Allen S. Whiting, 'The PLA and China's Threat Perceptions', *China Quarterly*, No. 146 (June 1996), p. 609.
37. Gao Heng, 'Future Military Trends', in Michael Pillsbury (ed.), *Chinese Views of Future Warfare* (Washington, DC: National Defense University Press, 1998), p. 93.
38. Greg Austin, *China's Ocean Frontier: International Law, Military Force and National Development* (St Leonards, Australia: Allen & Unwin, 1998), pp. 163–4.
39. Jean-Marc F. Blanchard, 'The US Role in the Sino-Japanese Dispute Over the Diaoyu (Senkaku) Islands 1945–1971', *China Quarterly*, No. 161 (Mar. 2000), p. 95.
40. Whiting, 'The PLA and China's Threat Perceptions', p. 611.
41. Richard Sharpe, *Jane's Fighting Ships 1999–2000* (Coulsdon, Surrey: Jane's Information Group, 1999), pp. 114, 374.
42. Whiting, 'The PLA and China's Threat Perceptions', pp. 610–11.
43. Ibid., p. 610.
44. Anon., 'China Urges Japan to Handle Shrine Visit "Cautiously"', *BBC Summary of World Broadcasts*, FE/3918 (14 Aug. 2000), p. G/1.
45. Chalmers Johnson, *Blowback: The Costs and Consequences of American Empire* (London: Little, Brown, 2000), p. 59.
46. Whiting, 'The PLA and China's Threat Perceptions', p. 609.
47. Anon., 'China Says "Irrelevant Issues" Should Not Stop Japanese Aid Loans', *BBC Summary of World Broadcasts*, FE/3918 (14 Aug. 2000), p. G/1.
48. Sumihiko Kawamura, Soushi (Isoko Sunakawa, trans.), glocomnet.or.jp/okazaki-inst/ (Mar. 2000).
49. Neil Renwick and Jason Abbott, 'Piratical Violence and Maritime Security in Southeast Asia', *Security Dialogue*, Vol. 30, No. 2 (June 1999), p. 184.
50. George Friedman and Meredith Lebard, *The Coming War with Japan* (New York: St Martin's Press, 1991), p. 280.
51. Whiting, 'The PLA and China's Threat Perceptions', p. 611.
52. Anon., 'China Says US Presence', p. G/4.
53. Morihiro Hosokawa, 'Are US Troops in Japan Needed?', *Foreign Affairs*, Vol. 77, No. 4 (July–Aug. 1998), pp. 2–6.
54. Whiting, 'The PLA and China's Threat Perceptions', p. 609.
55. Anon., 'Chinese, Japanese Foreign Ministers Praise "Friendly" Relations', *BBC Summary of World Broadcasts*, FE/3906 (31 July 2000), p. G/2.
56. Johnson, *Blowback*, p. 59.
57. Anon., 'China Says "Irrelevant"', G/1.
58. Anon., 'China Prepares for War', *Insight*, www.insightmag.com/archive/200003057.shtml, p. 11.
59. Dennis J. Blasko, Philip T. Klapakis and John F. Corbett Jr, 'Training Tomorrow's PLA: A Mixed Bag of Tricks', *China Quarterly*, No. 146 (June 1996), p. 488.
60. Anon., 'Yang Shangkun Comments on Reunification', in Peter R. Moody Jr (ed.), *China Documents Annual 1990: The Continuing Crisis* (Gulf Breeze, FL: Academic International Press, 1990, p. 407.
61. Michael G. Gallagher, 'China's Illusory Threat to the South China Sea',

International Security, Vol. 19, No. 1 (Summer 1994), p. 171.

62. Renwick and Abbott, 'Piratical Violence', p. 185.
63. John McBeth, 'Troubled Waters', *Far Eastern Economic Review*, Vol. 158, No. 1 (5 Jan. 1995), p. 18.
64. Nayan Chanda, 'Fear of the Dragon', *Far Eastern Economic Review*, Vol. 158, No. 15 (13 Apr. 1995), p. 28.
65. Nayan Chanda, 'Divide and Rule', *Far Eastern Economic Review* (11 Aug. 1994), p. 18.
66. Ibid.
67. Ibid.
68. Stein Tonnesson, 'Can Conflicts Be Solved by Shelving Disputes?', *Security Dialogue*, Vol. 30, No. 2 (June 1999), pp. 179–80.
69. Anon., 'Government Says South China Sea Issue Cannot Be Hurried', *BBC Summary of World Broadcasts*, FE/3893 (15 July 2000), p. G/4.
70. Ibid., p. G/5.
71. Anon., 'China Spokesman on South China Sea Issue', *BBC Summary of World Broadcasts*, FE/3893 (15 July 2000), p. G/4.
72. 'Government Says South', p. G/5.
73. Anon., 'Chinese, Laotian Presidents Hold Talks in Beijing', *BBC Summary of World Broadcasts*, FE/3894 (17 July 2000), p. G/3.
74. Anon., 'Malaysian Navy Chief, Chinese Fleet Delegation Discuss Relations', *BBC Summary of World Broadcasts*, FE/3893 (15 July 2000), p. B/3.
75. Anon., 'President Stresses Friendship with China', *BBC Summary of World Broadcasts*, FE/3918 (14 Aug. 2000), p. B/13.
76. Nayan Chanda, Rigoberto Tiglao and John McBeth, 'Territorial Imperative', *Far Eastern Economic Review* (23 Feb. 1995), p. 14.
77. Anon., 'What the Others Say', *Business Times* (as reported on LEXIS-NEXIS) (28 July 1992), p. 10.
78. Chanda, Tiglao and McBeth, 'Territorial Imperative', p. 14.
79. Ibid.
80. Tonnesson, 'Can Conflicts Be Solved by Shelving Disputes?', p. 180.
81. James A. Gregor, *Arming the Dragon* (Lanham, MD: University Press of America, 1987), p. 83.
82. Wu Hongbo, Shi Changxue and Pan Hongxin, 'Navy Takes Part in Building up Garrison off Paracel Islands', *FBIS-CHI-94-202* (19 Oct. 1994), p. 34.
83. Kevin L. Falk, *Why Nations Put To Sea: Technology and the Changing Character of Sea Power in the Twenty-First Century* (New York: Garland Publishing, 2000), pp. 68–9.
84. Ibid., p. 69.
85. Renwick and Abbott, 'Piratical Violence', pp. 186–7.
86. Ibid., p. 187.
87. Ibid.
88. C.Y. Chang, 'Overseas Chinese in China's Policy', *China Quarterly*, No. 82 (June 1980), p. 302.
89. Ibid., pp. 286–7. The decrees in question forbade alien residents from opening stores in rural areas. Many Indonesian citizens of Chinese descent feared that the government would close down their businesses as well.
90. Ibid., p. 296.
91. Chanda, Tiglao and McBeth, 'Territorial Imperative', p. 14.
92. Tetsuro Doshita. 'Regional Security Links Between Japan and the United States', *US Naval Institute Proceedings* (Mar. 1995), p. 51.
93. Anon., 'Military Chief Rejects Idea of US Bases', *FBIS-EAS-94-224* (21 Nov. 1994), p. 57.

94. Dewin Perira, 'Minister Opposes US Bases', *FBIS-EAS-94-238* (10 Dec. 1994), p. 68.
95. Anon., 'Mahathir Sees "No Need" For Foreign Bases', *FBIS-EAS-94-215* (7 Nov. 1994), p. 67.
96. Elaine Sciolino, 'With Thai Rebuff, US Defers Plan for Navy Depot in Asia', *New York Times* (12 Nov. 1994), Section 1, p. 6.
97. Anon., 'Article Reviewing Status of Relations Between US and Bangkok', *FBIS-EAS-94-226* (23 Nov. 1994), p. 50.
98. John McBeth, 'Troubled Waters', p. 18.
99. Sharpe, *Jane's Fighting Ships 1999–2000*, p. 77.
100. Tim Huxley and Susan Willett, *Arming East Asia* (Oxford: Oxford University Press, 1999), p. 15.
101. Richard Sharpe, *Jane's Fighting Ships, 1994–1995* (Surrey: Jane's Information Group, 1994), p. 122.
102. Anon., 'Article Reviewing Status of Relations Between US and Bangkok', *FBIS-EAS-94-226* (23 Nov. 1994), p. 51.
103. Dewin Perira, 'Minister Sees No Security Threat From People's Republic of China', *FBIS-EAS-94-238* (10 Dec. 1994), p. 69.
104. Dewin Perira, 'Minister Discusses Defense Ties With Singapore', *FBIS-EAS-94-238* (10 Dec. 1994), p. 69.
105. Anon., 'Malaysian Navy Chief, Chinese Army Chief, Indonesian Navy Head Discuss Taiwan Cooperation', *BBC Summary of World Broadcasts*, FE/3891 (13 July 2000), p. G/3.
106. Anon., 'Armed Forces To "Protect" Territorial Waters', *FBIS-EAS-94-216* (8 Nov. 1994), p. 88.
107. Anon., 'Article Reviewing Status', p. 51.
108. Sharpe, *Jane's Fighting Ships 1999–2000*, p. 83; Huxley and Willett, *Arming East Asia*, p. 20.
109. Mohan Malik, 'Burma Slides Under China's Shadow', *Jane's Intelligence Review*, Vol. 9, No. 7 (1 July 1997) (electronically accessed), p. 4.
110. Arthur A. Stahnke, 'Diplomatic Triangle: China's Policies Toward India and Pakistan in the 1960s', in Jerome Alan Cohen (ed.), *The Dynamics of China's Foreign Relations* (Cambridge, MA: Harvard University Press, 1970), p. 21.
111. Anon., 'Pakistani Envoy Predicts Closer Ties with China', *BBC Summary of World Broadcasts*, FE/3918 (14 Aug. 2000), p. G/2.
112. Ibid.
113. Stahnke, 'Diplomatic Triangle', in Cohen (ed.), *Dynamics*, p. 25.
114. Anon., 'Foreign Minister Says Missile Cooperation with China within Law', *BBC Summary of World Broadcasts*, FE/3917 (12 Aug. 2000), p. A/4.
115. Rahul Bedi and Duncan Lennox, 'Pakistan's First Test of its New Ballistic Missile', *Jane's Defence Weekly*, Vol. 29, No. 15 (15 April 1998), p. 4.
116. Malik, 'Burma Slides Under China's Shadow', p. 2.
117. Ibid., p. 3.
118. Ibid.
119. Ibid., p. 2.
120. Ibid., p. 4.
121. Bates R. Gill, *Chinese Arms Transfers* (Westport, CT: Praeger, 1992), p. 160.
122. Alfred Thayer Mahan, *The Problem of Asia and its Effect Upon International Politics* (Boston, MA: Little, Brown, 1905), p. 28.
123. Ibid., see especially p. 67.
124. George T. Yu, 'China's Competitive Diplomacy in Africa', in Cohen (ed.), *Dynamics*, p. 70.
125. Anon., 'Naval Task Group Begins Visit to South Africa', *BBC Summary of World Broadcasts*, FE/3917 (12 Aug. 2000), p. G/1.

126. Sharpe, *Jane's Fighting Ships 1999–2000*, p. 187; Hugo Gordon, 'US Plans to Sell Missile Know-How to China', *Daily Telegraph*, No. 1028, www.telegraph.co.uk (19 Mar. 1998).
127. Christina Lamb, 'China Puts "700,000 Troops" on Sudan Alert', *Daily Telegraph*, No. 1920, www.telegraph.co.uk (27 Aug. 2000).
128. Ibid.
129. Anon., 'China to Acquire Israeli Radar System', *Asian Defence Journal*, Vol. 7, No. 1 (Dec. 1999), p. 84.
130. Anon., 'Parliament Leader Meets Jordanian Speaker, Condemns Iraq Sanctions', *BBC Summary of World Broadcasts*, FE/3906 (31 July 2000), p. G/2.
131. Anon., 'Spokesman Says Yasir Arafat to Visit 14th August', *BBC Summary of World Broadcasts*, FE/3918 (14 Aug. 2000), p. G/1.
132. Anon., 'Parliament Leader Meets Jordanian', p. G/2.
133. Anon., 'Army Deputy Chief Meets Syrian Army Delegation', *BBC Summary of World Broadcasts*, FE/3914 (9 Aug. 2000), p. G/1
134. Gordon, 'US Plans to Sell Missile Know-How to China', accessed electronically.
135. Anon., 'Full Text of China–Iran Joint Communique', *BBC Summary of World Broadcasts*, FE/3876 (26 June 2000), p. G/1.
136. Sharpe, *Jane's Fighting Ships 1999–2000*, p. 335; Bedi and Lennox, 'Pakistan's First Test', p. 4.
137. Anon., 'Full Text of China–Iran', p. G/1.
138. Ibid.
139. Anon., 'Chinese, Iranian Defence Ministers Meet, "New Chapter" in Ties Declared', *BBC Summary of World Broadcasts*, FE/3876 (26 June 2000), p. G/3.
140. John W. Lewis and Xue Litai, *China's Strategic Seapower* (Stanford, CA: Stanford University Press, 1994), p. 229.
141. Barry Turner (ed.), *The Statesman's Yearbook: The Essential Political and Economic Guide to all the Countries of the World 1998–1999* (London: Macmillan, 1998), p. 1210.
142. Anon., 'Chinese General Signs Agreement, Ends Visit', *BBC Summary of World Broadcasts*, FE/3891 (13 July 2000), p. C/3.
143. Anon., 'Premier Reaffirms One-China Policy', *BBC Summary of World Broadcasts*, FE/3891 (13 July 2000), p. C/3.
144. Daniel Tretiak, 'China's Relations with Latin America Revolutionary Theory in a Distant Milieu', in Cohen (ed.), *Dynamics*, p. 98.
145. Anon., 'China to Build ELINT Facility and Modernize Cuba's Satellite Tracking Base', *China Reform Monitor*, No. 201, www.afpc.org/crm/crm201.htm (11 May 1999).
146. Harold W. Rood, *Kingdoms of the Blind: How the Great Democracies Have Resumed the Follies that so nearly Cost Them Their Life* (Durham, NC: Carolina Academic Press, 1980), pp. 112–22.
147. Tom Raum, 'Is the Panama Canal in Jeopardy?', bergen.com/molenews/uspanama199910233.htm (23 Oct. 1999).
148. Anon., 'President Meets South American Rio Group Foreign Ministers', *BBC Summary of World Broadcasts*, FE/3908 (2 Aug. 2000), p. G/1.
149. Anon., 'Chilean Foreign Minister Calls for More Cooperation with China', *BBC Summary of World Broadcasts*, FE/3909 (3 Aug. 2000), p. G/1.
150. Arthur Lall, *How Communist China Negotiates* (New York: Columbia University Press, 1968), p. 36.
151. Chris Patten, *East and West: The Last Governor of Hong Kong on Power, Freedom and the Future* (London: Macmillan, 1998), pp. 309–19.
152. Ibid., p. 311.

7

Conclusion

History, current events, Western strategic theory and Chinese military writings all point to the same conclusions. The Peoples' Republic of China is systematically using the resources at its disposal to build up its power upon the seas. Beijing's maritime expansion is central to a larger policy aimed at putting China among the foremost global powers. This policy has evolved over the course of generations, and although China's leaders have repeatedly demonstrated their ability to act swiftly when circumstances permit them, they are almost certainly prepared to follow such policies patiently for generations to come.

Having observed these facts, one must take care not to exaggerate or oversimplify them. China's regime is following a general course of action aimed at general goals, but there are few clues to predict exactly how it will handle any particular future crisis. Chinese leaders have applied a broad set of strategic ideas quite successfully over the past half-century, but the influence of any particular strategic concept is apt to wax and wane over time, in China as elsewhere. One must remember also that both China's regime and China's circumstances might change. A change in either might affect the PRC's actions.

Nevertheless, even a rough understanding of China's strategic methods provides insights into where Beijing's current actions might lead. China appears to be following an updated version of Mao's protracted war theory on a global scale. One of its chief objectives is to create conditions in which it can act as a maritime power. To summarize, China's strategy includes the following key features:

- China's leaders seek power in its most tangible form, and seek to maximize the ability of their regime to wield this power for its own purposes.
- For geographic reasons, China's maritime capabilities depend on China's position in numerous ocean areas, constrained by a variety of islands and peninsulas under a variety of governments. To realize its full potential as a seapower, China must organize these regions into a system that supports its needs.
- The PRC will attempt to build so-called United Fronts of countries

who share common interests on matters of importance to China. Some of these coalitions will be considerably more enduring and comprehensive than others. With regard to maritime strategy, China will seek friendly relations with powers on its landward flank, and with the countries that can offer the PLAN port facilities in strategic locations.

- Beijing will use all means at its disposal to assert its own power over other countries, and to render them dependent on China. When China cannot dominate a country, it will attempt to detach it from outside allies, rendering it neutral. The PRC's policies in the South China Sea are a clear example of this principle in action, but China will probably follow a similar course of action in Africa, the Pacific, South Asia, Central Asia, Latin America and the Middle East as circumstances allow.

- China will attempt to neutralize rivals through balance-of-power politics. For Beijing, the balance of power is not a system for achieving the so-called 'stability' beloved of Western international-relations theorists, but a way of turning other countries' energies against each other, so that China may reign supreme.

- Beijing recognizes that some of its potential opponents have an overwhelming military advantage over Chinese forces. China's leaders use a variety of techniques to limit their interference in Chinese affairs. These methods range from conciliation to nuclear saber-rattling, but the most satisfactory one tends to be that of detaching them from the allies who give them the bases and rationale to intervene in international matters.

- China recognizes that it needs to support many of these methods with capable armed forces. Nevertheless, none of its specific objectives are individually important enough to be worth fighting a major war in the near future. Therefore, China can afford to experiment with new ways of fighting, and to develop weapons systems which may take decades to perfect. China can also afford to give civilian economic development short-term precedence over military needs.

- China aspires to seize the initiative in strategic contests. Since the first step in taking the initiative is to develop the means to do so, China will continue to pursue greater industrial capacity. Although the Chinese regime currently gives general development a higher priority than direct military expansion, the '16-character' policy indicates what the purpose of such economic improvement is.

- China has geared its naval forces toward providing oceanic mobility for joint operations, and toward threatening the mobility of others, rather than toward gaining absolute dominance at sea. Although the Chinese suffer from severe naval weaknesses, they seek to maximize the advantages of their areas of strength. Against a more developed naval power, China will seek both military and diplomatic ways to limit the scope of the fighting. In this fashion, the Chinese hope to avoid an all-out war of the sort their forces would certainly lose.

- Although the Chinese make great use of cautious, indirect and so-called asymmetric strategies, they follow this approach because of their current position, not because of any inherent preference. They recognize that such methods are often the weaker form of warfare, and hope to put themselves in a position where they can act more directly.

China uses these methods and others like them as opportunities arise. Nevertheless, their policy consists of more than mere opportunism. If one follows the development of their armed forces and their foreign policy, one sees that they have systematically improved their position, incrementally putting themselves in a position to secure greater and more general gains. Although the Chinese prefer the path of least resistance, their actions are far from random.

In certain periods, such as the early 1990s, Beijing has acted rapidly to advance its policies in a great many ways at once. There are obvious parallels between these phases of China's foreign policy and the more aggressive military tactics that Mao recommends for the later stages of a guerrilla war. Just as guerrillas become able to step up their activity when their enemies become overstretched and must pull back, China gains the ability to act more directly in international affairs when other world powers withdraw from previous commitments. The break-up of the Soviet Union and the United States' subsequent re-evaluation of its foreign policy was a particularly dramatic example of such withdrawal. China's rhetoric about multipolarity and anti-hegemonism sounds like a call for more of the same.

There are reasons to question whether China will be able to continue with this strategy. Some suggest that the PRC's regime cannot last in anything like its current form. Many variants of this proposition exist. Certain authors believe that commerce is becoming so critical to every nation's economy that China's leaders will eventually abandon their current political ambitions in order to obtain more of it, whereas others maintain that the Chinese people will eventually find Western ways of living so attractive that they will replace the current government with a more liberal one. Others suggest that problems such as fuel shortages, food shortages, bureaucratic corruption and administrative incompetence will cripple the regime, if not destroy it outright.

Mahan anticipated many of these propositions, both in general and in the specific case of China. Not only did he say that commercial, republican regimes had a long-term advantage in acquiring seapower, he suggested that Western ideas in the form of Christianity could lead to a 'happy renewal' in Asia.¹ Just as many today believe that the idea of liberalism is irresistibly contagious, Mahan assured readers that Christianity leads to 'an ever-swelling volume of inbred spiritual conviction and transmitted habits of thought, which, by their growth from generation to generation attest their unimpaired vitality'.² Missionary work, in his view seems to have been a precursor of the current idea that the West can tame China by 'engaging' it.

China's leaders are aware of these possibilities, and are taking concrete action to protect themselves. The PRC regulates business enterprises, promotes its own ideology and suppresses subversive ideas, including religious ones. Not only did China crush the Tiananmen Square protest of 1989, but it has built up its security forces in order to deal with future unrest even more effectively. Perhaps, despite these efforts, the regime will eventually fall. Nothing is certain in politics, for China or for any nation. One can only observe that Beijing's methods have worked for decades, that it appears to be responding to potential threats intelligently, and that it appears strong now.

Even if the Chinese regime remains in power, the current weakness of the PLAN and the Chinese defense industry raise doubts about China's ability to become a military power in the future. There is no doubt that, if the PRC is to dominate Japan or India, much less the Western powers, it will have to develop its military establishment considerably. China's leaders appear to grasp this, and are attempting to reform both their fleet and their defense industry accordingly. Observers must also remember that Beijing does not even expect its current fleet to fight the US Navy on the open sea, or to conduct other operations for which it is patently unsuited. One must judge the PLAN, not merely on the basis of how it compares to Western navies, but on the basis of how well it supports the rest of China's foreign policy.

A WESTERN RESPONSE

Despite the PRC's potential handicaps, citizens of Western countries have every reason to view China's grand strategy with alarm. The fact that the Chinese regime so vehemently opposes liberal political ideals and the liberal world order should heighten their concern. Few today worry that the PRC will impose its own dictatorship upon unwilling peoples in a literal sense, except, perhaps, in the more remote regions of the world. Nevertheless, China intends to revise the international understandings that have served Europe, the United States and much of maritime Asia so well. China does not merely seek to redress inequities, it seeks to increase its own influence at the expense of the West.

Western countries cannot afford to be generous in this regard. To give up influence is to lose a little of one's ability to live the way one chooses to live. In the short term, the losses will be tiny. For decades, perhaps, Europe and the United States will notice China's demands only as minor crises and minor inconveniences. Asian nations will feel Beijing's pressure more acutely, as will all less-developed countries which might have chosen to adopt liberal institutions.

Eventually, these states will have to choose between the West and China's 'new order'. Liberal countries will have to decide how aggressively to promote their own cause. People may not understand the full consequences of such choices until many years after they have made them. Gradually, the political, economic and military landscape will change, until things which seem absurd in the first decade of the twenty-first century come to seem frightening and imminent. Just how much will change, and how quickly the changes will come, must remain a matter of speculation.

Those who care about the future of their countries will prefer to head off China's bid for influence now, when the liberal countries are at the height of their power, rather than later, when both their credibility and their capabilities may have declined. This raises the question of how the West should respond to the People's Republic of China. Policy analysts tend to present two broad options, which go by the names of engagement and containment.[3] The former means promoting trade and other forms of interaction with China, in the hopes that the Chinese will find more advantages in cooperating with the liberal world than with opposing it. The latter means applying some version of Cold War foreign policy to China.

Neither of these policies seems particularly promising. There may be sound economic and humanitarian reasons to engage China, but the strategic logic is dubious. China's leaders are on guard against the dangers of 'peaceful evolution' and 'bourgeois liberalization'. There have been few signs since 1989 that any influential segment of the population opposes the government in this regard. The idea that Western ideas are so appealing that they will transform China despite China's best efforts to resist them seems unlikely, not to mention arrogant.

Containment, likewise, seems to underestimate China's resource-fulness. If one sees Cold War containment in terms of the Pacto-mania of the 1950s, in which the United States formed mutual defense agreements with nations around the world, one must observe that the Asian and the Middle Eastern treaties collapsed in some of the United States' greatest failures. Beijing has demonstrated its ability to harass Japan and Taiwan, despite the United States' formal and informal commitments to those nations. In Southeast Asia, China has proved that it already has the ability to discourage its smaller neighbors from aligning themselves with Washington.

The very word containment implies a passive approach, which seeks only to minimize the effects of a bad situation. This is an unfortunate way to frame a policy. Passivity inspires neither fear in potential opponents nor confidence in potential allies. Furthermore, there is little diplomatic sense in declaring hostility toward another country unless one is prepared to follow up that declaration with demands or action.

There may be no effective way to modify China's behavior. The Chinese regime will do what it feels it must do, and although this need not always be hostile to the West, it will seldom be entirely in the West's interests either. By understanding China's approach to strategy, we in the liberal nations can craft more effective responses to Beijing's gambits. Britain and the United States have already taken steps to remind the Southeast Asian states that they stand by their military commitments in the Western Pacific.[4] Nevertheless, the strategic future of the Western countries ultimately depends less on their ability to interfere with China's world order than on their ability to promote their own.

China's leaders appear to have identified national assets and diplomatic ties that will allow them to project influence abroad. They seek these advantages with patience and determination. The liberal countries already possess an abundance of such resources and relationships. If they wish to maintain their position, they must acknowledge, protect and expand their assets as assiduously as their opponents attempt to undermine them.

This is why it is important to study the details of grand strategy, as well as the broad outlines. Relying only on a vague intention to protect one's own, one suffers from all the handicaps of the containment policy. It will be essential to be watchful everywhere, without being completely ready for action, materially or psychologically, anywhere. Opponents will always be able to find special cases that test a country's resolve and abilities at their weakest points. If the People's Republic of China is indeed following a modern variant of its protracted war doctrine, this is exactly the sort of situation it is prepared to capitalize on.

If, on the other hand, grand strategy is approached with a sense of what specific advantages one holds in given theaters of action, and how opponents may seek to wrest those advantages away, it is possible to perceive the larger significance of particular cases, and act accordingly. If, for instance, Korea is seen as a 'dagger and a bridge' between the aspiring maritime power of China and China's potential rival in Japan, then deeper insight is gained into the likely outcome of withdrawing US forces from Korea, not only for Northeast Asia, but for global naval strategy. It is possible to conclude that even larger issues demand that the United States withdraw its bases anyway, but at least one will be better prepared to plan against the likely consequences. One will be able to judge how the

Korea policy connects to the Southeast Asian and Middle Eastern policies, and establish priorities in that light.

This study has sought to show how China's actions concerning a variety of specific issues combine to form a unified grand strategy. The author hopes that, by revealing the larger significance of China's policies on certain matters, he can help Westerners act wisely in these areas as well. Moreover, Westerners might hope to emulate the best features of Beijing's statecraft. Just as the Chinese can combine specific policies to achieve more general political goals, so, too, can the liberal powers. Similar principles of geography, strategy and diplomacy will apply.

In this fashion, the liberal nations can preserve their freedom of action and maintain the global community they have created. This need not reflect any ill-will toward China. The Western nations have established certain standards of international conduct which, while controversial in some quarters, have much to recommend them. These standards encourage prosperity, good government and fair play for all nations, the PRC included. A successful Western strategy need not constrain Beijing, save only in its ambition to constrain others.

NOTES

1. Alfred Thayer Mahan, *The Problem of Asia and its Effect Upon International Politics* (Boston, MA: Little, Brown, 1905), p. 163.
2. Ibid., p.91.
3. A. James Gregor, 'Qualified Engagement: US China Policy and Security Concerns', *Naval War College Review*, Vol. 52, No. 2 (Spring 1999), p. 69.
4. Eric Grove, 'Britain's Continued Strategic Interest in the Region', *Asia-Pacific Defence Reporter*, Vol. 24, No. 2 (Feb.–Mar. 1998), pp. 6–7.

Bibliography

BOOKS

Anon., *The Communist Bloc and the Western Alliance: The Military Balance 1961–1962* (London: ISS, 1961)

Anon.. *China In Crisis* (Coulsdon, Surrey: Jane's Information Group, 1989).

Austin, Greg, *China's Ocean Frontier: International Law, Military Force and National Development* (St Leonards, Australia: Allen & Unwin, 1998), pp. 163–4.

Barnett, A. Doak, *The Making of Foreign Policy in China: Structure and Process* (London: I.B. Tauris & Co., 1985).

Baskin, Wade (ed.), *Classics in Chinese Philosophy* (New York: Philosophical Library, 1972).

Blechman, Barry M., and Berman, Robert P., *A Guide to Far Eastern Navies* (Annapolis, MD: United States Naval Institute Press, 1978).

Binnendijk, Hans, and Montaperto, Ronald N. (eds), *Strategic Trends in China* (Washington, DC: US Government Printing Office, 1998).

Bonavia, David, *Deng* (Hong Kong: Longman Group, 1989).

Bozeman, Adda B., *Strategic Intelligence and Statecraft* (Washington, DC: Brassey's (US), 1992).

Callwell, Charles E., *Military Operations and Maritime Preponderance: Their Relations and Interdependence* (Annapolis, MD: Naval Institute Press, 1996 (originally published 1905)).

Cheung, Tai Ming, *Growth of Chinese Naval Power* (Singapore: Institute of Southeast Asian Studies, 1990)

Christensen, Thomas J., *Useful Adversaries: Grand Strategy, Domestic Mobilization and Sino-American Conflict, 1947–1958* (Princeton, NJ: Princeton University Press, 1996).

Clausewitz, Carl von, *On War*, trans. and ed. Michael Howard and Peter Paret (Princeton, NJ: Princeton University Press, 1976).

Cohen, Jerome Alan (ed.), *The Dynamics of China's Foreign Relations* (Cambridge, MA: Harvard University Press, 1970).

Corbett, Julian S., *Some Principles of Maritime Strategy* (Annapolis, MD: Naval Institute Press, 1988 (originally published, 1911)).

Eftimiades, Nicholas, *Chinese Intelligence Operations* (Annapolis, MD: Naval Institute Press, 1994).

Falk, Kevin L., *Why Nations Put to Sea: Technology and the Changing Character of Sea Power in the Twenty-First Century* (New York: Garland Publishing, 2000).

Friedman, George, and Lebard, Meredith, *The Coming War With Japan* (New York: St Martin's Press, 1991).

Gernet, Jacques, *A History of Chinese Civilization*, trans. J.R. Foster (Cambridge: Cambridge University Press, 1972).

Gill, Bates R., *Chinese Arms Transfers* (Westport, CT: Praeger's, 1992), p. 160.

Golitsyn, Anatoly, *The Perestroika Deception: The World's Slide Toward the Second October Revolution [Weltoktober]* (London: Edward Halle, 1995).

Goodman, David S.G., and Segal, Gerald (eds), *China Rising: Nationalism and Interdependence* (London: Routledge, 1997).

Gray, Colin S., *The Leverage of Seapower: The Strategic Advantage of Navies in War* (New York: Free Press, 1992).

Gray, Colin S., *The Navy in the Post-Cold War World: The Uses and Value of Strategic Sea Power* (University Park, PA: Pennsylvania State University Press, 1994).

Griffith II, Samuel B., *Peking and People's Wars: An Analysis of Statements by Official Spokesmen of the Chinese Communist Party on the Subject of Revolutionary Strategy* (London: Pall Mall Press, 1966).

Gregor, James A., *Arming the Dragon* (Lanham, MD: University Press of America, 1987).

Gurtov, Melvin, and Hwang, Byong-Moo, *China Under Threat: The Politics of Strategy and Diplomacy* (Baltimore, MD: Johns Hopkins University Press, 1980)

Harvey, Brian, *The Chinese Space Program: From Conception to Future Capabilities* (Chichester: John Wiley, 1998).

Hattendorf, John B. (ed.), *The Influence of History On Mahan: The Proceedings of a Conference Marking the Centenary of Alfred Thayer Mahan's The Influence of Sea Power Upon History, 1600–1783* (Newport, RI: Naval War College Press, 1991).

Holborn, Hajo, 'The Prusso-German School: Moltke and the Rise of the General Staff', in Peter Paret (ed.), *Makers of Modern Strategy From Machiavelli to the Nuclear Age* (Princeton, NJ: Princeton University Press, 1986), pp. 281–95.

Hsu, Immanuel C.Y., *The Rise of Modern China* (Oxford: Oxford University Press, 1970)

Huxley, Tim, and Willett, Susan, *Arming East Asia* (Oxford: Oxford University Press, 1999).

International Institute for Strategic Studies, *The Military Balance 1994–1995* (London: Brassey's, 1994).

Johnston, Alastair Ian, *Cultural Realism: Strategic Culture and Grand Strategy in Chinese History* (Princeton, NJ: Princeton University Press, 1995).

Johnson, Chalmers, *Blowback: The Costs and Consequences of American Empire* (London: Little, Brown, 2000).

Kennedy, Paul, *The Rise and Fall of British Naval Mastery* (New York: Charles Scribner's Sons, 1976).

Khalizad, Zalmay M., Shulsky, Abram N., Byman, Daniel L., Cliff, Roger, Orletsky, David T., Shlapak, David, Tellis, Ashley J., *The United States and a Rising China: Strategic and Military Implications* (Santa Monica, CA: RAND, 1999).

Kierman Jr, Frank A., and Fairbank, John K. (eds), *Chinese Ways in Warfare* (Cambridge, MA: Harvard University Press, 1974).

Lall, Arthur, *How Communist China Negotiates* (New York: Columbia University Press, 1968).

Lewis, John W., and Xue Litai, *China's Strategic Seapower* (Stanford, CA: Stanford University Press, 1994).

Li Jijun, *Traditional Military Thinking and the Defensive Strategy of China* (Carlisle Barracks, PA: Strategic Studies Institute, 1997).

Lo-Shu Fu, *A Documentary Chronicle of Sino-Western Relations (1644–1820)* (Tuscon, AZ: University of Arizona Press, 1966).

Luttwak, Edward N., *The Grand Strategy of the Roman Empire* (Baltimore, MD: Johns Hopkins University Press, 1976).

MacFarquhar, Roderick (ed.), *The Politics of China: The Eras of Mao and Deng* (Cambridge: Cambridge University Press, 1993).

Mahan, Alfred Thayer, *The Influence of Sea Power Upon History, 1660–1783* (Boston, MA: S.J. Parkhill, 1890).

Mahan, Alfred Thayer, *The Problem of Asia and its Effect Upon International Politics* (Boston, MA: Little Brown, 1905).

Mao Zedong, *Selected Works of Mao Tse-Tung, Volume Two* (London: Lawrence & Wishart, 1954)

Mattern, Susan P., *Rome and the Enemy: Imperial Strategy in the Principate* (Berkeley, CA: University of California Press, 1999).

Moody Jr, Peter R. (ed.), *China Documents Annual 1989: The Crisis of Reform* (Gulf Breeze, FL: Academic International Press, 1992).

Moody Jr, Peter R. (ed.), *China Documents Annual 1990: The Continuing Crisis* (Gulf Breeze, FL: Academic International Press, 1994).

Needham, Joseph, Wang Ling and Lu Gwei-Djen, *Science and Civilisation in China, Vol. 4* (Cambridge: Cambridge University Press, 1971).

Paret, Peter (ed.), *Makers of Modern Strategy from Machiavelli to the Nuclear Age* (Princeton, NJ: Princeton University Press, 1986).

Patten, Chris, *East and West: The Last Governor of Hong Kong on Power, Freedom and the Future* (London: Macmillan, 1998).

Pillsbury, Michael (ed.), *Chinese Views of Future Warfare* (Washington, DC: National Defense University Press, 1998).

Plato, *Plato's Statesman*, trans. J.B. Skemp (London: Routledge & Kegan Paul, 1952).

Rawlinson, John L., *China's Struggle for Naval Development 1839–1895* (Cambridge, MA: Harvard University Press, 1967).

Rood, Harold W., *Kingdoms of the Blind: How the Great Democracies Have Resumed the Follies that so Nearly Cost Them Their Life* (Durham, NC: Carolina Academic Press, 1980).

Samson, George, *A History of Japan to 1334* (London: Cresset Press, 1958).

Sawyer, Ralph D., *One Hundred Unorthodox Strategies: Battle and Tactics of Chinese Warfare* (Boulder, CO: Westview Press, 1996).

Scales Jr, Robert H., and Wortzel, Larry M., *The Future US Military Presence in Asia: Landpower and the Geostrategy of American Commitment* (Carlisle, PA: Strategic Studies Institute, 1999).

Sharpe, Richard, *Jane's Fighting Ships, 1994–1995* (Coulsdon, Surrey: Jane's Information Group, 1994).

Sharpe, Richard, *Jane's Fighting Ships, 1999–2000* (Coulsdon, Surrey: Jane's Information Group, 1999).

Shoalwater, Dennis E., *The Wars of Frederick the Great* (Harlow: Longman Group, 1996).

Stone, Deborah A., *Policy Paradox and Political Reason* (New York: HarperCollins, 1988).

Sumida, Jon Tetsuro, *Inventing Grand Strategy and Teaching Command: The Classic Works of Alfred Thayer Mahan Reconsidered* (Baltimore, MD: Johns Hopkins University Press, 1997).

Sun Tzu, *Sun Tzu's Art of War: The Modern Chinese Interpretation*, trans. Yuan Shibing, commentary Tao Hanzhang (New York: Sterling Publishing, 1987).

Swaine, Michael D., and Tellis, Ashley J., *Interpreting China's Grand Strategy: Past, Present and Future* (Santa Monica, CA: RAND, 2000).

Turner, Barry (ed.), *The Statesman's Yearbook: The Essential Political and Economic Guide to All the Countries of the World 1998–1999* (London: Macmillan, 1998).

Waley, Arthur, *Three Ways of Thought in Ancient China* (London: George Allen & Unwin, 1939).

Walsh, Kathleen A., *US Commercial Technology Transfers to The People's Republic of China* (Washington, DC: US Department of Commerce, 1999), pp. iv–v.

Wilhelm, Richard, *A Short History of Chinese Civilization*, trans. Joan Joshua (London: George G. Harrap, 1929).

Wortzel, Larry M. (ed.), *The Chinese Armed Forces in the 21st Century* (Carlisle, PA: Strategic Studies Institute, 1999).

ARTICLES

Anon., 'Mahathir Sees "No Need" For Foreign Bases', *FBIS-EAS-94-215* (7 Nov. 1994), p. 67.

Anon., 'Russian Navy Chief Reveals Cooperation Pact', *FBIS-CHI-94-216* (8 Nov. 1994), p. 11.

Anon., 'Armed Forces To "Protect" Territorial Waters', *FBIS-EAS-94-216* (8 Nov. 1994), p. 88.

Anon., 'Military Chief Rejects Idea of US Bases', *FBIS-EAS-94-224* (21 Nov. 1994), p. 57.

Anon., 'Article Reviewing Status of Relations Between US and Bangkok', *FBIS-EAS-94-226* (23 Nov. 1994), pp. 50, 51.

Anon., 'Beijing to Build More Ports With Foreign Capital', *FBIS-CHI-94-236* (7 Dec. 1994), p. 27.

Anon., 'Rapid Deployment Key to PLA Modernisation', *Jane's Defence Weekly*, Vol. 29, No. 15 (15 Apr. 1998), pp. 30–2.

Anon., 'China's Hubei Develops Passenger Ekranoplan', *Flight International* (25 Nov.–1 Dec. 1998), p. 8.

Anon., 'China to Acquire Israeli Radar System', *Asian Defence Journal*, Vol. 7, No. 1 (Dec. 1999), p. 84.

Anon., 'Industry Embraces Market Forces', *Jane's Defence Weekly* (16 Dec. 1998), p. 28.

Anon., 'PLA Tests Invisible Destroyer', *Asian Defence Journal*, Vol. 6, No. 9 (Aug. 1999), p. 56.

Anon., 'China to Acquire 60 SU-30 Fighter-Bombers', *Asian Defence Journal*, Vol. 6, No. 11 (Oct. 1999), p. 70.

Anon., 'China to Acquire Israeli Radar System', *Asian Defence Journal*, Vol. 7, No. 1 (Dec. 1999), p. 84.

Anon., 'Full Text of China–Iran Joint Communique', *BBC Summary of World Broadcasts*, FE/3876 (26 June 2000), pp. G/1–G/2.

Anon., 'Congress Leader Li Peng Meets Azerbaijan Premier', *BBC Summary of World Broadcasts*, FE/3876 (26 June 2000), pp.G/5–G/6.

Anon., 'Chinese, Iranian Defence Ministers Meet: "New Chapter"' in ties declared', *BBC Summary of World Broadcasts*, FE/3876 (26 June 2000), p. G/3.

Anon., 'PLA Air Growth "Set to Change Balance of Power"', *Flight International*, Vol. 4, No. 10 (July 2000), p. 16.

Anon., 'Spokesman on Central Asian Summit, Russian Ties', *BBC Summary of World Broadcasts*, FE/3885 (6 July 2000), p. G/1.

Anon., 'Shanghai Five Sign Declaration in Tajik Capital', *BBC Summary of World Broadcasts*, FE/3885 (6 July 2000), p. G/2.

Anon., 'President Puts Forward Proposal to Improve Shanghai Five Cooperation', *BBC Summary of World Broadcasts*, FE/3885 (6 July 2000), pp. G/1–G/2.

Anon., 'Chinese, Turkmen Presidents Agree to Expand Economic, Trade Cooperation', *BBC Summary of World Broadcasts*, FE/3887 (8 July 2000), p. G/1.

Anon., 'President Has Talks with Turkmen Counterpart, Stresses "New World Order"', *BBC Summary of World Broadcasts*, FE/3887 (8 July 2000), pp. G/1–G/2.

Anon., 'China Says US Presence Hinders Korean Unification', *BBC Summary of World Broadcasts*, FE/3890 (12 July 2000), pp. G/3–G/4.

Anon., 'Malaysian Navy Chief, Chinese Army Chief, Indonesian Navy Head Discuss Taiwan Cooperation', *BBC Summary of World Broadcasts*, FE/3891 (13 July 2000), p. G/3.

Anon., 'Premier Reaffirms One-China Policy', *BBC Summary of World Broadcasts*, FE/3891 (13 July 2000), C/3.

Anon., 'Chinese General Signs Agreement, Ends Visit', *BBC Summary of World Broadcasts*, FE/3891 (13 July 2000), p. C/3.

Anon., 'Tajik President to Extend Further Military Cooperation with China', *BBC Summary of World Broadcasts*, FE/3893 (15 July 2000), p. G/5–G/6.

Anon., 'Government Says South China Sea Issue Cannot Be Hurried', *BBC Summary of World Broadcasts*, FE/3893 (15 July 2000), pp. G/4–G/5.

Anon., 'Malaysian Navy Chief, Chinese Fleet Delegation Discuss Relations', *BBC Summary of World Broadcasts*, FE/3893 (15 July 2000), pp. B/3–B/4.

Anon., 'China Spokesman on South China Sea Issue', *BBC Summary of World Broadcasts*, FE/3893 (15 July 2000), p. G/4.

Anon., 'Chinese, Laotian Presidents Hold Talks in Beijing', *BBC Summary of World Broadcasts*, FE/3894 (17 July 2000), pp. G/3–G/4.

Anon., 'Russia Taking Positive Measures to Enhance Inter-Korean Dialogue', *BBC Summary of World Broadcasts*, FE/3895 (18 July 2000), p. G/3.

Anon., 'China, Russia Share "Common Position" on Security – Putin', *BBC Summary of World Broadcasts*, FE/3896 (19 July 2000), p. G/4.

Anon., 'Russian President Comments on US Presence on Peninsula', *BBC Summary of World Broadcasts*, FE/3896 (19 July 2000), p. D11.

Anon., 'Chinese, Russian Leaders Reportedly Held Secret Talks on Opposing US Hegemonism', *BBC Summary of World Broadcasts*, FE/3902 (26 July 2000), p. G/11.

Anon., 'Envoys of Two Koreas Hold First Official Meeting in Beijing', *BBC Summary of World Broadcasts*, FE/3903 (27 July 2000), p. D/1.

Anon., 'Vice-President, Belarussian President Discuss Deepening Bilateral Ties', *BBC Summary of World Broadcasts*, FE/3904 (28 July 2000), pp. G/2–G/3.

Anon., 'Chinese, Russian Presidents Discuss Ties, North Korea Trip Over Hotline', *BBC Summary of World Broadcasts*, FE/3904 (28 July 2000), p. G/2.

Anon., 'Consultative Council Official Urges Adherence to United Front Policy', *BBC Summary of World Broadcasts*, FE/3906 (31 July 2000), pp. G/3–G/4.

Anon., 'Parliament Leader Meets Jordanian Speaker, Condemns Iraq Sanctions', *BBC Summary of World Broadcasts*, FE/3906 (31 July 2000), pp. G/2–G/3.

Anon., 'Chinese, Japanese Foreign Ministers Praise "Friendly" Relations', *BBC Summary of World Broadcasts*, FE/3906 (31 July 2000), p. G/2.

Anon., 'President Meets South American Rio Group Foreign Ministers', *BBC Summary of World Broadcasts*, FE/3908 (2 Aug. 2000), p. G/1.

Anon., 'Chilean Foreign Minister Calls for More Cooperation with China', *BBC Summary of World Broadcasts*, FE/3909 (3 Aug. 2000), p. G/1.

Anon., 'China and Belarus Boost Defense Industry Cooperation', *BBC Summary of World Broadcasts*, FE/3909 (3 Aug. 2000), p. G/1.

Anon., 'Inter-Korean Trade in First Half Year up by over 20 per cent', *BBC Summary of World Broadcasts*, FEW/0652 (9 Aug. 2000), p. WD/1.

Anon., 'Good Prospects for Reconnecting Korean Railway to Trans-Siberian Railroad', *BBC Summary of World Broadcasts*, FEW/0652 (9 Aug. 2000), p. WD/1.

Anon., 'Army Deputy Chief Meets Syrian Army Delegation', *BBC Summary of World Broadcasts*, FE/3914 (9 Aug. 2000), p. G/1

Anon., 'Li Peng Discusses Ties with Georgian Speaker', *BBC Summary of World Broadcasts*, FE/3917 (12 Aug. 2000), p. G/1.

Anon., 'Naval Task Group Begins Visit to South Africa', *BBC Summary of World Broadcasts*, FE/3917 (12 Aug. 2000), pp. G/1–G/2.

Anon., 'Pakistani Envoy Predicts Closer Ties with China', *BBC Summary of World Broadcasts*, FE/3918 (14 Aug. 2000), p. G/2.

Anon., 'Spokesman Says Yasir Arafat to Visit 14th August', *BBC Summary of World Broadcasts*, FE/3918 (14 Aug. 2000), p. G/1.

Anon., 'China Urges Japan to Handle Shrine Visit "Cautiously"', *BBC Summary of World Broadcasts*, FE/3918 (14 Aug. 2000), p. G/1.

Anon., 'President Stresses Friendship with China', *BBC Summary of World Broadcasts*, FE/3918 (14 Aug. 2000), p. B/13.

Anon., 'China Says "Irrelevant Issues" Should Not Stop Japanese Aid Loans', *BBC Summary of World Broadcasts*, FE/3918 (14 Aug. 2000), p. G/1.

Bedi, Rahul, and Lennox, Duncan, 'Pakistan's First Test of its New Ballistic Missile', *Jane's Defence Weekly*, Vol. 29, No. 15 (15 Apr. 1998), p. 4.

Blanchard, Jean-Marc F., 'The US Role in the Sino-Japanese Dispute Over the Diaoyu (Senkaku) Islands 1945–1971', *China Quarterly*, No. 161 (Mar. 2000), pp. 95–123.

Blasko, Dennis J., 'Evaluating Chinese Military Procurement from Russia', *Joint Forces Quarterly*, No. 17 (Autumn/Winter 1997–98), pp. 91–6.

Blasko, Dennis J., Klapakis, Philip T., and Corbett Jr, John F., 'Training Tomorrow's PLA: A Mixed Bag of Tricks', *China Quarterly*, No. 146 (June 1996), pp. 488–524.

Chanda, Nayan, 'Divide and Rule', *Far Eastern Economic Review* (11 Aug. 1994), p. 18.

Chanda, Nayan, 'Aiming High', *Far Eastern Economic Review*, Vol. 157, No. 2 (20 Oct. 1994).

Chanda, Nayan , 'Fear of the Dragon', *Far Eastern Economic Review*, Vol. 158, No. 15 (13 Apr. 1995), pp. 24–8.

Chanda, Nayan, Tiglao, Rigoberto, and McBeth, John, 'Territorial Imperative', *Far Eastern Economic Review* (23 Feb. 1995), p. 14.

Chang, C.Y., 'Overseas Chinese in China's Policy', *China Quarterly*, No. 82 (June 1980), pp. 281–303.

Dawnay, Ivo, 'China Plots to Bug West's Defences', *Sunday Telegraph* (17 June 1997), p. 33.

Doshita, Tetsuro, 'Regional Security Links Between Japan and the United States', *US Naval Institute Proceedings* (Mar. 1995), pp. 51–4.

Edmunds, Keith W., 'ASW – Current and Future Trends', *Defense Analysis*, Vol. 16, No. 1 (Apr. 2000), pp. 73–87.

Frankenstein, John, and Bates, Gill, 'Current and Future Challenges Facing Chinese Defence Industries', *China Quarterly*, No. 146 (June 1996), pp. 394–427.

Gaddis, John L., 'International Relations Theory and the End of the Cold War', *International Security*, Vol. 17, No. 3 (Winter 1992–93), pp. 5–58.

Gaddis, John L., and Hopf, Ted, 'Getting the End of the Cold War Wrong', *International Security*, Vol. 18, No. 2 (Fall 1993), pp. 202–15.

Gallagher, Michael G., 'China's Illusory Threat to the South China Sea', *International Security*, Vol. 19, No. 1 (Summer 1994), pp. 169–94.

Godwin, Paul H.B., 'Chinese Concepts of Doctrine, Strategy and Operations in the Chinese Peoples' Liberation Army 1978–87', *China Quarterly*, No. 112 (Dec. 1987), pp. 464–87.

Goldman, Merle, 'China's Anti-Confucian Campaign 1973–1974', *China Quarterly*, No. 63 (Sept. 1975), pp. 435–62.

Gregor, A. James, 'Qualified Engagement: US China Policy and Security Concerns', *Naval War College Review*, Vol. 52, No. 2 (Spring 1999), pp. 69–88.

Grove, Eric, 'Britain's Continued Strategic Interest in the Region', *Asia-Pacific Defence Reporter*, Vol. 24, No. 2 (Feb.–Mar. 1998), pp. 6–7.

Heuser, Robert, 'Chinese Law of Foreign Trade: An Interview', *China Quarterly*, No. 73 (Mar. 1978), pp. 159–65.

Hosokawa, Morihiro, 'Are US Troops in Japan Needed?', *Foreign Affairs*, Vol. 77, No. 4 (July–Aug. 1998), pp. 2–5.

Jensen, Peter, 'Chinese Sea Power and American Strategy', *Strategic Review*, Vol. 28, No. 3 (Summer 2000), pp. 18–26.

Jung-Pang Lo, 'The Emergence of China as a Sea Power During the Late Sung and Early Yuan Periods', *Far Eastern Quarterly*, Vol. 14, Issue 4, Special Number on Chinese History and Society (Aug. 1955), pp. 489–503.

Kamminga, Menno T. , 'Building "Railroads on the Sea": China's Attitude towards Maritime Law', *China Quarterly*, No. 59 (Sept. 1974), pp. 544–58.

Kaye, Lincoln, 'Courtship Dance', *Far Eastern Economic Review*, Vol. 157, No. 21 (26 May 1994), p. 24.

Kearsley, Harold J., 'An Analysis of the Military Threats Across the Taiwan Strait: Fact or Fiction', *Comparative Strategy*, Vol. 19, No. 2 (Apr.–June 2000), pp. 103–16.

Kennan, George ('X'), 'The Sources of Soviet Conduct', *Foreign Affairs*, Vol. 25, No. 4 (July 1947), pp. 566–82.

Khanua, R.P., 'Impact of China's Ambition to be a Regional Superpower', *Asian Defence Journal*, Vol. 6, No. 9 (Aug. 1999), pp. 6–9.

Li Cheng, 'Jiang Zemin's Successors: The Rise of the Fourth Generation of Leaders in the PRC', *China Quarterly*, No. 161 (Mar. 2000), pp. 1–40.

Li Ning, '30 Years of Development in Space Technology', *Beijing Review*, Vol. 43, No. 25 (19 June 2000), pp. 12–16.

Malik, Mohan, 'Burma Slides Under China's Shadow', *Jane's Intelligence Review*, Vol. 9, No. 7 (1 July 1997), electronically accessed.

McBeth, John, 'Troubled Waters', *Far Eastern Economic Review*, Vol. 158, No. 1 (5 Jan. 1995), pp. 18–19.

Murray, Laura K., 'China's Psychological Warfare', *Military Review*, Vol. 79, No. 5 (Sept.–Oct. 1999), pp. 13–22.

Nan Li, 'The PLA's Evolving Warfighting Doctrine, Strategy and Tactics, 1985–95: A Chinese Perspective', *China Quarterly*, No. 146 (June 1996), pp. 443–63.

Novichkov, Nikolai, and Zhang, Yihong, 'Russia Discusses AWE&C Lease to China and India', *Jane's Defence Weekly* (28 June 2000), p. 5.

Ogden, Suzanne, 'The Approach of the Chinese Communists to the Study of International Law, State Sovereignty and the International System', *China Quarterly*, No. 70 (June 1977), pp. 315–37.

Opall-Rome, Barbara, 'DoD Rings Alarm on Chinese Antisatellite Plans', *Defense News* (2–8 Nov. 1998), p. 6.

Perira, Dewin, 'Minister Discusses Defense Ties With Singapore', *FBIS-EAS-94-238* (10 Dec. 1994), p. 69.

Perira, Dewin, 'Minister Opposes US Bases', *FBIS-EAS-94-238* (10 Dec. 1994), p. 68.

Perira, Dewin, 'Minister Sees No Security Threat From People's Republic of China', *FBIS-EAS-94-238* (10 Dec. 1994), p. 69.

Renwick, Neil, and Abbott, Jason, 'Piratical Violence and Maritime Security in Southeast Asia', *Security Dialogue*, Vol. 30, No. 2 (June 1999), pp. 183–96.

Robertson, J. Michael, 'Alfred Thayer Mahan and the Geopolitics of Asia', *Comparative Strategy*, Vol. 15, No. 4 (Oct.–Dec. 1996), pp. 353–66.

Sciolino, Elaine, 'With Thai Rebuff, US Defers Plan For Navy Depot in Asia', *New York Times* (12 Nov. 1994), Section 1, p. 6.

Segal, Gerald, 'East Asia and the "Constrainment" of China', *International Security*, Vol. 20, No. 4 (Spring 1996), p. 132.

Segal, Gerald, 'Does China Matter?', *Foreign Affairs*, Vol. 78. No. 5 (Sept.–Oct. 1999), pp. 24–36.

Sengupta, Prasun K., 'PLA Force Modernisation Activities and Future Plans', *Asian Defence Journal*, Vol. 6, No. 5 (Apr. 1999), pp. 21–4.

Shambaugh, David, 'China's Security Strategy in the Post-Cold War Era', *Survival*, Vol. 34, No. 2 (Summer 1992), pp. 88–106.

Swaine, Michael D., 'The Modernization of the Chinese People's Liberation Army: Prospects and Implications in Northeast Asia', *National Bureau of Asian Research Analysis*, Vol. 5, No. 3 (Oct. 1994).

Tanner, Murray Scot, 'The Erosion of Communist Party Control Over Lawmaking In China', *China Quarterly*, No. 138 (June 1994), pp. 381–403.

Tonnesson, Stein, 'Can Conflicts Be Solved by Shelving Disputes?', *Security Dialogue*, Vol. 30. No. 2 (June 1999), pp. 179–82.

Tseng Hui-Yeh, 'Shandong Faction Reportedly Controls Military', *FBIS-CHI-94-204* (21 Oct. 1994), p. 34.

Whiting, Allen S., 'Chinese Nationalism and Foreign Policy After Deng', *China Quarterly*, No. 142 (June 1995), pp. 295–316.

Whiting, Allen S., 'The PLA and China's Threat Perceptions', *China Quarterly*, No. 146 (June 1996), pp. 596–615.

Wortzel, Larry M., 'China Pursues Traditional Great-Power Status', *Orbis*, Vol. 38, No. 2 (Spring 1994), pp. 157–75.

Wu Hongbo, Shi Changxue and Pan Hongxin, 'Navy Takes Part In Building Up Garrison Off Paracel Islands', *FBIS-CHI-94-202* (19 Oct. 1994), p. 34.

Yahuda, Michael , 'Deng Xiaoping: The Statesman', *China Quarterly*, No. 135 (Sept. 1993), pp. 551–72.

Zarzeck, Thomas W., 'Weaponry and War: Are Arms Transfers From the Former Soviet Union a Security Threat? The Case of Combat Aircraft', *Journal of Slavic Military Studies*, Vol. 12, No. 1 (Mar. 1999), pp. 124–48.

Zhang Xuebin, 'Two "isms" on the Same Vine', reprinted in *BBC Summary of World Broadcasts*, FE/3758 (8 Feb. 2000), pp. G/2–G/3.

ONLINE SOURCES

Anon., 'What the Others Say', *Business Times* (as reported on LEXIS–NEXIS) (28 July 1992).

Anon., 'Naval Modernization', *BBC Summary of World Broadcasts* (as reported on LEXIS-NEXIS) (12 Jan. 1993).

Anon., '"Largest-Scale" Military Naval Exercises Held Off Zhejiang', *BBC Summary of World Broadcasts* (as reported on LEXIS-NEXIS) (21 Sept. 1994).

Anon., 'China to Build ELINT Facility and Modernize Cuba's Satellite Tracking Base', *China Reform Monitor*, No. 201, www.afpc.org/crm/crm201.htm (11 May 1999).

Anon., 'Russia, China Hold First Ever Joint Naval Maneuvers', WorldTribune.com (1 Oct. 1999).

Cox Report, www.house.gov/coxreport/chapfs/ch1 html (Summer 2000).

Gesteland, Lester J., 'China: China Naval Experts Ponder Need for Aircraft Carrier', *ChinaOnline News*, http://www.chinaonline.com (12 Feb. 1999).

Gordon, Hugo, 'US Plans to Sell Missile Know-How to China', *Daily Telegraph*, No. 1028, www.telegraph.co.uk (19 Mar. 1998).

Kyodo News Service, 'Chinese Naval Vessel Arrives at Bombay Port', *Japan Economic Newswire* (as reported on LEXIS-NEXIS) (15 Nov. 1993).

Lamb, Christina, 'China Puts "700,000 Troops" on Sudan Alert', *Daily Telegraph*, No. 1920, www.telegraph.co.uk (27 Aug. 2000).

Raum, Tom, 'Is the Panama Canal in Jeopardy?', bergen.com/molenews/uspanama199910233.htm. (23 Oct. 1999).

Smith, Charles, 'China's Newest Secret Weapon', *World Net Daily*, www.worldnetdaily.com (30 Nov. 1999).

Sumihiko Kawamura, Soushi (Isoko Sunakawa, trans.), glocomnet.or.jp/okazaki-inst/ (Mar. 2000).

Index